The Editors of
ROLLING STONE

How to Get Off on
DRUGS

Written by
Ira Mothner and Alan Weitz

Foreword by William Nolen, M.D.

A ROLLING STONE PRESS BOOK/SIMON AND SCHUSTER

3 5 7 9 10 8 6 4

3 5 7 9 10 8 6 4 2 pbk.

Library of Congress Cataloging in Publication Data
Mothner, Ira
How to get off drugs.
"A Rolling Stone Press book."
"Information and referral sources": p.
Includes index.
1. Substance abuse. I. Weitz, Alan. II. Rolling
stone. III. Title.
RC564.M68 1984   616.86'306   84-1334
ISBN 0-671-49208-X
ISBN 0-671-46676-3 (pbk)

Grateful acknowledgment is made for permission to excerpt from:

I'm Dancing As Fast As I Can by Barbara Gordon. Copyright © 1979 by Barbara Gordon. Reprinted by permission of Harper & Row, Publishers, Inc.

Edie: An American Biography by Jean Stein, with George Plimpton. Copyright © 1982 by Jean Stein and George Plimpton. Reprinted by permission of Alfred A. Knopf, Inc.

Straight Life: The Story of Art Pepper by Art and Laurie Pepper. Copyright © 1979 by Schirmer Books, a Division of Macmillan Publishing Company. Reprinted by permission of the publisher.

Case Studies in Abnormal Psychology by John M. Neale, Thomas F. Oltmanns and Gerald C. Davison. Copyright © 1982 by John Wiley & Sons, Inc. Reprinted by permission of John Wiley & Sons, Inc.

Naked Lunch by William Burroughs. Copyright © 1959 by William Burroughs. Reprinted by permission of Grove Press, Inc., and John Calder (Publishers) Ltd.

" 'I'm Not Worth a Damn' " by Don Reese with John Underwood. Reprinted courtesy of *Sports Illustrated* from the June 14, 1982 issue. © Time Inc.

ACKNOWLEDGMENTS

Were it not for the many scholars, physicians, and drug abuse professionals who have contributed to the growing body of knowledge about psychoactive drugs and their abuse, this book could never have been written. We are grateful to the many authors whose work has guided us and to the experts whose advice we sought: Dr. Mitchell S. Rosenthal of Phoenix House, who enabled us to understand the causes of and the treatment for drug abuse; Dr. Stephen Pittel, who helped devise the book's drug involvement tests and was an invaluable guide to treatment approaches; Drs. George DeLeon and David Deitch, who suggested a number of ways to determine treatment criteria; and Dr. Ronald K. Siegel, whose thoughts on various aspects of drug abuse were most helpful.

We want to acknowledge the substantial contributions of Jann Wenner, the publisher and editor of *Rolling Stone,* whose ideas and insights added a significant dimension to the book, and those of Patty Romanowski, editor of Rolling Stone Press, Sarah Lazin and Jonathan Wells, the past and present directors, respectively, of Rolling Stone Press, and Bob Bender, senior editor of Simon and Schuster.

Finally, we would like to express our deep appreciation to Paul Fishbein, who contributed far more to the book than his solid research. His knowledge and his understanding of both drug abuse and drug abusers are reflected in each chapter, and Jason Forsythe, whose passion for accuracy has, we hope, saved us from more than a modest number of errors.

CONTENTS

PREFACE

This is not another book *about* drug use. It doesn't dwell on crime, the horrors of addiction or how drugs are destroying schools, families and the fabric of American life.

It is a book *for* drug users.

Mostly, it is for men and women (children too) who are thinking about quitting. If you have already tried and failed, or gotten off drugs and found yourself unable to stay off, or even if you still believe you can stop whenever you choose, then this book is for you. It is full of those things drug users ought to know about the drugs they take—predictable effects, immediate risks and long-term dangers, patterns of abuse and warning signs, how dependency works and how it can be managed, the limits of self-help and what else may be needed to get off and stay off. It is also a book for the husbands, wives, lovers, friends and families of drug users. It tells what you can do to help someone you love get off drugs.

Not every mind-altering and mood-changing substance is covered, but the book does deal with all illicit psychoactive drugs, from marijuana, hashish and cocaine to narcotics. It looks at misuse of alcohol, of prescription drugs—the tranquilizers, sedatives and hypnotics that come from the neighborhood pharmacy—and at drugs that fall between the cracks in substance control regulations, like nitrous oxide and butyl nitrite.

In addition to the drugs themselves, the book focuses on the context

9

of drug use—the "where" and "when" and "with whom" drugs are used. It looks at who uses drugs, and what kinds of treatment are available to the abuser. It discusses the complicated relationship between the drug user and those people close to him or her—how they can help and how they may reinforce drug use. It tries to answer the question: How can I get off drugs?

Although we have tried to resist drawing conclusions, a good many caveats have crept into the text, as have some biases. So, let us acknowledge up front that we do not consider drugs a valid route to self-knowledge or any other kind of enlightenment. Nor do we feel they are psychologically, socially or sexually useful for most people. But the belief—or bias—that most clearly has shaped this book is an unshakable conviction that everything comes with a price tag. "There ain't no such thing as a free lunch."

If you want to smoke cigarettes or drink or do drugs, it will eventually cost you something in health, safety, stability or performance. The trouble is that not everyone pays the same price for the same excess. It is another way in which life is not fair. Some people go years before any payment comes due; others never seem to see a bill. But these lucky types are balanced by those who get stuck with a devastating tab early on.

You take your chances. You may even get away with it. Only you never know just what your particular indulgence is going to end up costing or when you may have to start paying. With drugs, you may not even notice that the bill has arrived. It isn't only your health or your safety that's at risk, and you may easily miss the point at which drugs begin taking something else away from your career, your relationships or your life.

A note about the organization of this book. While you may be tempted to skip ahead to the chapter on your drug of abuse, it is important to put drug use in context. A knowledge of how drugs work, a look at treatment options, definitions of basic terms—some of the subjects covered in the opening section of this book—will help you understand what you need to know about getting off drugs. In addition, while drugs differ in what they do and may produce different symptoms when you stop taking them, the road to getting off drugs is basically the same whether your drug of abuse is amphetamine, marijuana, heroin, alcohol or cocaine.

FOREWORD

Drug abuse has changed considerably in the last twenty years, and not for the better. In fact, it has become more widespread than ever before. Now there are more drugs to which people become addicted, and addiction is no longer limited to the slums of the big cities. In 1984, it is found among the middle class and the wealthy as well as among the poor.

With the new class of patients and the new drugs, another problem has arisen—identification. When I was a surgical resident at Bellevue between 1953 and 1960, it was easy to spot the addicts who, with no accessible veins left on their bodies, were forced to inject heroin beneath the skin. But nowadays it is not easy to recognize the housewife who is taking 10 or 15 milligrams of Valium whenever she feels "tense" or the man who snorts a couple of lines of cocaine two or three times a day. The lady who knocks back three shots of vodka before she comes to a cocktail party may seem a bit more jovial than expected, but one would be hard pressed to identify her as an alcoholic. In fact, in the 1980s, thousands of people with severe drug habits "pass" for normal every day, at their offices, at parties, in their homes. Often, for months or even years, the only person who truly knows that he or she has a damaging drug habit is the user. Friends, relatives and even the patient's doctor may suspect, but getting hard evidence of drug abuse may be difficult.

The typical doctor may not be interested in diagnosing drug habituation, let alone curing an addict or reforming an alcoholic. Addicts are not like patients with appendicitis who can be cured in an hour or patients with pneumonia who can be cured in a week. The patient with a drug habit may need months of help and, even under optimal conditions, may regress just when it seems that he or she has "made it." Doctors may avoid these patients, thinking they are too much trouble.

Which often means that the user who wants to get off drugs may well have to make the diagnosis and arrange for a treatment plan himself. To do this, he or she will need guidance.

That is what *How to Get Off Drugs* provides. In very clear language, this book tells the reader how to decide whether he or she is hooked on a drug. It then tells the reader how to get off the drug. The authors don't equivocate. There is no pretending that kicking a drug habit will be easy, no suggestion that a drug problem can be taken lightly. The book emphasizes that treatment options vary with individual resources. For example, the user with a close family support group may be able to get off drugs without hospitalization; but if the support group is lacking, only a fool will try to break with drugs as an outpatient. This book is not of the *How to Lose Twenty Pounds in Twenty Days While Eating Constantly* genre. It is not a book that offers false hope.

It is a book that offers real hope. Over the last twenty years we have made substantial progress in dealing with drug problems. We've learned how valuable support groups can be. We've learned when drug substitution is appropriate and when it isn't. We've learned—to put it succinctly —that treating drug addiction is not the futile venture it once seemed. We know that, with appropriate help, drug habits can be broken and that patients who get off drugs can stay clean. One of the major remaining challenges is disseminating that knowledge to those who need it.

This is a role that *How to Get Off Drugs* can play. Filled with up-to-date, accurate information, it is a book that has been long overdue. It should not only be read by drug users and their families but should also be part of every doctor's library. I recommend it without reservation.

—WILLIAM NOLEN, M.D.

PART ONE

Getting Off Drugs: What You Need to Know

1

DRUG USE AND DRUG RISK

Society does not use drugs—people do. And the decision to use or not to use remains an individual one, no matter how society views the issue. Nevertheless, at any given moment, it is the cultural context that most influences individual choice.

Over the past two decades, drugs have increasingly become a part of everyday American life. The reasons for this are not very hard to see. We have the appropriate attitudes—"to live for the moment . . . to live for yourself," as Christopher Lasch puts it in *The Culture of Narcissism* —and we plainly have access. A gram of cocaine is as easy to come by as a six-pack of beer, whether you live in New York, Los Angeles, Atlanta or Kalamazoo. Narcotics, especially heroin, are readily available on the streets of major cities and a number of mid-size ones as well. And there is no place in the country where marijuana is not grown or flown.

Drugs have also achieved surprising visibility considering their illegality. Special-interest magazines now exist, and the specialty stores that cater to users have moved from grimy inner-city streets to shopping centers and suburban malls. Drugs have made for memorable moments in film—Woody Allen sneezing away a gram of coke in *Annie Hall* and Kris Kristofferson tooting with both nostrils in the latest remake of *A Star Is Born*. Even television is not immune, and one 1983 sitcom episode focused on efforts to save a threatened marijuana crop. As for popular music, the drug references that were once slyly coded for the knowing

15

are now openly there for all to hear, and drug use is taken for granted by both audiences and performers.

It isn't just that drug use is common today. Drugs have glamour—because glamorous people use them: athletes, entertainers and politicians. The great Capitol Hill cocaine scandal of 1982 may not have turned up many snorting congressmen, but the use of drugs among the Sunday heroes of the National Football League proved just as widespread as defensive lineman Don Reese had claimed in his 1982 first-person account in *Sports Illustrated,* with sizable drug-using contingents on a number of teams. And football is not an exception. Baseball and basketball stars have also had problems with drugs.

Be they famous or not, more than 57 million Americans have used some illicit drug. Most have done little more than smoke pot, but better than 22 million have at least tried cocaine and more than 5 million have sampled narcotics. The most telling statistics, however, show the increase in drug use over the past two decades. For example, the number of eighteen- to twenty-five-year-olds who have used marijuana jumped from a mere 4 percent to 64 percent, while harder drug use in this age group climbed from 3 percent to 30 percent. During the 1970s cocaine use among young adults tripled, from less than 10 percent to nearly 30 percent, while close to 12 percent have now used some narcotic drug.

Drug use has spread geographically, economically and chronologically. Although researchers for the National Institute on Drug Abuse (NIDA) are finding that the growth rate of drug use in metropolitan areas is finally slowing down, growth in rural areas is holding steady and seems likely to eventually reach parity with metropolitan levels. While drugs and drugs users were once concentrated in poor urban areas, drug use today is far from a prerogative of the poor. Studies in New York State show that upper-income families are now the most likely to be involved. As for the age spread, it is increasing as the "age of onset"—the point at which youngsters have their initial drug experiences—continues to fall. Today, 5 percent of the nation's twelve- and thirteen-year-olds have already smoked their first joints, as have one third of the fourteen- and fifteen-year-olds and better than half the sixteen- and seventeen-year-olds. Among high school seniors, 59 percent have used marijuana, 28 percent smoke regularly, and 6 percent smoke heavily.

Tracing the dramatic rise in drug use from the 1960s, we can easily spot other changes in our society that have made this increase possible —and probably inevitable. The way we live and where we live, changing values, the makeup of the population, the state of the economy, and the mechanisms of social control, all go a long way toward explaining why there are so many more drug users today. Nevertheless, the reasons why any single individual uses drugs are no different from what they were twenty or forty or four hundred years ago.

Why Drugs Are Used

Drugs provide some response to most of man's fundamental longings, and these have changed very little over the years. Britain's Victorian poet Matthew Arnold neatly capsuled them toward the end of his poem, "Dover Beach":

> *Ah, love, let us be true*
> *To one another! for the world, which seems*
> *To lie before us like a land of dreams,*
> *So various, so beautiful, so new,*
> *Hath really neither joy, nor love, nor light,*
> *Nor certitude, nor peace, nor help for pain.*

Drugs respond, in one way or another, to all these lacks. If they do not provide true joy, they do offer sensations so pleasurable that the chief obstacle to reduced use or abstinence is the overwhelming sense of pleasure denied. As for love, drugs enhance intimacy, loosen inhibitions and dampen anxiety. They shed light of a kind, too, and many users will swear to the validity of drug-derived insights and revelations. Although real certitude and peace are unlikely to be achieved through drugs, the absence of certitude and peace is far more easily tolerated with psychoactives that buffer the impact of uncomfortable realities. And "help for pain" is one of the oldest reasons for drug use.

Of course, drugs vary, use varies, and needs change throughout life, according to psychiatrist Jared R. Tinklenberg of the Stanford University Medical Center, who notes how many younger users prefer drugs that stimulate the central nervous system. "However, when the youthful drug user reaches his thirties or forties, his pattern of use often changes," says Tinklenberg. "He is less attracted to exciting, exhilarating stimulants and is more likely to prefer central nervous system depressants—alcohol, barbiturates and opiates."

The reasons youngsters start using drugs have long concerned researchers, for the clearest signals of future compulsive use can be seen during this earliest phase, and a sizable amount of government money has been invested in attempting to discover the origins of drug-taking. Curiosity clearly draws the young. Our society makes much of drugs, and their glamour has allure. So have their well-publicized dangers, for thrill-seeking and risk-taking are characteristic of adolescence. Indeed, a certain amount of youthful drug use seems to be "counterphobic"—that is, many kids will keep on using drugs not *in spite* of their fears but *because* of them. This may explain why young users continue to smoke pot even when the experience is unpleasant. Studies during the 1960s and early 1970s showed that nearly two out of five users were often depressed or unhappy after smoking, and most admitted to sometimes feeling insecure.

Peer pressure certainly plays a role in introducing many young people to drugs, as well as encouraging continued use. Drugs may be the price of admission to a social set or clique; and "turning on," some researchers maintain, has become a kind of "puberty rite," a way of marking or celebrating entry into adolescence.

A number of young people face unusual pressures during adolescence —family troubles, emotional problems, frustrations in school or social life. During these years of rapid and dramatic change, when a full-scale personality overhaul is under way, additional burdens make youngsters particularly vulnerable, and psychiatrists have found they will use drugs to compensate for "temporary ego weakness."

Although youthful motives for drug-taking are somewhat different from adult motives, both younger and older users find drugs do the same kinds of things for them. They provide pleasure and pleasurable sensations, feelings of exhilaration and various levels of intoxication. They are social lubricants, diminishing the frictions of social contact, relieving anxieties of the shy and inhibitions of the ill-at-ease. They also have a ritual role for those who believe drugs supply the shortcut to inner truths and insights (although hallucinogens are taken as often by thrill-seekers as by those in search of self-knowledge).

Self-medication is what a good many users are after. They will take drugs to counter sleeplessness, depression or anxiety, to raise energy levels or to overcome more specific complaints like impotence. And they will turn to drugs to relieve pain—any kind of physical or emotional pain. The great pain-killers, like heroin, are also great time-killers. Among the inner-city unemployed they are often used as antidotes for boredom and frustration as well as psychic pain.

The Costs of Drug Use

Almost no one who uses drugs starts out anticipating much in the way of cost. They count on benefits, for drugs almost always deliver. Although the range of responses is broad indeed (and many users have disappointing initial responses), few users are cheated of the drug experience. Costs, however, are allocated much less evenhandedly. When it comes to downside effects, "a small percentage will be particularly vulnerable," says Tinklenberg, "and others will be relatively immune." The seemingly random nature of drug risk and the fact that different drugs carry different risks make it hard for many users to realize that *all* drugs come with a price—a set of physical, psychological and social costs—that *any* user may have to pay at *any* time. For our purposes it's useful to categorize these costs, for though one may be more applicable than another to a specific drug, they are almost all true of all drugs.

Acute Toxic Effects

This is poisoning, pure and simple. A "toxic reaction," however, is no different *in kind* from the milder "intoxication" caused by a drug. It is just more—far too much—of what the user is seeking, the result of too large or too potent a dose or a drug interaction. Take too much or too pure a helping of narcotics and you overdose. Mix a sedative with alcohol and the combined depressant effect can put you into a coma or halt breathing completely. Almost any drug will display toxic properties when consumed in sufficiently large quantities. Even too much coffee can result in "acute caffeine poisoning."

Long-Term Physical Dangers

Here, the case against alcohol is most clear. Prolonged use of booze hits the body hard—degeneration of nerves in the arms and legs, destruction of brain cells, as well as severe liver damage. Glue sniffing, which can have devastating effects on the kidneys and cell membranes in the brain, has also been linked to certain forms of leukemia. Cocaine can weaken the heart, and amphetamines can do permanent brain damage. But there have been few long-term epidemiological studies in this area; and as Dr. Tinklenberg warns, there is "a considerable time lag between widespread use of a drug and the recognition of long-term deleterious effects. This time lag is best exemplified by the extensive, prolonged use of tobacco before association with lung cancer, coronary artery disease, and other disorders was established."

Somewhat easier to spot are effects of drug-induced behavior and damage done by the way different drugs are consumed. Sustained use of narcotics, cocaine and amphetamine, as well as alcohol, often leads to malnutrition and resulting vulnerability to infection and disease, while marijuana's strongest long-term risk is to the lungs and respiratory system, the result of regularly inhaling (and inhaling deeply) a highly irritating gas with a higher concentration of carcinogens than tobacco smoke. Narcotic users who favor injection risk hepatitis and endocarditis (inflammation of the heart's lining and valves) from unsterilized needles and syringes, particularly if they share equipment with friends. Cocaine, if sniffed with any frequency, can tear up the nasal passages pretty badly.

Today, there is a growing concern about the danger that psychoactive drugs pose to unborn children. Pregnant women are urged to reduce drinking and quit smoking. The placental barrier has proven no obstacle for narcotics, and children of addicts are born with drug cravings just as pronounced as their mother's and with considerably less capacity to withstand withdrawal. THC, the primary psychoactive component of marijuana, also crosses the placental barrier with ease and settles into the fatty tissues (brain, reproductive organs, etc.) of the unborn. Not only do the children of marijuana-using mothers experience a mild sedative withdrawal after birth, they may also get a flying start on longer-term health risks of pot.

Psychological Effects

Ignoring, for now, the results of drug dependence and focusing on direct effects of prolonged drug use on the mind, the best (or worst) example would seem to be the organic psychosis of longtime alcoholics, the permanent disorganization of thought that results from physical damage to the brain. Other drugs, too, can cause chronic mental impairment, as well as a wide variety of less permanently disorganizing effects.

There is the "panic reaction" even seasoned marijuana smokers sometimes experience, and the paranoia that grass, cocaine and amphetamines occasionally trigger. Toxic psychosis, which appears much like paranoid schizophrenia and often lasts as long as a week, can afflict amphetamine users. More profound drug-induced psychosis, also often mistaken for schizophrenia, may last for several weeks when the inducing drug is a hallucinogen like PCP or LSD. And LSD users are vulnerable, as well, to "flashbacks," which may occur as long as a full year after a drug-taking episode.

Behavioral Toxicity

This designation covers the ways drugs affect judgment and performance and includes impairment of perception and motor skills, loss of short-term memory and coordination. When an LSD or PCP user dives out a six-story window—and the intent is not to commit suicide—that is a fatal and extreme example of behavioral toxicity. More common are the accidents caused by drugs or alcohol. While it's hard to know for sure just how many car crashes are caused by drivers who are stoned (since few suspects are willing to submit to blood or urine tests), indications are strong that guilty drivers in fatal crashes are just as likely to be impaired by marijuana as by alcohol and that grass is to blame for as many as 12 percent of *all* highway accidents.

What is dangerous on the highway is no less dangerous in the shop or factory, and there is reason to believe that alcohol and other drugs are to blame for as many as half of all industrial accidents. Skiing accidents, boating accidents and drownings are also often the result of behavioral toxicity. Each year, drugs claim a sizable number of midnight swimmers who find themselves high and far from shore, unable to gauge distance, poorly coordinated, and with a faulty sense of their own body's position in the water. Drugs like PCP, which raise body temperature and give the skin a hot, dry feeling, actually inspire a desire to swim—and half of all PCP deaths are drownings.

Developmental Effects

The ability of psychoactive drugs to alter feelings and perceptions makes it possible for users to avoid dealing with unpleasant realities and to mask or dull pain and distress. While this is clearly useful in the treatment of emotional disorders, it has a considerable downside, for stress and pain are essential ingredients of normal life. They are signals that warn us when parts of our bodies or our lives aren't working as they should. They are also the natural concomitants of growth and development of almost every kind.

Young drug users can escape the stress that is part of the maturation process. But emotional storms of the teenage years are a necessary rite of passage, during which lifelong attitudes are developed and responsible ways of dealing with the world are acquired. Young people learn to make long-range plans, defer gratification, and accommodate their own desires and needs to the desires and needs of others. Regular drug use can inhibit this process. Indeed, a good many adolescent heavy users have trouble thinking far ahead or deferring pleasure or sustaining mature relationships.

Both young users and older ones who count on drugs to relieve pressure or pain find it difficult coming to grips with emotionally troubling situations. Young users may fail to ever develop adult coping mechanisms, while older ones easily slide into a pattern of avoidance, losing the capability to cope as they lose the willingness to confront difficult or complicated situations.

Interpersonal Costs

These are ways drug use can sap or strain personal relationships and influence other social contact. Clearly, the failure of some users to develop or to sustain adult coping skills affects their capacity to maintain relationships. They are unlikely to deal responsibly with partners—husbands, wives or lovers—or to play appropriately supportive roles within families or communities.

While drugs can and do enhance intimacy, they rarely help relationships endure. When both participants count on this kind of chemical enhancement, the relationship itself can be said to be "drug-dependent" and unlikely to stand up to real life demands.

Sex itself, often facilitated by drugs, can eventually become a cost of sustained use. Different drugs interfere in the sexual process in different ways, but cocaine takes a particularly heavy toll. "When you first start using coke," one male heavy user explains, "you can't get it down. Then, you can't get it up." Most drugs diminish sexual desire. But beyond this, if drugs are your recourse in emotionally troubled times, you won't be able to confront the loss of intimacy or diminished sexual activity and work out solutions with your partner.

The influence of drugs on social activity is complex, for the setting (where and with whom drugs are used) is an important aspect of drug-taking. Users often choose friends because of the drugs they use, or choose to use drugs because it is the practice of their friends. Social drug use can limit the range of social contacts, while solitary use may well lead to reduced contact and isolation.

Drug Dependence

Drug dependence exacts the highest personal costs from most users and involves a far more complex set of reactions than had been previously realized. It is a vital process for drug users to understand, and that means defining some language—such words as *drug abuse* and *addiction* —and recognizing some of the ways drugs work on the mind and in the body—psychological and physical phenomena like reinforcement, rebound and withdrawal.

Drug abuse is a fairly imprecise term with an unsavory past that has been used at various times to mean just about any kind of drug-taking perceived (usually by hostile observers) as harmful. Not long ago, to most

Americans it meant nothing less than the nonmedical use of any psychoactive drug with the possible exception of alcohol. For our purposes, the concept of drug abuse becomes most useful when its meaning is limited to *the compulsive use of a psychoactive substance that endangers physical or mental health*. Compulsive use, within this definition, means uncontrollable use, even irrational use.

Once we've got a handle on drug abuse, it becomes possible to focus on those drugs that have a capacity for abuse and can rightly be called *drugs of abuse*. This means something quite specific and measurable. It is not the physical or mental harm they are capable of causing that gives drugs an abuse potential. It is their ability to provide sensory rewards, the effects they have on the pleasure centers of the brain.

Different drugs stimulate different pleasure centers (located in concentrations of brain cells called nuclei) and produce different effects, depending upon the particular center stimulated and the strength of the stimulation. Because the "rush" of injected heroin or amphetamine, for example, mimics the intense pleasurable sensations of orgasm, these drugs have high abuse potential. On the other hand, volatile solvents like glue, which offer little in the way of bliss, have a relatively low abuse potential (not that this has prevented compulsive use of volatile solvents by thrill-seekers with a self-destructive bent).

Pharmacologists can get a fairly precise reading on the abuse potential of a drug by testing it on laboratory animals. The subject, often a rat, gets a dose of a drug after performing a specific act, like shoving against a push bar. In this way, the rat learns to self-administer the drug. Push the bar, get the drug. The pleasurable sensations the drug produces are the reward that *reinforces* bar-pushing behavior by the rat. In the same way, the rush is the reinforcement for heroin-shooting behavior in humans. Both the rat and the heroin user are being conditioned through reinforcement to continue self-administering drugs.

The behavior of laboratory animals, then, is not all that different from human behavior when it comes to drugs. What makes drug-taking different from most other forms of human behavior is the nature of the reinforcement. We all can be conditioned to do things that are rewarding, even activities that are initially difficult, painful or awkward. We are rewarded for hard work or diligence or thoughtfulness with praise, self-esteem, high grades, raises, promotions, friendship, affection and even love. Drug-taking, however, is *self-reinforcing*. The payoff is the drug experience itself, nothing more.

Reinforcement in humans can be helped along and amplified by *secondary conditioning*—the association of drug use with particular settings, sights and sounds, or even smells. A whiff of morning coffee can trigger an urge for nicotine. The sight of rolling paper in a store may set off the desire for grass. The corner bar, with its cast of sustaining characters and rich, beery smells says "booze" to drinkers, while a lover's bedroom may channel a user's thoughts to cocaine.

Never underestimate the power of reinforcement, for it can lead to *psychological dependency.* This is the conviction on the part of a drug user that the effects of his or her drug of choice are necessary to maintain a feeling of well-being. Psychological dependency can be just as direct a route to compulsive use as physical dependency. Cocaine, for example, while it seems to create no true physical dependency (and there is now some debate about this), is so powerfully reinforcing that users often become deeply depressed as the effects of the drug diminish. They may consume huge amounts over prolonged periods of time to sustain euphoria. Julia Phillips, who produced *The Sting* and *Close Encounters of the Third Kind,* figures she spent about $1 million on cocaine to feed a growing psychological dependency. At the end, she was smoking freebase cocaine, staying up for seventy-two hours at a stretch, then sleeping for twenty-four. Never a heavy woman, her weight dropped to ninety-three pounds. "I looked like someone out of Dachau," she recalls.

Physical dependency occurs when body cells are so changed by constant exposure to a drug that they become incapable of functioning properly when deprived of it. While drug researchers were once fairly positive about which drugs created physical dependencies and which did not, there is now growing uncertainty in this area. There is some question, for example, about amphetamine; though most researchers still believe it creates no physical dependency, amphetamine users do develop *tolerance* to that drug. They need increasingly larger amounts to achieve the same effects, and their systems can safely handle doses that would prove fatal to users with no tolerance.

To make the matter even more confusing, users of drugs to which no true tolerance is developed also will boost the amounts they use, even though their original dosage remains just as effective. This is called *experiential tolerance,* the desire for a higher "high," a more profound and possibly longer-lasting drug experience.

The basis of physical dependence for most drugs is not easy to understand unless you realize that the body is a highly efficient little chemical factory. It produces an extraordinary amount and an incredible number of substances for its sophisticated communication system. Chemicals dash here and there through the bloodstream delivering messages that tell organs and glands, brain cells and nerve cells what to do and how to respond to changing conditions and to both internal and external stimuli.

Basically, the body is a very conservative organism; most of its efforts are devoted to maintaining the status quo and keeping things as they are.

For this reason, when the central nervous system is continually being stimulated by a drug, the body will attempt to counteract this foreign influence. As a user of depressants is loading up with barbiturates, the brain will struggle to function normally. While the drug is telling the appropriate parts of the brain to slow down, the body's own chemical messengers are carrying a "stay-alert" message to the affected nerve tracts and brain nuclei. As the user is dumping in sedatives, the body is attempting to jam the sedative signals with its own homemade stimulants. As a result, it takes greater amounts of barbiturates to achieve the same degree of sedation.

But when the barbiturate user suddenly quits cold, the body's "stay-alert" messages continue to flow. This phenomenon is called *rebound*. The brain is stimulated to hypersensitivity. With no external sedatives to reduce this stimulation, the user experiences an "abstinence syndrome," known as *withdrawal*. For barbiturates, symptoms range from discomfort and nervousness to extreme agitation and even life-threatening convulsions.

The existence of an abstinence syndrome was long associated almost exclusively with opiate use. However, tolerance can be developed and withdrawal suffered by users of such other drugs as alcohol, amphetamines, barbiturates, tranquilizers and even caffeine. A coffee drinker with a daily multicup habit will actually suffer headaches if abruptly deprived of coffee.

A point to remember about physical dependency is the need to sustain drug use to avoid the discomfort created by rebound or withdrawal symptoms. Heroin users, in particular, can insist with good reason that they need the drug, not for any euphoria, but in order to "stay straight," to feel normal.

With all the new information we have about the mechanics of psychoactive drugs, the old concept of addiction has had to be scrapped. Originally, it referred to physical dependency as observed in narcotic addicts. Today, physicians rarely use the term *addiction*. Instead, they talk about "dependence" of one kind or another. They will call heavy cocaine use "dependence of the amphetamine type," and overindulgence in tranquilizers "dependence of the sedative-hypnotic type."

Still, *addiction* has not disappeared from the vocabulary of drug use. It has come to mean an extreme form of compulsive use. At the farthest reaches of addiction, drugs become central to the user's life. There is a preoccupation with getting and taking drugs, no capacity to limit use, and continued use in spite of obviously adverse effects. Addicts will steal to pay for drugs and will persist in drug use even when it endangers them or plainly is destroying other aspects of their lives. They will resume use after withdrawal and periods of abstinence.

Vulnerability and the Personality of Abusers

Who has to pay the steep costs of drug use? While every user is at risk, some run more risk than others, for the less controlled and more compulsive drug use becomes, the greater the exposure to danger.

"There are many people who take drugs in moderation," Tinklenberg explains, "a few people who use drugs excessively, and a very few who chronically abuse drugs." The incidence of excessive and compulsive use is statistically predictable and is roughly the same in every drug-using society. "Abusers constitute a small percentage of the total population of drug users, generally about 3 to 7 percent," according to Tinklenberg.

But while the overall incidence of abuse is predictable, the likelihood of any particular user becoming an abuser is not. This problem has fascinated behavioral scientists for years, and the attempt to discover what it is that predisposes an individual to abuse drugs—the search for the "addictive personality"—still goes on. These days, however, there seems to be a growing recognition that, among men and women who have both access to drugs and drug experience, no single set of psychiatric characteristics separates the potential abuser from the rest of the crowd.

Alan R. Lang, a professor of psychology at Florida State University, wrote the section on addictive personality in the 1983 report of the National Academy of Science's Committee on Substance Abuse and Habitual Behavior. While Lang allows that there is "no single unique personality entity," he does point to "significant personality factors" that contribute to addictions of all kinds (drugs and alcohol, food, gambling, etc.).

High on Lang's list are impulsive behavior, difficulty in delaying gratification, and sensation-seeking. He has found that an antisocial personality, nonconformist values, and little regard for goals generally valued by society indicate potential for addiction, as do a sense of alienation and great tolerance for deviant behavior. To these Lang adds heightened feelings of stress.

Looking at the differences between drug abusers and nonabusing users, other researchers have stressed the abuser's limited capacity for affection and small tolerance for frustration. Abusers also often have had more family problems and feelings of hostility toward their fathers that frequently translate into negative attitudes about authority.

There are aspects of compulsive use, however, that no personality profile can encompass. For example, many cases of drug abuse derive simply from extreme sensitivity to drug effects. Drugs, after all, do not have the same impact on all users. The range of responses is a broad one, and some users will feel far greater euphoria or experience far more relief as a result of their drug use. They will get more powerful reinforcement, build tolerance more rapidly, increase dosage more quickly, and suffer more profound distress when they attempt to limit use.

Similarly, it is hard to fit into the parameters of an "addictive personality" users who are essentially self-medicating, taking drugs to relieve the symptoms of real physical or psychological disorders. For example, a certain number of cocaine users—but relatively few—may well have discovered their own means of treating organic depression. While a physician might prescribe a more appropriate and less hazardous medication, like an antidepressant, cocaine will also raise flagging spirits. But using cocaine to control depression is a nearly certain route to abuse. There is no question that self-medicators usually take drugs that are more harmful than useful; many may need nothing more than vitamin supplements. Still, their motivation for what often becomes compulsive use is no more complex than the desire to avoid pain, insomnia and depression, to feel more energetic or control anxiety.

Drug abuse also has an external context, for drugs really cannot be separated from the rest of life. Daily demands of work and family and other essential activities compete for the drug user's time and attention. When competing activities are lacking, when users are unemployed or marginally employed and have no family responsibilities, then the potential for compulsive use is great.

The concentration of so much drug abuse in the inner city reflects both high rates of unemployment and fragile family relationships. Addiction has long been recognized as a response to the loss of status as well as the boredom that accompanies joblessness. But other factors are in play here as well. Researchers have noted "a sharply qualitative difference in opiate abuse in minority communities" and have suggested that such abuse "may be less a response designed to meet the pathology of the individual than a response designed to meet the pathology of the community." Heroin is so pervasive in certain inner-city neighborhoods that, to some extent, its use has become a symbol of belonging and is reinforced by the culture itself.

As community attitudes contribute to and reinforce abuse, so do the attitudes and actions of individuals, families and friends of users—parents, husbands, wives, lovers, roommates, colleagues and co-workers. Alcoholics Anonymous has long used the term *enabler* to denote individuals who contribute, most often passively, to another's alcohol abuse. Most drug abusers, too, have enablers in their lives.

An enabler might be a parent who fails to confront a young drug user and hopes the symptoms he or she observes will go away in time. Husbands and wives become enablers when they make scenes and elicit promises of change but invariably forgive and tolerate compulsive drug use. Friends who lend money and overlook outrageous behavior, colleagues who cover for, and co-workers who protect the abuser—all are enablers. They let the abuser off the hook, let him get away with actions or omissions that should simply not be tolerated.

Drug abuse is far from character building. Because of their preoccupation with drugs, abusers are undependable and irresponsible. The more dependent will cheat and steal, most often from family and friends. They will let you down. To put up with this kind of behavior and sustain a relationship in spite of it is, in a very real sense, to "enable" the abuser to continue compulsive drug use or to ease the movement of a nonabusing user toward drug abuse.

With all we know about vulnerability—the characteristics that reveal a predisposition toward compulsive use, the differences in drug effects, access to drugs, and the lure of self-medication—the point to remember is the essential unpredictability of abuse. You may have none or few traits of the addictive personality, plenty of activity to compete with drug-taking, little tolerance for deviance in your community, and no tolerance for irresponsibility or outrageous behavior among your friends or in your family. Still, you may well find yourself using drugs more often than makes you comfortable and unable to cut back. There are simply no guarantees. *Anyone* can become an abuser and exposed to more than the normal risk of drug use. Anyone can become dependent. No one sets out to be a drug addict.

Minimizing Risks

If in spite of all the dangers you are going to use drugs, then you should realize that you are engaged, to some extent, in risk management. This means discovering what is high-risk use for you and what is low-risk, and recognizing that there is no such thing as no-risk use.

High-risk use is not difficult to determine. Uncontrolled use, whether or not it is already demonstrably harmful, involves an unacceptable level of risk, and so does most regular use—drug-taking that occurs at predictable intervals. Low-risk use is harder to pin down. While the occasional use, in a social or intimate setting, of a substance such as marijuana would seem a low-risk activity, there are men and women whose sensitivity to the drug is so great that even this much involvement is high-risk. Nevertheless, for large numbers of users, this occasional, social use is within the low-risk range. The difficulty is keeping it there, avoiding incremental increases in dosage and finding more occasions to use, thus starting a slow slide toward compulsive use.

Learning to control drug use is not simple. Drug users do not have the cultural edge that drinkers enjoy. Most young people in our society are exposed to a wide variety of drinking behavior as they grow up. There are, as Dr. Norman E. Zinberg of Harvard's medical school describes, "various role models the alcohol user learns to avoid (an alcoholic relative) and to emulate (people who confine their drinking to cocktails before dinner)." In this way, alcohol education is acquired almost unconsciously and, as Zinberg puts it, "the informal rituals attendant upon alcohol control appear casual."

Drug-taking, too, involves a great many rituals, but rarely do they help limit use, for they are not usually based upon what Zinberg calls "limiting sanctions." Maintaining control is not simple and not just a matter of rationing intake. It includes restricting drug-taking to certain settings, being aware and prepared to deal with "untoward" drug reactions, and compartmentalizing use—segregating it from the rest of your life. The catch is that such control requires a high level of self-awareness, a capacity that is almost invariably diminished by drug use. Few users remain capable enough of honest self-scrutiny to sustain it.

Recognizing Costs

Reality is not the drug user's strong suit. Most regular-to-heavy users lie a lot. They will lie to their bosses, to their husbands or wives, friends and lovers. Most of all, they will lie to themselves.

They don't see how their lives are changing, and they don't listen to what their friends are saying. Among other costs, drugs seem to rob them of whatever capacity they had for self-appraisal.

It isn't that drug users are stupid. They just get caught up in drug-taking. Compulsive use takes over and orients the rest of their lives. There are flashes, though, moments when even users who are almost out of control catch a glimpse of how their lives have changed—moments when they look around a room and at the crew with whom they are turning on. "Hey," they may say, "who the hell are these people? Would I know them in any other context? Would I want to know them?"

It's also easy to see costs reflected in the disappointment or anguish of someone close to you. It's not as though there's any shortage of clues. Nor can users continue to ignore costs once they become high enough and obvious enough. That's when they will do whatever they can to make things right—short of giving up drugs. Unfortunately, that alternative often isn't faced until crisis time, when things fall apart—when jobs are lost or illness sets in.

By this time drugs are firmly in control. It is the early signs that drug users must recognize, signs they rarely are willing to see. They need to perceive increased use itself as involving increased risk, realize that at or near compulsive levels there is no way to avoid heavy costs.

What should you be looking for early on?

The following checklists are far from complete. Each drug has its own special signs. You can probably devise more appropriate questions of your own. But these should give you a clue to what you ought to be asking yourself about your drug use and its impact on the rest of your life.

Drug Use Checklist

1. Do you use drugs when you are alone?
2. Can you turn down a joint or a line of coke if it is offered?
3. Do you get high before seeing nonusing friends?
4. Do you need *something* (a joint, a tranquilizer or something stronger) before going to sleep?
5. Do you ever take something (a drink, a joint, a stimulant) first thing in the morning?
6. Do you feel flat and dull when you are not using?
7. How large a supply do you keep, and how concerned do you become when you start to run out?
8. Can you get through a full day without drugs and feel no distress?
9. Is it becoming difficult to pay for all the drugs you want?

Impact Checklist

1. Do you have many nonusing friends?
2. How many of your drug buddies would you want as friends if you stopped using?
3. Is there more friction in your dealings with colleagues and co-workers than before you used drugs?

4. Is your boss (teacher) less interested in your work?
5. Are your grades falling?
6. Did you get the last raise you thought you deserved?
7. Do you have less patience for detail and find it harder to master new material?
8. Do you often find yourself rereading the same page?
9. Are there times when you lose track of conversations?
10. Do you believe sex is better when you are high?
11. Are you sexually aroused less frequently?
12. Are you capable of an erection, an orgasm?
13. Are you interested in sustaining a relationship?
14. Do you feel you give as much as your partner to your marriage or relationship?
15. How does he or she feel about your drug use and your relationship?

The wrong answers are obvious. Any wrong answer should cause you to question how much control you are exercising over drug use and how other parts of your life are being affected. Some answers may indicate other problems. Clearly, if you spend a good part of your time high or often become intoxicated, miss work a lot or go off on binges, no checklist is needed.

Drugs and the Mind

Before moving on to the subject of how to get off drugs, it is important to discuss how drugs work and to define some additional terms that will be used in the chapters to come.

Basically, psychoactive drugs alter mood and affect the mind by interfering with the central nervous system's signal system. Communications is the brain's major industry; there are about 13 billion brain cells and each one may be in some kind of contact with as many as sixty thousand others. Whole systems are involved in regulating different aspects of personality and bodily functions. The limbic system, for example, which includes a number of pleasure centers and other nuclei (concentrations of brain cells), has a lot to do with regulating emotion. Because benzodiazepine tranquilizers such as Valium and Librium manage to slow down communication in this system, they can relieve symptoms of anxiety without interfering with other activity.

Drugs get to the central nervous system (the brain and the spinal column) via the bloodstream, which they enter directly (by injection into a vein) or indirectly (by injection under the skin or by absorption through membranes in the nose, in the bowels, in the lungs, or in the stomach). The speed with which drug effects are felt and the degree of the effect depend, in large measure, on how much of the drug gets to the central nervous system and how quickly it gets there. The way a drug is taken helps determine speed and extent of reaction. Certain drugs rarely are taken orally because they are not readily absorbed by the digestive tract or because, when taken orally, they can be diverted or altered in the liver. For example, little morphine survives passage through the liver, whereas codeine finds the liver a far more hospitable place, and some of it is actually converted to morphine there.

Once in the bloodstream, drugs go almost everywhere in the body, but they are effective only at those sites where they find receptors. The one exception to this "free-passage" rule is the difficulty some drugs have crossing the *blood-brain barrier* that protects the central nervous system. Penicillin cannot easily penetrate the barrier, which makes it difficult to treat infections in the brain, while heroin passes through easily, far more rapidly and in much greater force than morphine does.

In the central nervous system, most psychoactive drugs head for the *synapses,* gaps between cells in the neural pathways along which the brain signals (actually electric impulses) travel. Impulses—which may be thoughts, feelings or commands—do not simply jump these gaps before speeding on their way. Often, they must wait until chemicals (called *neurotransmitters*) stored at the synapses are released, flooding the gap and allowing them to pass across.

Drugs can stimulate or inhibit the release of neurotransmitters or keep them in place. For example, one group of neurotransmitters, the monoamines, are pumped in and out of the synaptic gap. They are essentially recycled. Cocaine and the tricyclic antidepressants appear to block the pumps, keeping the synapses flooded and impulses flowing, replaying their messages. But the body has a way to counter the buildup of monoamines by producing an enzyme that destroys them. Another type of antidepressant, the MAO (monoamine oxidase) inhibitors, interferes with this enzyme action.

Not all neurotransmitters work the same way. Some inhibit rather than convey impulses. Certain amino acids appear to function in an inhibitory manner and will reduce the rate at which impulses travel along the neural pathways. It is on these neurotransmitters that Valium acts to retard activity in the limbic system.

Although most drug action is focused at the synapses or near them, alcohol has little impact there. Instead, it appears to work on the nerve membrane, making it more flexible or fluid and reducing impulse flow in this way. The brain will counter this effect with its own chemicals that tend to make the membrane more rigid. As a result, the abstinence syndrome (alcohol withdrawal) is caused by nerve cells that are unnaturally rigid and excitable and accelerate the impulse flow.

Drug Responses and Interactions

Drugs do not strike all users the same way, and few have only a single effect. Nevertheless, we describe drugs by noting their *potency* in terms of the average effective dose—how much is required to produce the desired or primary effect in an average user. This can vary greatly among drugs that may appear quite similar, for potency is determined not only by a drug's ingredients but' also by how it is absorbed, how easily it penetrates the blood-brain barrier, what happens if it must pass through the liver, and how long it remains in the body.

A good many pharmacologists dismiss potency as unimportant, since it rarely matters much to a user if he must take 5 milligrams or 50, so long as he achieves the desired result. High potency is, in fact, often deemed more of a threat than a benefit, for a strong drug is likely to be more toxic and more dangerous to use.

Of greater significance than potency is a drug's maximum effect, the upper limit of reaction—the ultimate impact it is capable of producing in whatever amount it is taken. Caffeine, for example, will certainly stimulate the central nervous system, but no amount of caffeine will match the effect of amphetamine, just as no amount of aspirin will relieve as much pain as morphine.

For each drug and each of its effects, pharmacologists can chart a *response curve* showing the dosages needed to produce various levels of response. The steeper the slope of this curve—how quickly it rises from minimum to maximum effectiveness—the smaller the difference between the amount required to produce *any* effect and the amount that will produce *all* the effect of which the drug is capable. What a very steep slope, like those for many depressants, indicates is little margin for error and great potential for overdose.

Risk multiplies when more than one drug is used, but there are sometimes benefits to drug interaction, and it's useful to know the major ways drugs work in combination and opposition.

Potentiation. This is simply *synergism*—that is, adding one and one and coming up with more than just two—and the combined effect of drugs that interact this way is more than the sum of their individual effects.

Most often, potentiation involves drugs from two different classes that metabolize in different ways or behave differently in the bloodstream. The result of these differing actions is to release more of one or both drugs at the receptor sites.

Antagonism. The opposite of potentiation, this interaction results in *less* of an effect from a combination of two drugs than either would produce individually. It may involve drugs of the same or different classes and depends upon a number of different ways in which these drugs affect each other.

Cross-Tolerance. This does not involve the simultaneous use of two drugs, but refers instead to the use of drugs from the same class (narcotics, sedative-hypnotics, etc.) at different times. These drugs have similar effects on the central nervous system to which the body will respond in similar ways. Rebound for each is similar, and tolerance for one carries over to the other. For example, a heavy drinker may easily develop an unrecognized tolerance for sedatives and require a far larger dose than he would otherwise need to induce sleep.

Cross-Dependence. Similar to cross-tolerance, this refers to the ability of one drug to suppress the withdrawal symptoms of another. Methadone may suppress the abstinence syndrome for heroin users, and tranquilizers will do it for alcoholics. Although the use of these drugs will not, by itself, change a user's physical dependency, cross-dependence is a useful phenomenon and the basis for most of today's detoxification methods.

2

GETTING OFF SMARTLY

Getting off drugs can be one of the most difficult things you ever try to accomplish. It may involve real physical or psychological pain, possibly both. There are times when you may feel more alone than you have ever felt before, when you believe no one can know what you're going through. Yet, there are other people who do know what it's like, who are on the same road or have already traveled it. You can find help from treatment professionals, lovers, friends and family. You need not be as alone as you fear.

Getting off drugs is really no different from any of life's enterprises. You can increase or decrease your chances of success by the way you go about it. Learning how to get off drugs—getting off smartly—is the name of the game.

It's surprising that more people don't stop using drugs early in the game, for initial drug experiences are often unpleasant, different from one's expectations, or nothing much at all. Almost all narcotics beginners, for example, find the experience literally sickening. First-time marijuana smokers often don't feel anything, while the first snort of coke may have disappointingly subtle effects. Nevertheless, a good number of users still persist in taking drugs because of peer pressure, social needs or a stubborn conviction that they will eventually come to enjoy the experience. And many do.

If beginners who get no pleasure or reinforcement from drugs persist in using them, then imagine how much harder it is to quit if you enjoy using drugs, have become accustomed to that enjoyment and have developed considerable tolerance, as well. You are likely to resist quitting strongly, even if the need to quit is apparent. You may try instead to reduce use—to cut back.

It's not going to work. If you are a compulsive user, cutting back on drugs, lowering your level of consumption, won't solve the problem. If anything, it's just going to delay confronting it. You are already a high-risk user and you are not about to become a low-risk one. Abstinence is the only alternative for you. It's not any addictive traits or predispositions that preclude future drug use for you (although there may be deep emotional problems at the root of your compulsive drug-taking). On past performance alone, it should be evident that drug-taking is something you can't handle.

But you are unlikely to admit this, even if drugs start causing you real trouble. You will probably try cutting back. Even if you succeed, you haven't gained all that much. You have put off confronting the problem and prolonged your exposure to drug costs. The *nature* of your use isn't going to change (even if the amount you use varies some). The reality is that eventually you are going to have to quit, and you probably should not become involved in any elaborate scheme to ease yourself off drugs. For most users (but clearly not for users of heavy-duty sedatives or for many users of narcotics), the best approach is the simplest—to quit cold.

Now, we're talking real business. The most sensible first move you can make is to your doctor's office. You are going to need plenty of strength and stamina, so now is the time to discover if drug use has weakened you, done any physical harm. Malnutrition is common among compulsive users. Eating irregularly and erratically often results in vitamin and mineral deficiencies. Drug use may also have been masking symptoms of disease or concealing evidence of injury. You may even discover that compulsive use has been caused, at least in part, by physical or emotional illness for which a doctor can prescribe more suitable and less dangerous medication.

You may be embarrassed to talk about your drug use with your family or personal physician. And the average family doctor will not necessarily feel comfortable or competent to advise you; he or she may refer you to someone with a better understanding of your problem. Still, before you quit, it is useful to listen to what your doctor, or one with more experience handling drug dependency, has to say.

What you are likely to learn from a doctor, a therapist or a drug abuse professional is that there are four stages to the process of getting off drugs. The first is recognizing and admitting you have a drug problem, and deciding to stop using drugs. Second, there's separation from the drug itself—actually quitting—and getting through whatever brand of withdrawal your drug and your degree of dependency demand. This can be a hard time. Even if your withdrawal involves little physical distress, you may experience some severe psychological pain. Don't underrate it, but don't make too much of it either, for the worst is over fairly quickly (from a few days to a few weeks), and withdrawal has a tendency to live up to expectations (the worse you anticipate, the worse you're likely to experience). Think of this second stage as "starting off" drugs—taking the first big step. And recognize that the true challenge is the longer, third stage—making changes in your life.

Withdrawal behind you, you can start to deal with what getting off drugs is all about—making those changes in your life and in the ways you deal with yourself and the rest of the world that will enable you to remain drug-free. This is a hard period because change is hard. And though this third stage lacks the high drama of withdrawal, you are likely to feel fairly miserable much of the time, for depression may persist long after withdrawal ends. There will be a big hole in your life that drugs used to fill, and you may have trouble finding other sources of pleasure. You *will* miss drugs. Still, your expectations have a powerful influence on your feelings, and this part of the process does have its rewards. In fact, it *must* have them, for this is a time of growth and self-discovery, of taking advantage of opportunities to enrich your life and your relationships.

Can you do it on your own?

Basically, you *must* do it on your own, because nobody else will do it for you. "You alone can do it," is what they say in therapeutic communities, "but you can't do it alone." Some form of treatment is usually needed to get through this stage. For most users, it is far more important to have help at this time than during withdrawal (although medical care is essential for withdrawal from certain depressants).

Sure, you can try to go it alone. If your drug involvement is limited and your personal resources (family, home, friends, job) are strong, you may make it. But by the time most users are ready to quit, drug-taking has become too consuming and threatening. You are now well past the point at which you can get off easily. Your chances of succeeding solo are remote, and insisting upon going it alone is simply self-defeating.

Not that great individual effort isn't needed no matter how much help you get. You are the one who has to make the changes in your life, discover new ways to care for your body, to spend your time, to find pleasure, to relax, to deal with spouse, lover, family and friends.

Stage four, staying off drugs, is an open-ended part of the process. In a sense it is a continuation of stage three, getting along without drugs.

Many former users continue to count on formal supports (most often self-help groups similar to Alcoholics Anonymous) for the rest of their lives. Others phase themselves out or choose not to use support groups at all. Still, this is the time when you've got to cope with the problems created by your abstinence. Your life has changed. You may have changed for the better, but a good many people (many of them dear to you) have been accustomed to dealing with a different—a worse—you. While they may rejoice in the transformation, they can have difficulty adjusting to it. Now is the time to seek psychotherapeutic help in coming to grips with whatever emotional problems led to your drug use or were uncovered during the getting-off-drugs process.

Treatment Alternatives

The chapters on individual drugs that appear later in this book discuss ways of starting off and the specifics of withdrawal. They can help you determine the need for treatment and point out appropriate individual efforts for staying off drugs. The rest of this chapter gives you a broader look at treatment approaches and alternatives, the range of individual efforts that can help you through the change-making stage, and the role of spouses, lovers, friends and parents in the process of getting off drugs.

Although a great variety of treatments for drug abuse now exist throughout the United States, most people's options are limited to what is available locally. In any particular area, there may be many alternatives for certain abusers, and abusers of certain drugs, while relatively few for others.

The imbalance derives from an early emphasis on treatment for narcotic addiction to the exclusion of other drug dependencies and from the various factors that have tended to place drug abuse somewhere outside the area of traditional medical responsibility. These included the view, which doctors long shared with the general public, that addiction was essentially incurable. This view was buttressed by the failure of traditional psychotherapy and long-term hospitalization to produce many treatment successes. As a result, the treatment field was left open to nontraditional and innovative approaches.

A sizable public investment was made in treatment during the 1960s in response to political demands that "something" be done about heroin addicts. What we have today draws heavily on the trials and errors of that period. Treatment now ranges from minimal, short-term intervention to lifelong maintenance. Treatment may be chemically assisted, continuing administration of drugs long after withdrawal ends, or it may be drug-free, holding fast to a goal of total drug abstinence. It can be residential or outpatient; it may address specific dependencies or deal with all kinds of abuse.

The most generally useful of the new nonchemical approaches employs the concept of "self-help" as it was developed by groups like Alcoholics Anonymous and adapted to the treatment of other drug dependencies in "therapeutic communities." Many different kinds of drug abuse programs now use some therapeutic community (TC) methods and the concept of self-help. Self-help has little to do with going it alone. The "help" comes from membership in a group that provides mutual support to its members. The "self" refers to recognition of individual responsibility: "You are responsible for your drug use, and you are responsible for your cure." Emphasis is on the "here and now," on changing present behavior rather than on tracking down and coming to terms with whatever events in the past may have prompted it. Acting responsibly is the demand the group makes of the individual.

What self-help gives the drug abuser is a means of sustaining the commitment to quit drugs, an alternative social and physical setting (one that neither prompts nor tolerates drug use), a mechanism for problem-solving and self-examination, and a way to introduce and monitor new behavior. Most high-risk users find all of these useful or necessary to getting off drugs.

More and more individual physicians, therapists and private hospitals and clinics are offering treatment based on nontraditional approaches like self-help or developing innovative therapies of their own. While traditional psychotherapy, which focuses heavily on acquiring insight and an understanding of behavior, is not all that useful to someone getting off drugs, a good many psychiatrists and other conventionally trained therapists today are providing a brand of treatment that can be effective for many drug users. Most use "reality therapy" to help these people solve the specific problems that arise as they are getting off drugs.

Discovering what treatment is available to you is not always easy. Most often, you or your doctor will have to turn to a referral source—a drug abuse service or the agency that coordinates services in your state (a list of state agencies appears at the end of this book)—for local listings. Usually, treatment programs are classified rather than described, and generally listed as

- detoxification
- residential, drug-free
- outpatient, drug-free
- methadone maintenance

With the exception of methadone maintenance—which is useful only for narcotic dependency, and heavyweight dependency at that—these designations include a wide range of programs.

Detoxification

Detoxification is gradual withdrawal by physically dependent drug users, most often using decreasing amounts of either the specific drugs of dependence or cross-tolerant drugs. Although it is counted among treatment methods, detoxification is not generally considered a rehabilitative procedure. The goal of detoxification is usually too limited to provide users with the potent kind of intervention they need to stay off drugs. Yet detoxification is clearly the first step for many physically dependent users. It also offers access to other medical services, to counseling and to further treatment.

Detoxification starts by determining a user's level of tolerance (and any injuries or physical or emotional conditions) in order to establish a dosage sufficient to prevent withdrawal symptoms. Doctors are limited in their choice of drugs by federal controls; they must, for example, use either methadone (a synthetic narcotic) or a nonnarcotic psychoactive to detoxify heroin or morphine addicts. They generally prefer to use a long-acting drug to replace a shorter-acting one. In hospital programs, detoxification usually involves a 10 percent reduction in dosage each day until abstinence is achieved. At outpatient clinics, reductions tend to be smaller and the length of time needed to complete the process longer.

For multiple-drug users, detoxification can be somewhat more complicated. Narcotic abusers who take sedatives or tranquilizers are usually withdrawn from the sedatives or tranquilizers first, while receiving enough methadone to prevent narcotic withdrawal. If the user combines sedatives and alcohol, then the procedure is simpler, since these drugs are cross-tolerant, and a single drug like phenobarbital may be substituted for either or both.

Drugs are not always needed to aid withdrawal, and sometimes they are used to relieve symptoms unconnected with abstinence. For cocaine users (who do not *appear* to develop true physical dependencies), detoxification is usually achieved without any chemical support, although some users may be given antidepressants if their depression is "endogenous" (of physiological origin) and it predates their use of cocaine.

Drugs also are not the only way that withdrawal symptoms can be relieved. In recent years, acupuncture treatment has given considerable relief to some narcotic users. Acupuncture's ability to control the symptoms of narcotic withdrawal is most often attributed to neurochemical activity and the possibility that acupuncture may stimulate production of natural endorphins—the brain-produced chemical that has been called the body's own morphine.

Detoxification can be accomplished in an outpatient clinic, a hospital, or a residential treatment center. The choice depends mostly on the degree of risk and the amount of control needed to deny the patient access to drugs. Because withdrawal from sedatives and hypnotics (sleep-inducing drugs) is often severe and may be life-threatening, it rarely should be attempted outside a hospital.

For users with a strong desire to quit and little inclination to cheat, the close supervision of a hospital or residential facility may not be necessary. Still, where to detoxify is a decision that can best be made with the advice of a doctor who knows the nature and the extent of your drug dependency and can determine if other physical or emotional conditions might make it desirable for you to be carefully observed during withdrawal. Generally, detoxification is accomplished more quickly in a hospital or residential center, and is both safer and easier there.

If you are deciding for yourself which way to go, you should probably play it safe; an established detoxification unit with an experienced team in a teaching hospital would be your best bet. If you don't want to go through withdrawal on a full-time basis, check out an outpatient clinic. Make sure it has a properly certified and experienced medical staff. Look for a clinic that has been in existence for a while and one that has experience with detoxification from your particular drug of dependence.

Residential, Drug-Free

This no-nonsense, government designation is used to identify live-in treatment that offers no chemical support. Most residential drug-free programs are therapeutic communities or have adopted some therapeutic community or self-help method. Initially designed for narcotic addicts, the TC has proven remarkably flexible; most programs are now able to deal equally well with drug dependencies of all kinds and with most drug abusers who require a heavily structured environment (twenty-four-hour-a-day supervision and segregation from the rest of society) within which to break free from drugs and the patterns of behavior that reinforce drug use. The TC is often described as a "large family that provides physical and emotional support to all its members." It is a closely knit community where mutual concern is demonstrated and where "caring" relationships among residents and between residents and staff are the ideal, if not always the norm.

Yet, the TC is also a rigidly hierarchical structure where individual status is never in doubt. Newcomers, whatever their age or accomplishments in the outside world, occupy the bottom level of this hierarchy. They are expected to learn from everyone in the community. But movement up and down can be rapid, for it is based on responsibilities within the community (and there is little the community does not do for itself). Every resident has a job; they work in the kitchen, serve, clean, paint and repair. They run the offices, assist professionals who provide medical care, legal service, classroom instruction, or vocational counseling, and they act as staff aides and deputies. Good performance and attitude are quickly rewarded and reinforced with promotions. Poor performance and violations of house regulations—which start with two "cardinal rules," no violence and no drugs—are just as speedily punished.

At the top of the hierarchy are members of the TC staff, house directors and assistant directors, who are most often former drug abusers themselves, graduates of a TC who have been trained in its clinical methods. Their experience allows them to relate easily to the street experience of new residents. They know all the ways their charges are likely to resist new demands and cheat on new responsibilities. More important is their function as role models. They are proof that the TC works. The ways in which they have changed behavior—their self-assurance, sensitivity, judgment, openness and honesty—are attributes to be emulated. The use of paraprofessional staff in key clinical positions and the promotion of residents to responsible posts in the hierarchy do much to soften the line between residents and staff within the TC's rigid structure.

While clinicians do a considerable amount of individual counseling (aimed mostly at problem-solving), the basic therapeutic tool of the community is group therapy—"the mutually reinforcing self-help group," where responsibility lies as much with the group itself as with its leader. The TCs developed a rugged variety of self-help group, known as "the encounter," to break through the heavy defenses of longtime drug users. TC encounters are designed to encourage the kind of self-examination that leads to understanding and change.

TCs are remarkably successful with their graduates. In some programs, better than three fourths fulfill all three measurements of success —no use of illicit drugs, no criminal involvement, and full-time employment—according to a number of long-term outcome studies. These studies have followed graduates for as long as five and seven years after treatment, and those who are successful during their first posttreatment year appear likely to remain successful.

The trouble is that most therapeutic community residents do not hang in long enough to become graduates. Still, many who leave before this point are also successful. Follow-up studies of dropouts have found that those who remained in treatment for a year or more stand a fair chance of meeting all three indicators of success. What seems to count is not graduation or failure to graduate; it is time in treatment. The longer one remains in a TC, the better the chance of success and the greater the degree of psychological improvement as well.

The characteristics just described are found in older, established programs like Daytop Village in New York and Phoenix House in New York and California. But there are many programs that operate quite differently. No national organization accredits therapeutic communities, although there is a national association, Therapeutic Communities of America. So how can you tell if a particular therapeutic community is good for you—or any good at all? Size isn't important. But its age can tell you something. If it has been around for a while, and kept the same name, it is more likely to have a sound program, an experienced staff and a strong corps of senior residents. You should make sure that it is licensed or approved by your state's drug abuse agency, that it is a voluntary program and does not depend on physical coercion. Generally, the more effective TCs will also carefully screen candidates for admission, refer inappropriate applicants to other modalities and offer other treatment alternatives, including an outpatient program. Your safest guide will probably be your gut feelings about the place. Look it over carefully, ask to meet key members of the clinical staff, see if you are comfortable with them, if you can accept their authority and would be willing to share your problems with them. Talk with residents already in the program, if you can. Then go with the feeling—even if you have some reservations. Undue caution, at this point, may be simple avoidance.

Remember that "therapeutic community" is not a trademark. Any program can adopt the designation, and the model has been much modified. There are short-term TCs, which demand far less treatment time than veteran TC clinicians believe necessary. There have also been attempts to merge the TC with other approaches, creating a facility that offers both drug-free and chemically assisted treatment.

Today, TCs for special groups are popular. New York State has long had one operating within its prison system. Phoenix House runs a residential high school in New York and an adolescent unit in California, and a number of other residential programs have been started for young people.

In addition to drug-free residential programs that follow, strictly or otherwise, the TC approach, there are some that owe nothing at all to therapeutic communities, although they may well share certain self-help attributes. These programs will generally be shorter, anywhere from ninety days to six months, like the "recovery houses" that stick more closely to the Alcoholics and Narcotics Anonymous approach. Softer than the TC version, their therapy groups do not demand that participants reveal information they are unwilling to volunteer. These residences emphasize "reentry"—preparing to rejoin society—and aftercare, including the connection to support groups.

Religious, quasi-religious and even politically oriented groups may run residential treatment programs, too, and these often have a strong attraction for isolated drug users looking for someplace to belong. Bear in mind, though, that the kind of emotional pressures that can be brought to bear in such a community may come perilously close to "brainwashing" when the goal is not only freedom from drugs and more socially responsible behavior but also allegiance to a religious or political orthodoxy. On the other hand, if you need the company and support of a group of peers to feel comfortable and trusting, a residential program structured along those lines may be of help to you.

Finally, there are halfway houses found in most communities these days that serve as way stations for former criminal offenders or former mental patients returning to society from institutional life. These offer a stable living accommodation plus individual and group counseling and vocational training. Some drug abusers find that the combination of outpatient treatment and halfway house residence enhances their chances of getting off drugs.

Outpatient, Drug-Free

Another designation of bureaucratic origin, "outpatient, drug-free (OPDF) treatment," covers a number of approaches that have little in common with each other save that they are neither residential nor use chemical agents or other medication as part of the regular treatment regimen. OPDF services are provided by mental health agencies and multiservice drug abuse agencies. They can be found at drop-in "rap" centers that come in no standard shape or size and range from single storefronts staffed by volunteers to outreach outposts of larger agencies. Although many centers consider youngsters their target population, they serve as contact points for drug users of any age or type who are seeking help. "Free clinics" are another outlet for OPDF treatment, and many now exist to supply direct medical, dental and psychological services to drug abusers and offer drug information and counseling to young users mistrustful of both conventional drug education and traditional medical settings.

Because both counseling and group therapy are basic components of most outpatient programs, it helps to know what is meant by "counseling" and by "group therapy" in the treatment of drug abuse. Counseling might easily be called "psychotherapy" were it offered by a psychiatrist, psychologist or clinical social worker. It is the source of treatment, most often a paraprofessional clinician or "counselor," not the content, that determines the designation. Yet, neither the credentialed therapist nor the noncredentialed counselor is likely to get involved in the traditional psychotherapeutic search for insights during outpatient drug treatment. Both will probably concentrate on questions of social adjustment, relationships with family and friends, difficulties at school or on the job, and the setting of treatment goals.

Group therapy in OPDF treatment tends to be of the "mutual support, self-help" brand, although it rarely involves the potent dynamics of the TC encounter. Individuals find support for new behavior in the group, opportunities to share experiences, insights and goals, and ways to assess progress toward abstinence.

The relative importance assigned to counseling or to group therapy in outpatient programs depends almost entirely upon the origins of the particular program. Those that are part of a larger mental health system, or favor traditional mental health practices, give counseling far more weight than group therapy. Drs. Herbert D. Klebar and Franz Slobetz, of the School of Medicine at Yale, stick close to the mental health philosophy in their report on outpatient treatment for the National Institute of Drug Abuse, *Handbook on Drug Abuse*. There they maintain that "counseling is the backbone of most OPDF programs," although they do allow it can be "augmented" by group therapy.

OPDF treatment that derives from self-help programs and from residential drug-free treatment, on the other hand, tends to place priority on group therapy. Psychiatrist Mitchell S. Rosenthal, founder of Phoenix House and a pioneer in drug-free treatment, holds that "one-on-one interventions are really only ancillary to group therapy." The type of therapy he finds most useful places responsibility on the drug abuser for both his condition and his cure, and includes a major role for the former-abuser counselor, both as role model and as group leader and teacher. Rosenthal favors programs, like those of Phoenix House, that immediately bring clients together in groups and make the treatment process a collective undertaking from the outset.

While OPDF programs do not measure up to either residential programs or chemically assisted programs in long-term outcome studies, it's important to recognize that these studies were designed primarily to measure success with narcotic abusers. Abusers of other drugs and high-risk users who still are able to exercise a measure of control over their habits may find OPDF treatment far more valuable than the results of this research would indicate.

When it comes to choosing an OPDF program, there are lots of factors to consider. Programs that emphasize group therapy and family participation seem best suited for most drug abusers who have some structure in their lives—jobs, families or other responsibilities.

Programs that place less emphasis on the group process and take a mental health approach can also be useful and may well be appropriate for certain treatment candidates. If, for example, you reject the notion of uncredentialed counselors as "role models" and have reservations about their ability to lead groups, or reservations about the mutual support group itself, then you may well want to start treatment in a more traditional setting.

Comfort counts in treatment, and you should realize that your comfort within a self-help group will depend, to some extent, on the makeup of that group. A "peer group" requires peers, and a good many of today's drug abusers have had difficulty relating to groups composed primarily of more traditional drug-abusing types. Middle-class cocaine users or marijuana smokers, for example, may not feel comfortable in a group of heroin users off the street.

Finally, you should be aware that OPDF treatment is more likely to be effective if it demands regular, several-times-a-week participation in counseling or groups. It should also periodically include more intensive involvement on weekends. The measure of how well outpatient treatment is working for you is its impact on your overall behavior—not drug use alone—during the time you are away from the program.

Methadone Maintenance

Methadone maintenance, designed exclusively for narcotics addicts, involves the daily oral administration of methadone, a highly addictive synthetic narcotic, in order to suppress opioid drug craving and stave off withdrawal symptoms. There is a great variety among methadone clinics, and this is most apparent in the supportive services that all are required to provide. Some offer counseling that matches in quality the best OPDF clinics. One-on-one therapy is considered more significant than groups, and many counselors employed in methadone clinics are trained former abusers, some of whom are themselves methadone patients. Educational and vocational counseling is also available, and family counseling may be offered as well.

Methadone maintenance is not an alternative that should be considered by anyone to whom other forms of treatment offer a reasonable chance of achieving abstinence. It ought never to be a first choice, and probably should be reserved until there have been *several* treatment failures. It is best regarded as the treatment of last resort. (A more detailed discussion of methadone is included in Chapter 4, on narcotics.)

Other Treatment Methods and Aids

The kind of innovation that has characterized drug abuse treatment for the past two decades continues today. New approaches are tried and older ones studied and revised in the light of new knowledge about drug dependency and in response to new treatment needs. Although several of the strategies described below are not, by themselves, full treatment methods, they may enhance the effectiveness of other therapies.

Antagonist therapy is the use of one drug to block the effects of another by antagonist action—and not by high doses of a cross-tolerant drug like methadone. Antagonists are used exclusively to treat narcotic abusers, although some work has been done on antagonists for other drugs. What the therapy attempts to do is reverse the process of reinforcement. If a drug abuser takes heroin and experiences no pleasure, no euphoria—in fact, nothing at all—there is no longer a reward for drug-taking, and the pattern of stimulus and response can be broken (a process called "extinction"). Antagonists work by moving in on receptor sites in the brain so that the drug of abuse (most often heroin) can't make a connection. Since heroin produces its effect only by activating a receptor, it is rendered impotent by the antagonist. Narcotics and antagonists are not cross-tolerant; one cannot replace the other, so users must first be detoxified before starting antagonist therapy.

Although cyclazocine, the first antagonist tried, will block heroin for about twenty-four hours, its side effects include weakness, tiredness, irritability, tension, and reported instances of "weird" thoughts and "fuzzy thinking." Naloxone has none of these side effects, but it is too short-acting to be of use. At present, naltrexone is being tried. It seems relatively free from side effects, lasts twenty-four hours and is effective when taken orally (which naloxone is not).

Antagonist therapy has, thus far, shown little ability to retain patients. The reasons for this may include the lack of any inducement (like methadone's "glow") that might cause someone to take it and the lack of any penalty (like withdrawal) for not taking it. Not widely available, antagonist therapy is most often provided through a methadone or outpatient, drug-free clinic.

Behavior modification treatment attempts to reduce the reinforcing properties of drugs or create new patterns of behavior that make it impossible, unpleasant or unreasonable to take drugs—to attack the "conditioned response" responsible for compulsive drug use. One approach is to "desensitize" users by weakening the stimulus (the trigger mechanism of the conditioned response). Psychologists have reproduced "cues" (sights and sounds, settings and situations to which drug-taking is the response) and employed various means, including relaxation techniques and hypnosis, to prevent users from responding as they have been conditioned to respond—with anxiety and drug-taking.

"Counterconditioning" procedures are used not to weaken reinforcement but to create an aversion to the response. Drugs that cause vomiting, such as apomorphine and ipecac, have been given with a user's drug of dependence to recondition him, so that his response to drug-taking is nausea. Electric shock has also been used to make drug-taking unappealing. More recent is a technique known as "covert conditioning." This requires patients to replay in their head the entire process that leads to drug-taking, from the moment the initial craving is felt. They are then asked to imagine decidedly unpleasant consequences for drug-taking— violent illness in vivid colors. When they think about avoiding drugs, they are encouraged to imagine only pleasant scenes. The technique has worked on its own and in combination with hypnosis and chemical aversion techniques.

Hypnosis has been used in counterconditioning to link drug-taking with nausea, anxiety and other unattractive results. It has also provided substitute gratification for detoxification patients, allowing them to reexperience a "good trip" or satisfying drug reaction and relieving some of the depression and joylessness that accompany withdrawal.

Contingency management is a simple behaviorist carrot-and-stick technique, in which the carrot gets most of the attention. Desirable behavior is "bought" with whatever rewards are appropriate to the setting. Prisoner-addicts were found by one study to show far greater interest in group therapy and educational programs when participation bought points toward early release. In methadone programs, the right to take medication home has been used as the payoff for regular appearance at counseling sessions.

Contingency contracting is a new treatment technique that more or less uses self-blackmail to keep participants in outpatient treatment. On entering a program for cocaine users, participants "contract" to stick with the treatment and stay clear of cocaine for a set period of time (usually three months). Should they violate that contract, the clinic will mail letters written by the participant at the time the contract was signed. Letters contain confessions of drug use, and they can go to employers, professional associations, licensing boards, families, newspapers, or wherever else they will cause real trouble. They may also contain hefty contributions to causes that the participant violently opposes. A Reagan Republican might write a check to the Americans for Democratic Action, or a member of the ACLU to the American Nazi Party. A one-year test of the contracting process was run at two clinics operated by the University of Colorado School of Medicine. The results: more than 80 percent of the contract participants made it through three months of treatment with no use of cocaine, while no noncontracting participant stayed clean for more than four weeks and only one was in the program after two months.

Electrotherapy looks pretty mysterious. The "black box" is what users call a device developed by Scottish surgeon Margaret Patterson. She calls her approach to rapid narcotics detoxification NeuroElectric Therapy (NET). A boxlike device, which clips onto a user's belt, sends an electric current through wires to tiny electrodes placed over the mastoid bones behind the ears. The technique resembles, and indeed is based upon, the use of acupuncture with electrical stimulation.

NET uses prolonged periods of electrical stimulation (continuously during the initial state of treatment) at very low levels and is considered most effective when backed up with counseling, remedial services and a stable home environment. With detoxification patients in Europe (including Eric Clapton and Keith Richards), Dr. Patterson claims a 98 percent success rate. Peter Townshend credits her with pulling him out of a two-year bout with alcohol and drugs. Dr. Patterson contends that the device can be used for rapid withdrawal from *any* drug simply by varying the frequency of the electrical impulse.

Making Treatment Choices

Do you need treatment?

For the period of withdrawal, you should probably get a physician's advice about treatment if your drug of abuse produces serious physical dependency. But further treatment depends on a great many factors other than your drug of choice or degree of dependency. You also need to consider responsibilities to your family or your job or the demands of school or college.

Certainly, you want the most appropriate and useful kind of help. But the most appropriate should also be the least intrusive that will work for you. In general, the more demanding forms, such as long-term residential treatment, are most useful for younger users and for users with less social

Table 1. Abuse Potential by Drug Class: Risks and Consequences

	Opioids[1]	Sedatives[1]	Tranquilizers[2]	Stimulants[3]	Hallucinogens[4]	PCP	Marijuana[5]	Inhalants	Cocaine	Alcohol
Acute intoxication leading to life-threatening overdose	Yes	Yes	Possible (esp. if taken with alcohol)	Possible	Rare	Yes	None documented	Yes	Yes	Yes
Relative potential for dependence/addiction	High	Moderate to high	Low	High	Low	Low-high[6]	Low to moderate	Low	High	Moderate
Risk of progressive organ damage, possibly irreversible	Low[7]	Low to moderate	Low	Moderate	Low	High	Low	High	Moderate	High
"Flashbacks"	No	No	No	No	Yes	Yes	Yes	No	No	No
"Panic reactions" (acute toxic psychosis)	No	No	No	Yes	Yes	Yes	Yes	No	Yes	No
Persistent psychotic reaction	No	Yes	Possible	Yes	Yes	Yes	Possible	Possible	Possible	Yes
Risk of serious social dysfunction or "life-style consequences"	Very high	High	Low	Low to moderate	Low	High	Low to moderate	Low to moderate	Very high	Moderate to high
Organic brain syndrome (severe or long-lasting adverse mental or behavioral consequences)	Low to moderate	Low to moderate	Low	Moderate to high	High	Very high	Low	High	Moderate to high	High

1. Barbiturates, Quaaludes, and other "neo-barbiturates"
2. Valium, Tranxene, Ativan, etc.
3. Amphetamines and related stimulants (e.g., Preludin, Ritalin)
4. LSD, mescaline, "mushrooms," DOM, DOB, MDA, MDM, etc.
5. Marijuana and other Cannabis derivatives such as hashish and hash oil
6. Varies greatly: seems to have a particular abuse potential in adolescents and certain unstable adults
7. Low organ damage assumes the drug is given in a pure, known dosage form under sterile conditions to otherwise healthy individuals

stability (including fewer responsibilities and commitments). Older users with more in the way of personal resources are usually better candidates for less demanding treatment, the kind available at outpatient programs.

To give users some idea of treatment needs, a series of tests has been adapted from self-assessment scales developed by Dr. Stephen M. Pittel of the Wright Institute in California. (Dr. Pittel's scales are based on treatment referral manuals he has prepared for drug abuse service agencies that are used in more than thirty states.) The personal resources test can help you determine if your resources are strong, limited or weak. Used with the drug involvement tests in each drug chapter, it can help you decide what treatment options to consider first.

Personal Resources Test

	YES	NO
1. Do you have close friends you can count on?	—	—
2. Are you a regular member of a nondeviant social group?	—	—
3. Do you believe your family is supportive?	—	—
4. Do you live alone or with nonusers?	—	—
5. Are you a high school graduate?	—	—
6. Do you have a regular job you like?	—	—
7. Have you used drugs for less than one year?	—	—
8. Have you used drugs for less than three years?	—	—
9. Have you decided to get off drugs by yourself, with no external pressures?	—	—
10. Are you prepared to make significant changes in your life?	—	—

Count only your Yes answers. Seven or more means your personal resources are *strong*. Between six and four means they are *limited,* and fewer than four means they are *weak*. With only limited or weak personal resources, chances are you will need some form of treatment to quit—no matter what the extent of your drug involvement.

If you have strong personal resources, you may be able to get off drugs with no treatment at all, as long as your drug involvement is no more than moderate. If involvement is serious, however, you'd best think about some modest kind of intervention, like group therapy or counseling at an outpatient clinic. If your resources are only limited, then you should consider more structured or demanding treatment, no matter how moderate your drug involvement. You can't reasonably expect to make the kinds of changes drug abstinence demands on your own. You should seriously consider a therapeutic community if your personal resources are weak and you are seriously or profoundly drug-involved.

This personal resources test can only give a crude indication of what your resources might be. It is not a valid diagnostic instrument, and you will surely be able to get a much more accurate reading on both your resources and your treatment options from an experienced drug abuse counselor.

You should also realize that the test is designed primarily for adults. It will not give a worthwhile readout on an adolescent's resources, since these depend so much on the nature of the family and individual resources of its other members. However, it is not difficult to find trained counselors and youth workers in the school and in the community who can readily determine a young person's treatment needs, and there are a great many options for adolescents today, including school and after-school programs, day-long programs and special residential programs.

In addition, bear in mind that it is impossible to tell with any certainty what kind of treatment will prove successful with any given individual. There are just too many variables at work—type of drug, degree of dependence, numerous personal resources, age, social setting and environment, and underlying psychological or physical problems, to name some of the more obvious. Many of today's cocaine users, for example, look like excellent candidates for abstinence when motivated to get off drugs. Many hold good jobs and derive satisfaction from their work; they may come from stable family backgrounds, be well educated and have friends who are not drug users; they may even understand the dynamics of drug abuse. But all this does not automatically mean they will be able to get off drugs with little effort or that a specific type of treatment will work for them. When it comes to drugs, there are no guarantees.

Finally, it's important to recognize that treatment decisions are not easily made, but they can be easily changed. It is always possible to move from one program to another—and probably helpful to start with a less demanding one, since the first hurdle is accepting the need for *any* form of treatment. If you are dealing with professionals and conscientious drug abuse workers, they won't let you make any more mistakes than you must, and will try to guide you to the help you need.

Individual Efforts

Drug abuse may be a disease, but it does not yield to treatment alone. The traditional medical model—which demands little from the patient except payment and submission to therapy—doesn't work all that well. No matter how much treatment or what kind of treatment you opt for, there are efforts you must still make for yourself.

To get off drugs, with help or without it, means making real changes. Most often, these include

- overcoming conditioning, breaking the pattern of stimulus and response that leads to drug-taking
- restoring your body, taking care of it, strengthening it, using and enjoying it in new ways
- finding alternative activities, interests, pleasures and associations
- learning to handle anxiety and depression
- dealing with the changing relationships that are the result of both your drug abuse and your efforts to quit

Overcoming Conditioning

Drug-taking is a conditioned response. It is learned behavior. Men and women are conditioned, much as laboratory animals are, through reinforcement by euphoria or other pleasurable drug effects. There is also "secondary conditioning" that links drug use with specific settings or stimuli.

Drug experts agree that three variables determine how much control a user is able to exercise. These are the nature of the drug itself, the user's "set" (personality and attitudes about drug use), and the "setting" (the physical site and social framework within which drug use occurs).

Behavioral psychologists include in "setting" all the sights and sounds, smells and situations that may prompt drug use. These are the stimuli or "cues" that trigger the drug-taking response, and a major task of getting off drugs is learning how to deal with them. Suppose, for example, that you often snort coke or smoke a joint after work. You do this with a group of friends from your office or shop, in a back storeroom, a nearby park or the apartment of a friend. Now, there are a number of ways you can rearrange your life to avoid the after-work setting that is so strongly connected with drug-taking. You can leave for home as soon as work ends, choosing a route that will not take you past the drug-taking site. You can support this decision by signing up for a course or committing yourself to volunteer work that starts soon after working hours. Schedule other activities that start when work ends.

It will take time to recognize all the cues that trigger drug-taking, all the places, associations and activities that prompt you to use drugs. Avoidance is the best strategy, and you can reinforce new patterns by rewarding or punishing yourself for how well you steer clear of settings and avoid cues associated with drugs. If you do well, buy yourself a present. If you've been doing a bad job of it, assign yourself penalties— say, twenty-five pushups.

There are certain situations connected with drug use that you will be unable to avoid. If you feel nervous when you meet new people and this, in the past, has been a triggering situation, you needn't become a hermit to remain drug-free. Behavioral psychologists believe one way to handle this is through "cue exposure," which starts with discovering which situations are the most powerfully suggestive and which are the least powerful. Once you have established a hierarchy of cues, you can begin cautiously exposing yourself to those at the low end of the scale. If you overcome the prompting of these situations, you will feel more confident about confronting the more powerfully suggestive ones. In "desensitization" exercises, behaviorists use hypnosis and relaxation techniques to help weaken the effects of these cueing situations.

While cue exposure is a useful way of dealing with all kinds of compulsive behavior (overeating, gambling, drinking, smoking, etc.), there are limits to how it can be applied by drug users. Seeking out drug buddies and returning to the sites of drug use, handling drugs and drug paraphernalia are not activities that have a legitimate place in your new abstinent life. Exposing yourself to those situations because you feel some need to test yourself and prove you are strong enough to resist temptation is a mistake. Dr. Mark Gold, research director at Fair Oaks Hospital in New Jersey, believes a user who tries this is "orchestrating his own relapse."

Another means you can employ to help overcome conditioning is *aversion*. Since what you know and feel about drugs has considerable influence on your behavior, now is the time to dig out all the material about the downside of drug use that you either avoided reading before or only glanced at and dismissed. There's plenty of information on how men and women have destroyed their careers, families, lungs, livers and sex lives through drug use. Read about toxic effects, drug fatalities, and drug-induced psychoses. These "horror stories" can help weaken conditioning.

Among the techniques recommended by Dr. Peter Miller, who runs the Sea Pines Behavioral Institute in South Carolina and is coauthor of *Self-Watching* (a book about fighting addictions, habits and compulsions), are ways of talking to yourself and practicing self-restraint. Dr.

Miller advocates what he calls "controlled self-talk" that avoids negative thinking, self-doubts, and excuses. His rule for self-restraint is to "immediately impose a ten-minute delay on any decision regarding the temptation." This allows time for cravings to subside, and lets you consider the consequences of your actions so you can make a more logical decision.

Restoring Your Body

Drugs do not exact physical costs from everyone, but plenty of users find themselves run-down, malnourished and in generally awful shape when they finally decide to quit. Alcoholics and narcotic and stimulant abusers are likely to have dietary deficiencies and should consult a doctor. But for most former users, taking a vitamin and mineral supplement —a regular over-the-counter preparation that ensures minimum daily requirements are met—is probably a good idea.

Mood level can be affected by diet, and plenty of red meat can help relieve the depression that so often follows prolonged drug use. Certain drugs, such as PCP and amphetamines, that remain in the system for some time after use ends can be speeded out of the body with cranberry juice.

Getting off drugs involves the development of a whole new self-image, and this has to include a new awareness of your body. It's hard to develop positive feelings about yourself when you are run-down, overweight and out of shape. Exercise is the answer, and it will do lots more than just put you back in condition. It opens the way to a number of alternative activities. It's a means of expending energy and relieving feelings of tension and anxiety, and it, too, can raise mood levels.

Heavy, physically taxing exercise like weight lifting or body building is a good way to relieve tension. Sustained exercise like slow jogging and cycling, which puts a severe demand for oxygen on the body, helps counter depression. Long-distance running works particularly well for cocaine users; the "runner's high" that results resembles the high induced by coke.

Probably the most important aspect of your physical reconditioning is learning how to relax your body. There are a number of ways you can do this. Dr. Miller recommends a method that calls for progressively relaxing each set of muscles, from your toes to your face, by first tensing and then slowly loosening them. Stretching exercises for the back and shoulders can also help you relax and are taught by most physical therapists.

Transcendental meditation, which goes a bit beyond mere muscle control, is one means a number of users have found to deal with tension. Another is biofeedback. Often used as an aid to drug abuse treatment, biofeedback converts the electrical activity of muscles and brain waves or even body temperature into tones you can hear or visual displays you can watch. By observing what actions will alter the tone or the display, you can learn to control your body's responses.

Electromyography (EMG), which translates muscle activity into tones, is relatively simple to use. A few sessions are all it takes before you are able to loosen tightened muscles at will. This device has helped relieve the distress of withdrawal, and Drs. David E. Smith and Donald R. Wesson, who have used it with multidrug abusers in San Francisco, feel the kind of mastery it allows "is of great importance to an individual who has relinquished control of his/her feelings . . . to drugs."

Alternative Activity

What you need is activity that replaces not only drug-taking but all the time-consuming business that goes with it. Lethargy is the enemy. It gives you more opportunity to miss drugs and allows depression to settle in.

Exercise, of course, is one alternative, and there are ways to parlay your concern for a better body into a richer social life. Hiking, biking and running offer the opportunity to take part in races, excursions and other group activities. More adventurous undertakings, such as rock climbing, mountaineering and white water canoeing, can give you a risk-taking high, build confidence and expand your social contacts.

But you aren't about to become involved in anything so demanding the day after you quit drugs. In fact, the initial problem will be generating enough enthusiasm to move out of your chair and out of the house. Start simply. Ask yourself what you used to enjoy before you started using drugs, what you wanted to learn or what places you wanted to visit. You may need something that can hold your attention while making only minimal demands on you. Many users find it easiest at first to become involved in religious or political activity.

Build up to alternatives that are more challenging. Now may be the time to study cooking or photography. Mastering a new skill will give your ego a sizable and needed boost. Consider signing up for additional college or graduate credits; join a theater group or a choral society. The point is to fill your life and expand it as well.

Dealing with Anxiety and Depression

Handling stressful situations is a major challenge of getting off drugs, and one you shouldn't rush to confront. Wait until you feel fairly comfortable with your new abstinence. Even then, you may find that anxiety will trigger drug cravings. What you can do is use the "cue-exposure" strategy to cope, developing a hierarchy of situations and starting with those that are least threatening and will produce the weakest drug-taking stimuli.

If you are uncomfortable in social situations, feel insecure and ill-at-ease, it is not only the drug cue you must deal with but the source of the anxiety itself. One way is to initiate new behavior by "acting as if." If you try, modestly at first, to behave as though you were not insecure and uncomfortable, you may find others responding to you in ways that will actually reduce your level of anxiety.

In addition to its other benefits, exercise can also help you deal with anxiety, which results when you respond to a "flight-or-fight" signal from your brain. The body starts preparing to battle or flee, and all that surplus energy keeps you wound up and tense. Heavy, energy-demanding exercise is one way to wind down. Relaxation techniques, meditation, muscle relaxation, and biofeedback also help.

Depression thrives on inactivity. You won't feel like doing much when you are down. You won't really believe that anything is going to raise your spirits, either. This becomes a problem when drug use ends. Not that users are invariably depressed at this point, but many do feel a lack in their lives once they have given up the single most pleasure-producing activity they have known. What doctors call *anhedonia,* the inability to enjoy yourself or to experience pleasure, can result. The trick is to deny your expectations and start moving, start finding alternatives to drug use.

In time, you'll find that one useful tactic is to plan your week in advance. Fill your calendar with assignments and appointments; plan when you will go to the gym, when you will go to the library, meet friends at the movies or a restaurant. Don't leave empty periods of time for depression to claim.

It might also help to start considering what your requirements for happiness are. What do you need to enjoy life? Are your demands reasonable and appropriate ones? This is something you might want to discuss with your counselor or therapist or to raise in group therapy. It might be worth talking over with your spouse or lover.

Changing Relationships

A good many drug users tend to think of themselves as relatively helpless individuals. Indeed, they spend so much time feeling guilty or embarrassed by their behavior that they may well become easy to manipulate and control. If this is true of you, then getting off drugs will result in some major changes in the way you deal with friends and family, particularly the person closest to you—your husband, wife or lover.

This is not a good time, however, to think about changing basic relationships themselves—about breaking up, separating or divorcing, or even about changing jobs. That may follow, of course, but you've more than enough to handle already.

But you will have to deal with drug buddies—the friends and acquaintances you got high with—and it's easiest simply to drop them. No explanations are necessary. With people you are closer to, with real friends who may also use drugs, future relations will depend upon how they react to your decision to stop using drugs and how well you handle the situation. Don't be ambivalent about it. Make it clear that you are serious: You no longer use drugs and you expect them to respect that choice.

You may well need support from your friends, spouse or lover, and family to get off and stay off drugs. If you have succeeded in concealing your drug use from them until now, this may be the time to come out of the closet and let the people who care for you know the truth and help you. You may even make a formal contract with your spouse, lover or family (a variation of contingency contracting), publicly pledging to quit in exchange for their involvement in the process. This might mean allowing them to control your finances and deny you funds for drugs or supervise your activities and deny you opportunities for drug-taking.

Recognize that you are going to feel angry and resentful part of the time, and you've got to avoid taking this out on the people you care about and who are doing their best to help you. That's why it is so useful to involve them in whatever kind of treatment you choose. In many ways, it's roughest on them—because there's only so much they can do for you.

Notes for the Drug User's Partner or Parent

Like it or not, you are a part of the problem, and you must be a part of the solution, too.

If you yourself use drugs, then there's not much you can do to help your partner or child get straight or stay straight without dealing with your own drug use. Hard as it is to get off drugs by yourself, the problems increase geometrically when two are involved, for you constantly reinforce each other's drug use and can frustrate each other's efforts to quit.

If you are not a user, then you've got to examine the ways in which you might be contributing to—*facilitating* or *enabling* is what the experts call it—your partner's or child's drug use. A number of treatment organizations can help you deal with this problem once you realize it exists. For parents, there are many groups that have formed during the past several years to provide mutual support and information. These can be located through your local or state drug abuse agency. Although Al-Anon (part of Alcoholics Anonymous) is intended to aid families and partners of alcoholics, it is sometimes helpful when the problem is other drug use. More difficult to find than Al-Anon are branches of Nar-Anon (connected to Narcotics Anonymous), Pil-Anon (linked to Pills Anonymous), or Families Anonymous, which also will help with drug problems.

Understand that if your partner or child is using drugs regularly and you have not confronted the situation in any significant way, then you are indeed a party to it. No matter how much you may have disapproved, you have tolerated it. So, what do you do once you decide to take some responsibility for the situation?

Parents have a somewhat easier job than husbands, wives or lovers when it comes to convincing a user to quit. Not that children automatically respond to parental wishes. In fact, it usually takes a lot of time and patience to get the message across. It may also require some outside help, and since youngsters will often listen more readily to another adult in the family than they will listen to their parents, a trusted relative or older brother or sister might be called in before you reach out for professional assistance. Still, parents have controls that partners do not, and if they are willing to use all their muscle, they can make and enforce a demand of drug abstinence.

Husbands, wives and lovers must stick to persuasion. Threats are useful only if you intend to follow through, and that is a last resort. You can point out dangers and involve other concerned friends, but if the user refuses to quit and rejects the idea of seeking help, then your choices are limited.

You may choose to stick with your user even though he (or she) isn't yet willing to get straight. This is not an unreasonable decision if you care for him and if his drug use is still under control. But the issue will remain, and you must make it clear that you want him to quit and that you are no longer willing to support his use either financially or emotionally.

When your partner does choose to quit, however, you must realize that he may not succeed. It might take several attempts to get straight. There may be several periods of drug abstinence, each followed by relapse. As much as you love him, it will be hard to contain your anger when he fails, and you have got to make your own decisions about when to bail out of the marriage or relationship.

Getting off drugs is rough on both of you. There will be lots of anger flying around. Users are generally angry at the world for getting them into this predicament (even though they may be well aware of where the fault truly lies). Your drug-using lover or spouse may be angry with you (for not stopping him sooner), with his parents, or his employer or anyone else on whom he can pin some blame. He may respond to legitimate concern with hostility, convinced that you don't trust him and are checking up on him.

Before all of this gets under way, it's good to sit down and talk things out. Offer your support, but make clear how you feel—how lonely and hurt his drug-taking has made you feel. With luck, he'll be honest, too, and share some of his fears and frustrations. By sharing your feelings, becoming closer, you stand a better chance of making it through together. While you should participate in whatever treatment he agrees to accept, you shouldn't expect it to resolve problems in your relationship. These must wait until after drugs are no longer the issue.

Participation in a treatment program can help you deal with what he is going through. Many programs have groups that allow you to share your experiences with others who are also involved in helping a partner get off drugs. Programs for youngsters may include groups for parents, where they can work out with other parents ways of dealing with children in treatment and ways of helping the process along at home.

In general, you can help your spouse, lover or child best by supporting his or her individual efforts. You should be aware of drug-taking cues and help avoid them—not by saying, "Come right home after work," but by suggesting, "Why don't you meet me at the movies?"

Helping someone you love to fill the empty part of his life may be extremely frustrating at first, especially when he resists even the simplest effort to get him moving. But it can bring you closer together. You may well find new activities that both of you enjoy. There are dozens of ways to help and support a partner—and more specific issues are covered in the individual drug chapters. But you should keep in mind that what he needs least from you is more guilt, resentment or anger. He may already have more than he can handle. That doesn't mean swallowing anger when you feel it, but you should try to work out your problems in ways that underline your love and concern.

PART TWO

Getting Off Your Drug of Abuse

3

COCAINE

Cocaine has always been a mercurial drug. A century ago it became popular overnight and lost favor just as suddenly. Recently patterns of use and public perception of cocaine have undergone radical change. Just twenty years ago, cocaine was a rare drug of abuse, favored by a small number of artists and musicians, the convention-flouting rich and some narcotic addicts who combined it with heroin. Today it permeates almost every social and economic level of society. About 20 million Americans have tried it, and according to a survey by the polling firm of Yankelovich, Skelly and White, one out of every four adults in the United States knows someone, whom he or she considers "close to me," who has used cocaine.

More frightening is the belated recognition that cocaine is addicting. While it produces none of the physical symptoms of narcotic withdrawal, continued use—by snorting, smoking or shooting—can and does lead to severe dependency. Drug experts, while still unsure about the *kind* of dependency and tolerance cocaine produces, do agree that it can be a very dangerous drug. "Addiction is compulsion, loss of control and continued use in spite of the consequences," says Dr. David Smith, director of the Haight-Ashbury Free Medical Clinic in San Francisco. "Cocaine is very addicting." In the *Journal of Psychoactive Drugs,* Dr. Ronald Siegel, a faculty member of UCLA's School of Medicine, who has extensive experience with cocaine users, has written of "cocaine smoking withdrawal," which he maintains ". . . is clearly evident in abrupt cessation from chronic high doses." Dr. Siegel has witnessed the syndrome in regular snorters, too. And according to Dr. Mitchell Rosenthal of Phoenix House, "Of all drugs, cocaine is the most difficult to deal with."

Clearly we have come a long way in little time. The notion that cocaine is an addictive drug would have been dismissed by most users and researchers only a few short years ago. Socially, cocaine was the most glamorous recreational drug of the 1970s, used by stars of sports, film, music and industry. Its admirers argued that it was a "soft" drug that could be taken for years with little threat of danger either to the individual user or to society.

In retrospect, cocaine seems to have been a drug whose time had come. The feelings it produced—euphoria, energy, alertness and power—meshed perfectly with the tenor of the times, for this was an era of success-stressed, pleasure-packed, go-get-'em, everything-can-be-mine living. Cocaine became so accepted by the American public that Johnny Carson could joke about it on network television and the audience would laugh along knowingly, as if sharing some guilty secret.

There were, of course, casualties—users who couldn't handle the drug, who became consumed by it. But they were regarded as isolated cases. Most users believed that "it can't happen to me." And who could blame them? Coke seemed to be everywhere—in homes, schools, offices, factories. It carried little social stigma.

But with the 1980s came danger signs. Richard Pryor almost killed himself in an accident that occurred after a binge of coke smoking. "Ten million mothers freebase," he later joked, trying to make comedy out of tragedy, "and I blow up." Pro football player Don Reese, in a startling confession, admitted that cocaine "has dominated my life, one way or another, almost every minute since [1974]. Eventually, it took control and almost killed me. It may yet." Reese's former NFL colleague, Mercury Morris, was convicted of dealing coke—something he needed to do, he claimed, to support his habit. Morris is now serving a twenty-year jail term.

But it's not just the famous. Today, there is evidence of wreckage throughout society—failed careers, broken families and relationships, bankruptcy, prison terms, physical and emotional injury and even death.

While a great many Americans still find pleasure in occasional use of cocaine and are able to sustain this pattern and avoid high-risk use or dependency, others plainly cannot. Far from the relatively harmless substance it once was thought to be, cocaine has proven to be one of the most dangerous of drugs—often harder even than heroin to get off and stay off.

Early Use/Present Trends

When the Italian explorer Amerigo Vespucci reached the New World, hard on the heels of Christopher Columbus, he found that the natives of the South American mainland derived great satisfaction and refreshment from leaf-chewing. The greenery Vespucci observed being eaten in what is now northern Venezuela most likely came from the Bolivian coca plant, *Erythroxylon coca,* which thrives in the upper Amazon basin and the Andean highlands.

Among the Incas of Peru, the use of coca leaves was generally restricted to members of the court and other royal favorites. The practice also had a good deal of religious significance to the Incas, which at first prompted Spanish priests to prohibit it. The attitude of the church changed drastically, however, once it became clear that chewing coca leaves greatly increased the efficiency of Indian workers.

Cocaine, the principal alkaloid derived from coca leaves, was first successfully produced at Göttingen University, Germany, in 1860, and enthusiasm for the drug mounted sharply during most of the remainder of the nineteenth century. A potent local anesthetic, cocaine was also widely touted as a treatment for hay fever, catarrh (inflammation of mucous membranes) and the common cold. A famous booster of the new drug was Sigmund Freud, who was interested in the stimulant properties of cocaine and saw it as a means of overcoming depression, morphine addiction, writer's block and alcoholism. Freud ingested the drug himself, and in *On Coca,* his review of the literature on coca and cocaine, described how "a small dose lifted me to the heights in a wonderful fashion."

Soon cocaine was available in patent medicines and cordials—Angelo Mariani's wine and cocaine combination was endorsed by Pope Leo XIII —as well as in ointments, powders, sprays, lozenges, cigarettes and suppositories. John Styth Pemberton of Georgia introduced his French Wine of Coca, the Ideal Nerve Tonic and Stimulant, in 1885, and the following year produced the soft drink Coca-Cola, using a syrup made with both coca and caffeine.

But cocaine's popularity was short-lived. By 1890, doctors realized that cocaine not only was incapable of curing morphine addiction but had considerable abuse potential of its own. Freud's own attempts to wean a colleague from narcotics with cocaine failed, and the American surgeon William Stewart Halsted became one of the first victims of cocaine dependence, the result of experiments he carried out on himself.

The drug also lost some of its cachet as use spread down the social ladder. Lower-class drinkers began substituting cocaine for alcohol or mixing the two. Bars of the time sold a vicious combination of whiskey and coke—one pinch to one shot. By 1891, there were two hundred cases of death from cocaine poisoning, and a few states and local communities adopted ordinances to regulate its use—though this didn't stop the Coca-Cola Company, formed in 1892, from promoting its coca and caffeine soft drink as a "tonic for elderly people who are easily tired."

What did the most to end cocaine's popularity in America were rumors of widespread use by blacks. Fears of cocaine-inspired defiance and crime spread through the South. "So far, the evidence does not suggest that cocaine caused a crime wave," writes David Musto in *The American Disease*, "but rather the anticipation of black rebellion inspired white alarm. Anecdotes often told of super-human strength, cunning and efficiency resulting from cocaine. One of the most terrifying beliefs about cocaine was that it actually improved marksmanship. Another myth, that cocaine made blacks unaffected by mere .32 caliber bullets, is said to have caused Southern police departments to switch to .38 caliber revolvers." Pressured by Southern politicians, the Coca-Cola Company removed the cocaine from its cola in 1903.

Rigid controls were finally clamped on the sale and use of cocaine by the Harrison Act of 1914, which classified the drug as a narcotic and caused its use to drop sharply for decades to come. Indeed, cocaine did not again become a common drug of use in the United States until the 1970s, when government restrictions on amphetamines were being stiffened. Since certain effects of cocaine and amphetamines are quite similar —both produce energy, alertness and euphoria—it is likely that the difficulty of acquiring one sparked more demand for the other. In addition, as Dr. Ronald Siegel says, "As we moved into the Seventies there was a time of dropping back into society, and a concern with production and productivity. And cocaine was rediscovered as a recreational drug of choice because it fit very nicely into the Protestant ethic and the spirit of capitalism. It was a drug for producers and for producing."

At first, cocaine seemed to recognize no barriers of class, race or income. Between 1976 and 1982, however, use not only accelerated but became more stratified. In New York State, the number of first-time and regular users nearly tripled during this period. Patterns of use changed, too, with a fivefold increase in *both* once-a-month and more-than-ten-times-a-month users. So did the cocaine constituency. Racially, the mix changed from approximately 84 percent white, 10 percent black and 7 percent Hispanic to 92 percent white, 7 percent black and less than 1 percent Hispanic. While women made up only one third of the cocaine-using population in 1976, they had become the majority by 1981. And the rich were now more likely to do coke than the poor. Although better than half the regular users in 1976 had annual incomes below $15,000, by 1981 only one third had incomes that low, while users with incomes greater than $25,000 a year more than doubled their proportion of the user population, from 21 percent to 44 percent.

By 1981, cocaine use had grown to epidemic proportions and nearly fifty tons of cocaine a year were reaching U.S. dealers from South America, most of it in the form of cocaine salts (hydrochloride), about 90 percent pure. Contributing to the huge profits of this ever-growing illicit industry—with total sales estimated at better than $32 billion a year—is the cutting, or adulterating, of cocaine before distribution to street dealers, a process that increases the bulk by 400 to 800 percent, while reducing purity to between 22 and 11 percent. Adulterants may be simple fillers such as milk sugar or quinine, stimulants such as amphetamine or ephedrine, or local anesthetics such as lidocaine or procaine.

With this coke blizzard came changing patterns of use. While most regular users (about 80 percent according to Dr. Ronald Siegel) only snort coke, as the 1970s gave way to the 1980s an increasing number discovered the pleasures and dangers of smoking it in a highly potent chemically altered form called "freebase." A smaller group took to intravenous injection of the drug. Whatever the method of administration, about 11 percent of the American population had used cocaine as of 1982.

Cocaine is a short-acting stimulant that works on the central nervous system and a potent local anesthetic, unique in its dual ability to deaden feelings while constricting blood vessels. Although medical use of the drug diminished considerably during the early part of the century, it remained in the pharmacopoeia as a local anesthetic and is still used (although rarely) by ear, nose and throat (ENT) specialists and proctologists.

What some users seek from cocaine is relief from depression, for the drug acts on the central nervous system much as antidepressants do. Others use the drug to sharpen their performance on the job or on the social scene or during sex. And cocaine can, indeed, upgrade performance by increasing energy, creating a wide-awake-and-with-it feeling and masking depression. Everything appears sharper and clearer with coke; confidence rises and problems seem simpler.

Cocaine also has a reputation as an aphrodisiac that is not entirely unearned. Although these effects depend upon a great many factors, including how the drug is administered and the social setting, coke can enhance sexual prowess. Male users often report spontaneous erections and erections that persist after orgasm. In one test, half the twenty participants had spontaneous erections, one experienced a series of orgasms without loss of erection, and two others maintained erections for more than twenty-four hours (which proved exceedingly painful). Although coke is often used to overcome sexual anxieties, to increase intimacy and to intensify responses, the effects on sexual activity do not persist. After prolonged use, not only does sexual performance fall below precocaine levels, but desire tends to diminish as well.

For most users, what coke has to offer is euphoria. The coke high is achieved quickly and soon passes. Yet that brief period—usually not much longer than half an hour, sixty minutes at most—is powerfully reinforcing. It is hard to tell just what produces this reinforcement—the most potent elicited by any psychoactive drug. While it may be the euphoria itself, chances are greater that it results from both the rapid lift the user gets and the equally rapid descent—not back to normal levels, but into a deep depression, a dreary cheerless state the user is often desperate to escape.

So strong is the urge to get back "up" that cocaine is used in teaching laboratory animals how to self-administer drugs. Once they learn the routine, animals can then be used to test the abuse potential of other substances as well. In experiments that allow test animals to keep getting cocaine, record scores for abuse have been achieved. Monkeys will shove enthusiastically at push bars nearly thirteen thousand times for a single shot. They will keep pushing—not even pausing for a lunch break —when they are literally starving, and even when each push is accompanied by a "punishing" electric shock. When free to "earn" unlimited amounts of cocaine, monkeys have worked diligently until rewarded with enough of the drug to overdose and die—which they will *not* do when the payoff is heroin.

Still, there is some reason to believe that the expectations of users play as much of a role in cocaine reinforcement as do the properties of the drug. In a recent experiment, experienced cocaine users were unable to tell the difference between the effects of coke and the local anesthetic lidocaine, which looks and feels similar. But though lidocaine is sold as a cocaine substitute and has reportedly produced some stimulating effects, it is just not in the same psychoactive league as cocaine.

Cocaine has the potential for abuse, no matter how it's taken. Certainly the more rapid forms of administration—smoking and shooting— offer the greatest risk. But snorting coke or taking it orally does not mean you will automatically escape its dangers.

In this country, most users take cocaine intranasally, snorting into the nostrils, a process technically called "insufflation." Cocaine is readily absorbed by mucous membrane and easily reaches the bloodstream this way. Rarely is cocaine taken orally these days, although contrary to myth, it is just as effective when swallowed as when snorted. When taken orally its effects peak more slowly—roughly an hour after administration —and fall off less sharply. When the drug is snorted, a maximum response is usually achieved within the first ten minutes.

Smoking cocaine is rapidly gaining popularity. Some users simply sprinkle street coke on marijuana cigarettes, but this is not a very efficient way to use the drug. Smoking coca paste—the first crude extract of the cocaine-making process (after coca leaves have been mashed and steeped in kerosene, sulfuric acid and an alkaline to produce a white paste that is about 80 percent pure cocaine)—is popular in parts of South and Central America. Its failure to catch on here may simply be the result of scarcity, for coca paste is rarely smuggled into the United States.

What has caught on here is smoking freebase. This highly efficient and heavily reinforcing means of administration is almost as rapid a route as injecting the drug intravenously. Smoking freebase requires the conversion of cocaine back to its alkaloid form, purifying it in the process, which is most often done by boiling it with baking soda or using more explosive solvents.

Don Reese, who went from a snorter to a freebaser—and from a talented football player to a drug-dependent ex-con—vividly described his experiences with cocaine in a June 1982 article in *Sports Illustrated:*

> Cocaine arrived in my life with my first-round draft into the National Football League in 1974. It has dominated my life, one way or another, almost every minute since. Eventually, it took control and almost killed me. It may yet. . . . Users call cocaine "the lady." The lady has a widespread acceptance in the best of circles. However, those of us who are—or were—hooked can tell you it's no lady. And until I am cured, I consider myself hooked. Even now, talking about it makes me want it. I can feel the familiar signals going through my body, making my heart beat faster.
>
> I am 30 years old, and desperate. A 6′6″, 280-pound desperate man who should have known better. Who *knew* better, because I was raised better. Six weeks ago I took myself out of society (and out of football, which I don't intend to play again) to a rehabilitation hospital where help was available, and I think, I *pray,* I've seen the light. But to see it, I had to see a lot more.
>
> I had to see myself depicted in the press and on television and everywhere else as a drug dealer, even if my dealing was a silly one-shot kind of deal that was more naive than evil.

I had to see the jailhouse door slammed shut, and know I wouldn't walk free again for a year. As bad as that was, it still didn't cure me. I got worse *after* I was freed.

I had to see my family shy away from me, the wife I doubt I could live without grow disgusted, the mother and father I love and respect grow ashamed. I had to see players I considered close friends go through the same deterioration, their lives messed up, their talent blowing away.

I saw my own fortune wasted—thousands and thousands of dollars, down the drain. I now know the embarrassment of hiding from creditors, of having checks bounce and cars repossessed. I was like a man at his own funeral as my career as a defensive lineman went from what I thought was the brink of All-Pro in 1979 to the edge of oblivion in 1981.

And I saw more. . . . Twice I looked down the barrel of a loaded gun, held by men who said they would kill me if I didn't pay the debts I owed. Debts for cocaine. . . .

Here's what it's like to be a big-time football player in America and screwed up: In New Orleans, where the drugs got to be so bad in 1980, I began getting blackouts in my thinking. Like climbing a ladder with rungs missing. I couldn't hold conversations without my mind going off somewhere. I thought I was losing it. I was in a stupor much of the time. . . .

Football—the environment, not the game itself—as good as wrecked my life. I should have been smarter. I should have been stronger. I know that. But drugs dominate the game, and I got caught up in them, and before I knew it I was freebasing cocaine. And then I was a zombie.

The lady is a monster, a home wrecker and a life wrecker. In the body of a skilled athlete, she's a destroyer of talent. . . . But even if you don't give a damn about the players, if you care about the game you have to be alarmed. What you see on the tube on Sunday afternoon is often a lie. When players are messed up, the game is messed up. The outcome of games is dishonest when playing ability is impaired . . . you line up 11 guys who don't use drugs against 11 who do—and the guys who don't will win every time.

If you're a team on drugs, you'll never play up to your potential, at least not for more than a quarter or so. Then it's downhill fast. I've known times on the field when the whole stadium blacked out on me. Plays I should have made easily I couldn't make at all. I was too strung out from the cocaine. It was like playing in a dream. I didn't think anybody else was out there. . . . New Orleans lost 14 games in a row in 1980, when freebasing became a popular pastime in the NFL. New Orleans was a horror show. Players snorted coke in the locker room before games and again at halftime, and stayed up all hours of the night roaming the streets to get more stuff. I was one of them. . . .

I tried coke for the first time [the week the Miami Dolphins drafted me] . . . I tooted it through a straw. It seemed natural enough. I heard a lot of guys were doing it . . . I got a terrific tingling sensation. . . . I remember sitting there and thinking, "Dang, this is the best s—— I ever had."

The next week I tried it again, a little heavier. This time I *really* felt it—wiinnnnnngggg, opening up my nostrils and going right to my toes and back up again. From then on, I was available whenever *it* was available. By the time the season started, I was snorting at least once a week. . . .

And my want grew just like a cancer. I went up to two grams and then to what people called "eighths"—three and a half grams. An eighth is a "big snorter."

The popularity of cocaine got a dramatic boost in 1980. . . . And the big new item was freebasing . . . [The first time I tried it] I took one pull and threw up. I got sick like a dog. It tasted like raw chemicals. . . . [The next time] I liked it. It had a different taste—sweeter, actually. And it gave me the best high I ever had with drugs.

I inhaled it, and when I blew it out I got that ringing in my ears— wiinnnnnngggg, real high . . . I call it getting a ringer. When people ask me to describe the total experience of freebasing, I say it's like enjoying an all-league climax. The funny thing is . . . you usually can't get an erection. . . .

After a while, I stopped snorting altogether. All I wanted to do was freebase. And that meant an ever increasing expense. . . . I began making regular withdrawals from the bank, and when I stopped to figure it out, I had a habit that was costing me $1,500 to $1,800 a month. . . .

[Soon] my whole world was coming apart. . . . And for once I did the right thing. I checked into a hospital and finally got the help I needed. I know I *wanted* to be helped, and they told me that's the first big step.

Cocaine is hardly ever injected subcutaneously (under the skin) or intramuscularly, for its capacity to constrict blood vessels makes these decidely inefficient routes. Almost invariably, coke is mainlined—injected intravenously. Introduced directly into the bloodstream, cocaine delivers a maximum load to the central nervous system within minutes—and a nerve-jangling rush (much like what the freebaser feels) within seconds.

Although users who inject cocaine suffer an extremely abrupt descent, all users know the "crash" that follows the high, and all crave the same instant uplift. This makes cocaine a difficult drug to control, and users often trap themselves in "sprees," snorting a line every twenty or thirty minutes, or smoking or shooting at even more frequent intervals. Sprees usually last just as long as the user's money or supply does. Among freebasers and shooters, they have been known to go on for days and even weeks.

When a spree ends or when the crash runs its course, the exhausted user is rarely willing to endure the profound bout of depression that follows. To dull their sensibilities and hasten sleep, they will often turn to other drugs—usually alcohol, hypnotics, sedatives or tranquilizers. Some will use heroin. In general, there is a good deal of multidrug use among men and women who have made cocaine their psychoactive favorite.

Just how much potential for abuse does cocaine carry? Plenty.

It is difficult to say whether actual tolerance is created. But a great many users do increase their dosage. This may be no more than "experiential tolerance," the desire for a more profound drug effect. It may result from the cycle of highs and lows that experienced users try to ride but can never master. But it might well be the result, as some researchers now believe, of true tolerance to the drug's euphoric and stimulant effects, requiring increased doses to reproduce what was once achievable with smaller amounts.

A few researchers also now claim that cessation of cocaine-taking by regular users triggers an abstinence syndrome that is marked by severe depression, fatigue, hunger, chills, tremors and nausea. For some, the depression is far more distressing than the physical symptoms, and even after it lifts, many users continue to feel a pronounced craving for cocaine. Withdrawal appears to affect all kinds of users; Dr. Ronald Siegel says he has seen the symptoms in regular snorters (who average 1 gram of cocaine per week) as well as freebasers, who use much greater amounts.

As most researchers, Dr. Siegel prefers the word *dependency* to *addiction*. But whatever it is called, increasing evidence of tolerance and withdrawal make it clear that users can be well and truly hooked by cocaine.

Adverse Reactions

Regular cocaine users put up with a great many unpleasant drug effects. Restlessness, irritability and apprehension are common. Users tend to become suspicious and even display paranoid symptoms—frequently changing locks and phone numbers, doubting friends and showing inappropriate anger or jealousy. All this derives from cocaine's impact on the brain, where it wreaks havoc on the sympathetic nervous system—the network that controls "flight-or-fight" responses to fright. In addition, even at fairly low doses cocaine may cause tremors, cold sweats and grinding of teeth. At higher doses, vomiting and nausea may result, along with muscle pains, a disoriented feeling and dizziness—followed, in some cases, by life-threatening seizures.

Continued snorting also damages the nasal passages. Both abrasion of tissue and periodic constriction of blood vessels cause short-term injury, while the increased flow of blood to the mucous membranes that follows cocaine use often leads to chronic nasal and sinus congestion. Damage can also result from abrasive substances with which cocaine is cut.

The adverse effects of cocaine increase greatly during a spree. Users often work themselves into a highly agitated state, the most characteristic symptom of which is rapid speech. It seems impossible, at this point, for the user to get all his or her thoughts out fast enough. Some users have trouble breathing and sitting still. Then suspiciousness grows, and a feeling of panic begins. Users may experience a high level of anxiety and fears of losing control or "going crazy." Confusion and paranoia set in. Users need to get outside in order to breathe better but become fearful once they are on the street. They may decide to go somewhere but forget exactly how to get there. They may focus on one activity, only to abandon it, start again, and soon quit once more. Interestingly, a marked characteristic of this state is the conviction of some users that they are doing serious harm to themselves.

This is another point at which cocaine users turn to alcohol and other drugs. They will often try to bring themselves down with alcohol, sedatives or tranquilizers.

When dosage of cocaine reaches toxic levels, users are constantly nervous, unable to concentrate at all and severely depressed. Temperature rises, and users' distorted perceptions are likely to produce "pseudohallucinations"—not true hallucinations, perhaps (although some do experience these), but just as terrifying. Visual images include halos and psychedelic patterns, though some users have reported seeing faces, bodies, burglars. Tactile delusions are most often the "coke bugs" that appear to be crawling on or under the skin. The sensation is so real that users in this state will tear and scrape at their skin while trying to scratch and pick at these imaginary insects. One man observed by Dr. Siegel was convinced that tiny white snakes were crawling over his body. He picked these off his skin and put them in a vial. Later, the vial was found to contain only bits of dry skin.

Suspiciousness now blossoms into full-blown paranoia—a cardinal feature of cocaine's toxic psychosis. Its victims are filled with nameless dread, an overpowering fear of attack from which they feel incapable of protecting themselves. Medical treatment for this drug-induced psychosis normally involves an antipsychotic drug. Without treatment, the paranoia and hallucinations usually end within two to four days.

When an overdose reaches life-threatening proportions, there are the obvious signs of what physicians call "the adrenergic storm," the shorting-out of the sympathetic nervous system. There is loss of control over basic body functions, exaggerated reflexes, failure to respond to stimuli, and epilepsylike convulsions, which can range from one brief seizure to persistent convulsions that can cause brain damage.

Death is preceded by coma and loss of reflexes, and results either from brain damage so severe that nerve centers controlling respiration cease to function or from the direct effects of cocaine on the heart. Toxic doses can cause irregularities in heart rhythm and cardiac arrest. Cocaine fatalities are caused not only by the amount consumed but also by the rate at which drug levels in the blood have been increased. Indeed, some users have died with blood levels of cocaine lower than those they had previously handled easily. Although the average lethal dose of cocaine, according to Dr. Siegel, is 1.2 grams, he says he has witnessed users tolerate much greater amounts. While the rapid routes of administration —intravenous injection and freebasing—are clearly the most dangerous, lower-risk routes offer no guarantees.

Long-Term Effects

Cocaine is far from a physically low-cost drug, and not all of its direct and indirect long-term effects are reversible. While effects of malnutrition and physical deterioration, for example, often can be reversed, it is sometimes impossible to overcome *all* the damage that may result from cocaine abuse.

The most obvious long-term damage is done to the nose. Cocaine powder and even more abrasive adulterants wear away sensitive tissue that lines the nose. Coke's anesthetic effect may dull the pain and mask the degree of damage being done. In addition, its constriction of blood vessels reduces blood flow and prevents oxygen and the substances necessary for tissue repair to reach the damaged site. Unable to repair itself, mucous membrane is lost. After years of heavy use, continued abrasion can even, though rarely, result in perforation of the septum, the cartilage separating the nostrils.

Intravenous administration of the drug leaves the user prey to abscesses, cellulitis and other infections at the site of injection. And unsterilized needles or syringes can cause tetanus, hepatitis, and endocarditis (inflammation of membranes around the heart). Impurities in coke can threaten kidneys. The dangers of injection mount during sprees, when users become sloppy or careless—and inject themselves with far greater frequency than even longtime heroin addicts.

Recently, medical researchers have found evidence that smoking freebase may well diminish the lungs' capacity to do their job—supply the body with oxygen and rid it of carbon dioxide. More clearly established is the punishment cocaine inflicts on the heart. Toxic doses can cause irregularities in heart rhythm, and even moderate doses will sharply raise pulse rates and blood pressure.

The liver too is at risk. It can't always handle the large amounts of the drug that must be rapidly metabolized without suffering injury. However, liver damage from cocaine use is reversible. The brain damage caused by convulsions is not.

In very rare cases, cocaine-induced psychosis can lead to severe long-term emotional problems. While this is often more the result of preexisting psychological disorders than of cocaine use, the role of the drug can't be overlooked. However, cocaine users often become dependent on depressants that they use to take the edge off a high or actually bring it to an end.

Danger Signs

When does your use of cocaine become a problem? Since the great majority of users—and there are millions of them—take the drug experimentally (do it a few times and then stop), are social or occasional users, or do the drug for a specific purpose (to get through exams or meet a work deadline), the question needs to be asked. If you're smart and emotionally healthy, if you know yourself and your limits when it comes to drug use, and if you're lucky, cocaine may never become a problem. You may be able to enjoy it for the rest of your life and never pay its costs.

But you can't count on continued emotional health or sustaining self-awareness. Cocaine is a sly drug. It has a habit of sneaking up on you. With cocaine, probably more than any other drug, the line dividing low- and high-risk use is a fuzzy one. And cocaine's ability to make you feel more confident and secure, better able to handle any problem that comes along, may blind you to the fact that you are gradually losing control over your drug-taking or that your habits of drug-taking have changed.

Even if you feel that cocaine is not a problem in your life, remember that no one sets out to become dependent on a drug. People smarter and stronger and more together than you have gone from recreational use to addiction. People have gone from having little interest in coke to making it the center of their life.

Consider the following list of danger signs. If any of the points discussed sound familiar, you should think about stopping your cocaine use.

1. Can you imagine doing without cocaine? If you can't, if the thought of not being able to snort another line is a dismal prospect, you should reassess the value you place on the drug.

2. Do you have to have coke at a party? Many users equate coke with party time. If you have to snort a line before leaving for a party, make trips to the bathroom during the festivities to toot some more, or if things can't start for you until the person who's going to turn you on arrives, you have a habit—a pattern of behavior. The danger is that this habit may start moving into other areas of your life.

3. Do you do cocaine in the morning? Anyone who can't wait for the first toot of the day has established a dangerous pattern of behavior.

4. Do you spend much time just thinking about cocaine? You may not be using all that much or all that often. Maybe you do coke only on weekends. But if you daydream about it, go to sleep at night thinking about the drug or spend a good many of your working hours anticipating your next high, you've got a lot less control over your use than you might imagine.

5. Can you set limits? If you have trouble limiting the amount of coke you do or stopping once you've started—even if you don't indulge very often—if you can't resist a line even when you know you're stoned or are tempted to do coke at inappropriate times, you are on the way to compulsive, uncontrolled use.

6. Do you and your friends always talk about coke? If cocaine is the main topic of conversation among you and your friends, then the drug is becoming central to your life.

7. Do you often regret your behavior? If you say, act or do things you later regret, it's possible that coke is affecting your behavior more than you realize.

8. Are you selfish with your coke? Considering how expensive cocaine is, it's reasonable not to take it out in the middle of a party, but if you're no longer sharing lines with people you usually snort with, your pattern of use is changing for the worse.

9. Do you freebase or inject cocaine? If you are in the fast lanes, using routes of rapid administration, you are a high-risk user, exposing yourself to the most potent adverse effects—infection, disease, psychosis —and risking fatal overdose. While you may have been able to control cocaine when you were snorting, you have now moved into a different league where the reinforcement is so powerful and so pleasurable that you are unlikely ever to be content with snorting again. Odds are you will crave even better highs and want them more often. You will find runs and sprees harder to resist, for the crash from where coke now takes you is such a fearsome drop. What's more, you have crossed a line, violated a taboo. "You'll never catch me using a needle," you may have said, and probably promised yourself to stop well short of freebasing, too. Now you're beyond that, involved in a new set of drug-taking rituals— and rituals reinforce behavior. It often becomes as difficult to give up pipes and needles as it is to give up drugs themselves.

10. Are you getting high alone? Most users take cocaine socially. It's a shared experience, something you do with friends or, perhaps, at a party. It may even give you pleasure to spread a few lines out for your friends. Once you start getting high alone it becomes a different kind of activity. When you sneak off on your own, things aren't so much fun anymore. In fact, the tendency to withdraw comes with growing suspiciousness and is a sign that coke is beginning to influence your judgment and personality.

11. Are you starting to lie? If you've begun to lie about how much coke you are taking, you're exhibiting a classic danger sign that afflicts all drug users. If you're snorting a gram a week but telling friends you only do a line now or then, you probably know you're losing control but can't admit it—to friends or to yourself. And if you've started turning down dinner invitations with weak excuses because you'd rather be home doing coke or because you've just come off a run, cocaine is playing an awfully big role in your life. These are real danger signs. In addition, you're starting to fall into a pattern of dishonest behavior—and with close friends and loved ones. You're starting to push people away, and they're soon going to start repaying you in kind.

12. Have you become secretive? This too is part of cocaine's paranoid pattern, suddenly refusing to share thoughts and feelings with friends or lovers as you once willingly did. When coke no longer makes you talkative but causes you to clam up instead, you might well be down the high-risk road.

13. Are you spending more money than you can afford? If you've been making it from paycheck to paycheck or scrimping on food and clothes you are in trouble. You are out of control if you're running through your savings or have started borrowing money from friends, colleagues and people you hardly know. Or if you hock your possessions. Or if you steal goods. Or if you deal coke. But nothing will help. You are never going to have enough money to buy all the cocaine you want.

14. Are you using other drugs? While you might not enjoy the depression that follows the cocaine high, you can usually handle it at first. It's a price of drug use that you accept. When you are no longer willing to pay this price because the depression has become too heavy or the amount of cocaine you now use makes the crash too much to handle, you are likely to use other drugs to ease you down: alcohol, sedatives and tranquilizers, even narcotics. This is more than a sign that you're taking too much coke. What you have now is not one high-risk habit but possibly two.

15. Have you lost interest in sex? When whatever spice or increased capacity coke added to sex is gone and desire has diminished (along with potency for men), there's no way you can consider your drug use light, limited or low-risk. You are choosing drugs over sex, and that shows a powerful preference.

16. Is your work suffering? Cocaine can help you to be sharp and alert, look better on the job or at school, get a difficult assignment finished on schedule. But it will eventually—if you use it regularly—start to diminish rather than enhance performance, and it may be difficult for you to make a fair assessment of this. You're on dangerous ground when it starts taking you longer than necessary to get things done; when the great work you did after snorting some coke turns out to be mediocre; when lateness and missed appointments become a habit.

17. Do you have extreme mood swings? All psychoactive drugs will alter your mood. Cocaine does a particularly good job of it, and the more cocaine you use, the greater mood swings you will experience. Moments of soaring self-confidence, even grandiosity, give way to prolonged periods of depression. You are often irritable and defensive, and can be withdrawn and secretive. Expansiveness and even kindness can give way to anger and arguments with friends and colleagues. You might not be all that aware of these changes, but they're a sign cocaine's getting the best of you.

18. Are your close relationships deteriorating? Coke need not be the reason. You might even feel that cocaine is helping you deal with the tension of sustaining what has become an unhappy and painful relationship. But don't kid yourself. If you are choosing cocaine over a wife or husband or lover, spending time with drug buddies instead of with him or her, or going off alone to do coke, it's not the relationship that's determining your behavior, it's the coke.

In general, if your behavior is changing—if you relate to people differently, if your priorities have changed, if you're taking risks you previously never would have taken, if you've lost interest in things that once excited you and have become obsessed with the world of cocaine users and dealers—you're into high-risk use.

It's time to get off coke—and it's probably going to be difficult to do. You're going to have to stop denying you have a problem, stop taking the drug and make the changes in your life that will increase your chances of becoming and staying drug-free.

Starting Off

The first thing you have to do to get off cocaine is to admit and recognize you have a problem—that you're a high-risk user dependent on the drug—and decide to do something about it. Which means resolving to stop taking coke.

Even if you know coke is not doing you any good, and is not even giving you the lift it once did, you are going to be giving up something that once gave you immense pleasure. It will be very easy to remember the good times and forget the bad coke experiences. It will be hard to imagine life without cocaine. Chances are there is a good deal of the drug around you—where you work or study, among your friends and colleagues. They may be able to handle coke. You have to remember that, for you, cocaine is a problem.

There's no right or wrong here, no good or bad. You're not a worse person for not being able to control your cocaine use. You've got a problem, that's all. But you've got to admit that. You can't keep saying, "Hey, that's not me. I'm not strung out. That's the other guy."

The world is not going to fall apart because you've gotten messed up on coke, no matter how bleak things may seem. But you've got to start putting the pieces of your life back together again. Remember that you have lots of company. If you're the type of person who has trouble asking for aid, now is not the time to be too proud to accept it. Other people can help you. And you will need their help.

If you start wavering in your decision, now might be a good time to read up on all the harm cocaine can do to you, to listen to the voices you ignored for so long. A place to start is with the article on cocaine in the March 1982 issue of *Scientific American,* Don Reese's account of his troubles in the June 14, 1982, issue of *Sports Illustrated,* and Dr. Ronald Siegel's monograph in the October-December 1982 issue of the *Journal of Psychoactive Drugs.*

Now that you are ready to start, your first move should be to your doctor. You may be embarrassed about talking to your personal or family physician about your cocaine use, and he may not feel confident exploring the problem with you. Many doctors don't know a lot about cocaine or drug dependency. A referral to someone more knowledgeable may be in order.

Still, you need to know what kind of shape you're in, whether cocaine use has weakened you through malnutrition, infection or injury, or if you have any other medical problems. You may discover that you have been medicating yourself—inappropriately, to be sure—to relieve the symptoms of a real disease or disorder. Dr. Mark Gold of Fair Oaks Hospital in New Jersey has found that a number of cocaine users admitted to the institution's neuropsychiatric evaluation unit were treating themselves for weakness, lethargy and mood changes that were actually caused by thyroid disorders, vitamin deficiencies, anemia and even cancer.

What self-medication most often does, however, is relieve depression that is endogenous (of biological origin). But it is not clear how many cocaine users help precipitate endogenous depressions by their use of the drug. Nevertheless, Dr. David Smith at San Francisco's Haight-Ashbury Free Medical Clinic estimates that 10 percent of all cocaine users suffer this kind of depression—and that it can be relieved with antidepressant drugs that act on the central nervous system in much the same way cocaine does.

Ideally, your doctor will know both you and the field of cocaine treatment well enough to help you decide whether or not you need treatment and what kind of treatment will be most effective for you. As Dr. Siegel, who specializes in treating cocaine-dependent people, says, "Ideally, the treatment should be tailored to the individual."

The following test of drug involvement, when used with the personal resources test in Chapter 2, can help you decide if you need treatment and what kind of treatment might be appropriate.

Drug Involvement Test

Answer each question as honestly as you can, but don't trust yourself too much. Remember, honest self-assessment is not your strong suit. Ask someone close to you—your husband or wife, friend or lover—to check and correct your answers.

		YES	NO
1.	Do you inject or smoke cocaine?	—	—
2.	Do you use more than $200 worth of cocaine a week?	—	—
3.	Do you use at least $50 worth a week? (Answer Yes even if you have responded positively to the previous question.)	—	—
4.	Do you use cocaine more than three times a week?	—	—
5.	Do you use the drug more than once a week? (Answer Yes even if you have responded positively to the previous question.)	—	—
6.	Do you use it for four or more hours on any day of use?	—	—
7.	Do you use cocaine in binges three or more times a month?	—	—
8.	Do you use another drug or alcohol in combination with cocaine or to compensate for the effects of coke?	—	—
9.	Has your use of cocaine increased significantly during the past three months?	—	—
10.	Have you shown signs of paranoia (increased secretiveness or suspiciousness), displayed increased hostility or violence or been troubled by sleeplessness?	—	—

A Yes answer to Question 1 or 2 or a total of more than five Yes answers indicates *profound* drug involvement. Three to five Yes answers indicate *serious* involvement, and less than three *moderate* involvement.

Some form of treatment is advisable if your drug involvement is more than moderate, no matter what your personal resources may be—strong, limited or weak. And some treatment is advisable if your resources are less than strong, no matter what your drug involvement measures.

Treatment Alternatives

Treatment may become a concern even before you are ready to quit. You may need medical care for the adverse effects of cocaine use. Indeed, a good many users require medical attention when they become highly agitated and paranoid during a spree. But it's difficult to get them to seek help, and they are not likely to respond well to the atmosphere or the attitude in the average hospital emergency room. At the Haight-Ashbury Free Clinic, doctors work at regaining the trust of these patients. A "quiet room" with minimal stimuli is provided to reassure and encourage them to rest. In addition to prescribing tranquilizers, doctors count on "talking the patients down" to help them return to a calmer and more secure state.

Medical care is also necessary to control toxic psychosis induced by cocaine. Without treatment (usually involving an antipsychotic drug), the frightening psychosis can rage on for as long as four days. At present, doctors are also seeing a growing number of patients with what amounts to an ongoing toxic reaction, who show the distinctive tics and jerks brought on by too much cocaine and suffer distorted perceptions and paranoia. Recently, some of these patients have been treated with propranolol when the sympathetic nervous system starts behaving erratically. The drug, a partial antagonist which blocks many cocaine receptors, causes the physical signs to diminish. The euphoria—unaffected by the drug—reappears, and the patients quiet down. Dr. George Gay, at the Haight-Ashbury Clinic, uses propanolol in a long-term treatment plan that includes a special diet, vitamin supplements and psychological counseling. Although not many users with this degree of drug involvement are likely to quit using cocaine, propanolol may protect them from the potentially lethal effects of their next spree.

Drug treatment in the United States reflects an imbalance in favor of heroin and similar narcotics, with fewer treatment options for cocaine dependency or coke-related disorders. This is less the result of neglect than of limited need and limited experience. Today, however, because of the drug's popularity, more researchers are studying coke than ever before, and more doctors are becoming familiar with the problems it can create.

These experts do not always agree. Dr. Mark Gold is downright discouraging about treatment for freebase and intravenous users. "If you are looking for total abstinence as an outcome," he says, "then very few patients are going to succeed." Yet Dr. Ronald Siegel claims an 80 percent success rate for cocaine users tracked for two years after participation in his program.

But just because treatment doesn't provide easy answers or guarantees doesn't mean you can afford to pass it up. After all, treatment alone doesn't get you off drugs. You do that. Treatment can only help.

For all cocaine users, the best treatment will offer an individualized recovery plan based on your personal needs, education about cocaine abuse, and the use of therapy groups. Preferable is the self-help model, where emphasis is put on mutual support and individual responsibility for your actions; it's important to share your experiences, your difficulties and your strengths with others in the same bind. You should look for treatment that meets your needs—as determined by the self-assessment tests and the advice of a doctor and drug counselor—and is least intrusive. While you do not want to disturb the structure of your life more than is necessary, it is foolish to opt for treatment that will not do the job —bring about the cessation of drug use.

Residential treatment provides a potent form of intervention. Some drug researchers, among them Dr. Siegel, feel that only few cocaine users need this kind of setting. Nevertheless, there are a growing number of residential programs for cocaine users, many using the same brand of group therapy and the same self-help approach as therapeutic communities (TCs) without the commitment to long-term participation that most TCs demand.

However, the TCs themselves have proven remarkably effective in dealing with all forms of drug abuse—though they were designed for narcotic addicts—and if your cocaine use is profound or serious and your personal resources are weak, you may well need the eighteen months or more of residence most require. If you have few career or school responsibilities to consider, no family ties, and if drugs have been pretty much all you've been doing with your time, then a therapeutic community might be a good place to start restructuring your life.

If you are considering a TC (a more detailed discussion of them can be found in Chapter 2), you want to find one that is right for you. Size doesn't matter; a good TC can be quite small. What's important is continuity. Has the program been around for a while? Does it have an experienced staff? Is it licensed or approved by your state's drug abuse agency? Even if group therapy there involves confrontation, treatment should not include physical or other excessive forms of coercion. And you are best off with a program that carefully screens candidates for admission and offers a wide range of services, including outpatient treatment. You must be willing to trust the clinicians you meet there. At bottom, you have to trust your feelings about the place. If you don't think you'll be comfortable there, follow your instincts.

Less demanding forms of residential treatment are now becoming available in *hospitals*. These should be considered in those rare cases where your physician thinks your cocaine use has been so heavy that your body or mind needs attention, or if your drug involvement is more than moderate and your personal resources are limited. Clearly, a hospital or other residential environment will help you make a clean break with your immediate past and help you get away from drug friends, dealers, coke paraphernalia and all your other drug associations—the cues that can set off renewed cocaine use.

If you consider a hospital, make sure it has had experience treating cocaine users. Look for a treatment program that uses therapy groups and takes a self-help approach or emphasizes "here-and-now" problem-solving in counseling.

Outpatient clinics will be most useful for the greatest number of cocaine users. If your personal resources are strong, this is the type of treatment you should try first. Unfortunately, this category includes a confusingly wide variety of programs—from storefront or church-run "rap" centers to hospital and TC-affiliated programs. The most useful are likely to be those, like the ones Phoenix House operates in New York, that emphasize self-help, count heavily on mutual support groups and require participation by your spouse or lover and other significant people in your life. Other outpatient programs emphasize individual counseling rather than self-help and group support. Whichever you choose, your success will depend at least as much on what you bring to the program as what you get from it. At first, all you bring is your commitment and your willingness to participate, and initially this may mean just faithfully showing up at group sessions, meetings with your counselor and whatever more intensive activities may be scheduled. The greater your commitment, the more likely you are to succeed at the program.

You must keep in mind that not every program that uses self-help groups will work for every cocaine user. These groups are based upon the expectation that members will be open and honest and share their feelings and their problems. You may not be willing to do this. If you are successful professionally, for instance, you may have difficulty accepting a peer relationship with drug users off the street. If so, you've either got to find a self-help group where you will feel comfortable or choose a program that counts less on the group dynamic.

A good many well-credentialed therapists who have had little experience with drug dependency are now entering the treatment field. Some programs designed specifically for cocaine users are opening up. In California, particularly, cocaine treatment seems to be a growth industry, and you should check out any program as well as you can. A sure sign you've picked the wrong one is a treatment goal of something less than abstinence. When you hear that your coke problem can be solved by cutting down or switching from freebasing back to snorting, head for the exit. Forget about the possibility of returning to controlled use. It can hardly ever be done. It's no solution and will only prolong your problem.

There are also experts with a good deal of experience who are developing new programs. Dr. Siegel, for example, believes that most cocaine abusers—and he includes snorters as well as heavy freebasers—can solve their cocaine problem within ninety days. Dr. Siegel's program, as outlined in the *Journal of Psychoactive Drugs,* involves helping the user through withdrawal (the depression, fatigue and craving that follow cessation of the drug); preparing the patient for detoxification through self-control strategies that include fading (reducing dosage), contingency contracting, and stimulus-control methods designed to make the patient aware "of the specific environmental and internal cues associated" with cocaine use; support therapy on a daily basis during the first weeks of abstinence, with such exercise as long-distance running and, rarely, chemical treatment for depression; and to maintain abstinence, booster therapy sessions and regular telephone contact and support for a few months, plus exercise and other therapies as needed.

When assessing any treatment program remember:

1. Short-term treatment of one or two weeks with no subsequent aftercare is not likely to help most cocaine users.
2. Though individual counseling can be very helpful, it does not usually generate the kind of involvement that self-help programs do and may be less successful in holding clients in treatment.
3. Any program that offers the possibility of return to cocaine use will create more problems than it solves.

Some cocaine users can find effective treatment in *private therapy,* but usually only if they have strong personal resources and if the therapist sticks to "reality therapy" and avoids the lengthy search for insights. What you need is help in the day-to-day difficulties of getting off drugs. Deeper psychotherapy can come later, once you've stopped using coke and managed to stay away from it for a fair period of time.

While not necessarily treatment by themselves, a number of *behavior modification techniques* can be helpful to cocaine users eager to quit. "Desensitization" strategies weaken the conditioned response to drug-taking cues. "Aversion" strategies attempt to replace the pleasurable associations of coke with decidedly unpleasant ones. One popular behavioral approach uses "contingency contracting"; clients agree to remain in treatment and free of cocaine for a set period of time (usually three months) and sign letters that will be mailed should they drop out of treatment or resume cocaine use. In essence, this is blackmail, for the letters confess drug use to parents, employers or professional organizations and can cause the writer real trouble. Sometimes the letters contain generous contributions to causes or political groups the clients strongly oppose. (All these techniques are covered more fully in Chapter 2.)

Individual Efforts

A good many cocaine users who decide to quit try to stop without any treatment. The great majority are snorters who have never before had a drug problem. Because they usually do not fit the drug abuse stereotype —they are educated professionals or students, come from middle-class families—it is easy for them to believe that quitting involves nothing more than willpower. They rarely see themselves as having a real problem, and this perception has been reinforced by the popular view of cocaine as a relatively benign drug and certainly not addicting.

There are other reasons users have for not seeking treatment. The paranoia brought on by coke tends to make its victims mistrustful of doctors and other professionals who could help them. And Dr. Siegel has seen in cocaine smokers a "dissatisfaction with conventional [treatment] programs because of the uniform lack of knowledge regarding cocaine smoking, coupled with [the smokers'] individual beliefs that cocaine smoking represented a unique drug problem requiring special treatment methods. This lack of client trust in the conventional programs caused a high dropout rate among cocaine smokers."

Although cocaine smokers are a small minority, their attitude toward treatment probably reflects the feelings of most cocaine users. Indeed, the notion of "specialness" is all too common among drug users and reflects no more than what Dr. Mitchell Rosenthal calls "the reluctance of *all* users to give up their beloved drugs." So it would not be surprising if most tried to quit on their own—at least the first time around.

Even if you do seek treatment, the reality is that getting off coke is up to you, and you start simply by stopping. If your doctor hasn't suggested hospitalization and you're not entering a residential treatment program, the first few days of going without coke will be hard to get through alone. Don't expect the worst, for withdrawal has a way of living up to expectations, but do prepare for it. You are likely to be exhausted yet sleep restlessly, be irritable, depressed and anxious. Heavier users will often feel chills, tremors and muscle pains. Doctors are generally reluctant to prescribe medication to ease the restless sleep because they do not take coke's abstinence syndrome too seriously. Indeed, the withdrawal should pass after two to four days in even the most severe cases. Still, *you* should take all this very seriously, even if you escape the more uncomfortable symptoms, for the depression itself can go on long after the withdrawal has faded.

Recognize, too, that you are going to crave cocaine, possibly more than you have ever craved it before. This desire could well threaten your commitment. In the beginning, at least, you won't necessarily feel the rewards of what you are doing. In time, you will feel good about the changes you are making, but for a while you might be restless, irritable, angry, have trouble sleeping, feel constantly depressed and deprived of the release you've grown to count on.

Here are a few simple rules to help you get through this time:

1. Take time out: at least a week. You don't need the distractions of daily life. If you work, see if you can take some of your vacation time. If you're in school, find a way to clear your calendar or use a long holiday. If you can, find a place in the country where you can get some distance from your regular pressures and commitments.

2. Cut yourself off. Except for a spouse, lover or close friend who is willing to stay with you, don't let anyone know where you are. Certainly you don't want your dealer or drug buddies coming by. Even your non-using friends may be too much to handle; the odds are you're just going to want to be left alone. This isn't the time to explain what you're doing. Not to them, not to your parents, not to anyone else who may ask. There will be plenty of time for that. The point now is to feel as comfortable as you can.

3. Don't stay alone. Your partner's job is to take care of you—cook, clean, see that you eat and rest, answer the phone and door and turn away unwanted visitors. He or she is your safeguard in case you need medical attention and is there to reinforce your decision to stay clean.

4. Be sure your partner is prepared. If you were bad to live with before, you're likely to be worse to live with now. Make sure your partner is prepared for a wide range of emotions from you—rudeness, anger, hostility, guilt. Talk about all this before you quit. Make sure your partner knows that this isn't the time to let out his or her anger about your drug use. You won't be sleeping well, so your partner shouldn't be surprised if you want to sleep alone. This is your time. You may be asking a lot, but your partner is there to care for, comfort and help you.

5. *Quit cold*. Don't make a big deal about one last snort of coke. Now that you've made your decision to quit, don't continue to romanticize about cocaine.

6. *Clean out*. Get rid of every bit of cocaine paraphernalia in the house. Throw out all the reminders: razors, straws, pipes, syringes. All your drug books and magazines, too. You don't need those reminders of coke; you'll have enough memories to contend with.

7. *Set no goals*. You do this one day at a time. That's all you can ask of yourself. Just another day without cocaine.

8. *Give in to your feelings*. There's no need to keep up a front. You are going to be angry, sad, wretched and maybe sick. Yell if you want to, cry if you feel like it. You've been dealing with chemically induced feelings for a long time. This may be a chance to start getting in touch with your real feelings.

9. *Remember the bad times*. It's very easy to remember the pleasures of cocaine use and block out all the misery. Now's the time to forget how great it was to get high and focus on the depresssions that followed, the lethargy after a coke run, the paranoia, the coke bugs under your skin, the times you felt you couldn't breathe and the disorientation.

10. *Do what pleases you*. Do whatever makes you feel better, be it a hot bath or a run around the block as your strength starts returning. Remember, this is your time.

11. *Reward yourself*. Not for staying clean any set number of days, but for taking the initial step and getting it together as well as you have. Plan special treats—a great dinner, watching a movie on TV, whatever strength and access permit. It may sound simplistic, but you deserve it.

12. *Don't get overly confident*. A few days off coke is just one of the first steps. It's great you've taken it, but don't think you've gotten coke licked. Even if you feel terrific.

Withdrawal can be dramatic. But after it's over, you have to face the challenge of living normally with temptation close at hand. When the depression lifts, you may not feel much like your old pre-coke self. Most likely, you'll be pretty gloomy. After all, you've been manipulating your moods for a long time. You'll feel deprived, because something that was important is gone from your life. You may well experience what psychiatrists call *anhedonia,* which is not depression so much as the inability to be happy. This is when it becomes important to get the kind of support you can find in the right treatment program.

What you can do for yourself is keep busy. Any activity is better than none. The best will keep you physically active and involved with other people. Exercise is important. What's best for you is sustained exercise that increases oxygen demand—aerobic exercise, dancing, swimming, hiking, biking. These improve circulation and raise mood levels. Best of all for the former cocaine user is slow, long-distance running, which can give you a high of its own, not all that much different from coke's. Physical fitness can also be a way to expand your social contacts. Join a health club or a hiking, biking or camping group. (Additional information on these *individual efforts* is contained in Chapter 2.)

Breaking with your drug-using past can be hard. You may choose to move, find a new apartment far from the sites of your drug use and away from companions of your drug-using days. But this isn't a practical alternative for everyone. Most likely, you'll just have to rearrange your schedule, planning new activities for the times when you once used coke and new places to hang out or meet friends. It's important to let those drug-using friends who are more than just drug buddies know how you now feel about cocaine. If they can't respect your commitment and insist on using drugs while you're around, then it's best to let the relationships die. Sticking with friends like these makes no more sense than "testing yourself" by revisiting your old haunts or "proving" that you can handle cocaine and still turn it down. This is high-risk nonuse and often precedes relapse.

Staying Off

You've gotten off. You've made the changes you've had to make and become comfortable with them. You have a history, however brief, of drug freedom. You have a right to be proud but not complacent.

There are a good many threats to your abstinence. You may still be troubled by drug cravings. You may feel your post-coke life has not been as successful as you'd like. Untreated emotional problems can still threaten your freedom from drugs, and so can problems in your relationships that might have developed since you quit.

But you bring a lot to the battle with drug cravings now. When temptation calls, wait ten minutes, as Dr. Peter Miller suggests, before deciding to act. Now, you can think about more than just the future consequences. You can weigh your past successes too—the efforts you've made, the new way of life you've built, your new body, sense of self-confidence and new interests. There's a lot to throw onto the other side of the scales.

Nevertheless, you may want and need the kind of support you get in treatment—a group of caring men and women with similar problems and similar fears. A growing number of treatment programs now run aftercare groups, and there are other organizations as well, all based on the Alcoholics Anonymous model for self-help groups (covered in Chapter 7). Many local AA chapters will accept former drug users. Narcotics Anonymous, a smaller but similar organization, includes former cocaine users, too, and several chapters of a new Cocaine Anonymous organization have been formed in California and Chicago.

Basically, these groups demand little in either fees (usually nominal) or participation, although many participants do attend weekly meetings. What they provide is a support network, people you can turn to when you feel threatened or vulnerable, and groups in which you can work out problems in your new life.

Support groups help you to recognize that you remain vulnerable. You can't handle coke—and you should take that both figuratively and literally, for you should not risk exposure to strong drug-taking cues.

It is possible that you will slip, but the world will not end if you get high again. A spree, however, is something else and much harder to pick yourself up after. But relapse is common, and that's when a self-help support group comes through; to help you up and keep you steady until you feel more confident again.

Not all researchers, however, favor the Alcoholics Anonymous–based self-help groups. Dr. Siegel, for example, feels that attending meetings at which cocaine is the focus for extended periods of time may be more harmful than good. "I find this approach never allows people to leave [their past cocaine problem] alone, to move on with their lives," he says. "They're constantly stigmatized. I like my clients to look back at their period of involvement with cocaine as an interesting period. Fortunately they've survived it, and we want them to move on."

Another kind of help you may reach out for now is traditional psychotherapy. Getting off drugs meant dealing with a number of behavioral issues. Now is the time to look deeper, at the roots of the anxiety or depression, the feelings of inadequacy or resentment that were uncovered along the way. It may also be the time to find the professional help you may need to keep your marriage or other intimate relationship together.

You are now a different person from the one your spouse or lover, your boss or even your friends were used to dealing with. You feel less guilty, more entitled. Although your behavior is much improved, you are now making demands you might never have made before. You are taking charge of your life in a number of ways you probably left to others to handle. This all can be difficult to swallow for a partner who still may carry some resentments from your drug-abusing days and feels his or her role was pivotal to your success in quitting.

The trick for you is not to be any more burdened by gratitude than you are by guilt and to work out your problems on the basis of what is best for both of you right now.

Notes for the User's Partner

No one but the drug user can make up his (or her) mind to quit. When it comes to cocaine, even the urgings of a loved one may not be enough. Your spouse may love you, but may need and want coke more.

Still, the user's husband, wife or lover plays a vital role in the process of getting off drugs. It's hard for him to make it without your help, and it's almost impossible if both of you are into cocaine.

Your partner will probably stop using coke only when he decides to. There's very little you can do to influence the decision—though you can try. Try to convince him, gently, that the relationship will not last if he goes on snorting cocaine. (Real threats come later, when you decide there's nothing left to try and you've decided the relationship is only dragging you down.) Try to get him to see what coke is doing to his body, his mind and his career, if he doesn't seem to respond to arguments about the relationship.

Try to talk to him in a nonthreatening way that doesn't trigger defensiveness or guilt. This may be asking a lot of you, but for now it's the tack to take. And this isn't to say you shouldn't let him know that his cocaine use has built a wall between the two of you, and left you feeling lonely and hurt. But tell him, too, that you'll support any effort he makes at getting off drugs as best you can. Don't make threats about what will happen if he fails. Offer your help and hope he'll accept it. This may bring down some walls, and he might start confiding his own fears, frustrations and feelings.

Even if your partner does decide to quit, you are probably harboring a good many resentments about his drug use. You are not starting out with a clean slate. Still, if you believe in the relationship, you will want to provide all the support he needs.

While the first days can be trying if he goes through withdrawal at home, they may be lots simpler than what is to come. Be prepared for irritability, anger, and a depression which, while hardly ever suicidal, may leave him feeling he has little to live for. When this gives way, as withdrawal ends, to the empty feeling of anhedonia, he may become lethargic and lounge around the house doing little more than watching television. The only sign of life he may show is renewed appetite. Mostly, he will just want to be left alone, while you may feel renewed resentment because of his distance and the demands he makes on you.

If he is not in treatment already, now is the time to suggest it, not for *his* needs alone, but for *yours* as well. Participation in a treatment program that encourages family involvement can give you a chance to talk out your problems with others in the same bind. It offers the two of you a way to deal with the tensions that surround his efforts to get straight. But you should not expect a drug treatment program to tackle the deeper problems the two of you may have. Those must wait.

You can be trapped by your fear that he will go back to using cocaine, but you can't show too much anxiety or he will feel you are suspicious and mistrustful. If he is wavering, that might be all it takes to push him over the edge. It is a hard line to walk, and you will need all the help you can get in learning how to demonstrate concern without making him feel defensive or wronged.

4

NARCOTICS

Until recently, illicit drug use has meant narcotic abuse to most Americans—specifically heroin addiction. Even today, when a great variety of drugs are available—some more life-threatening or habit-reinforcing—heroin is still perceived as uniquely dangerous and dreadful. It cannot be produced, imported or prescribed for medical use in the United States. Heroin carries a stigma no other drug does, for it is linked in the public consciousness with crime, urban decay, vintage myths of instant dependency—"one shot and you're hooked"—unbearable withdrawal and incurable addiction.

During the past decade, however, public concern about heroin abuse has diminished. Heroin dependency is no longer perceived as the urgent social problem it was during the period of 1968 to 1972, when the drug spilled out of the inner city and spread through suburban white America and when use among soldiers in Vietnam made everyday news. In the late 1960s and early 1970s, heroin use was considered a crisis of epidemic proportions. Today, that perception has lessened, though there now are nearly as many heroin users—about 500,000, according to current estimates—as there were over a decade ago. (The numbers dropped off sharply during the mid-1970s, but picked up again at the end of the decade, when new sources of opium in the Middle East flooded the market with more potent and less expensive heroin.) Evidence of drug fatalities, emergency-room admissions and new treatment clients indicate that current use is near 1972 levels in many major cities, including New York, Chicago and Washington, where it reached an all-time high in early 1983.

While use of the drug remains heavily concentrated in ghetto areas, the number of white middle-class users continues to grow. Heroin has cashed in on cocaine's chic and is easily available in the clubs that cater to the new-wave cultural scene.

The drugs we call narcotics (from the Greek *narkoun,* meaning "to deaden or benumb") are more properly known these days as opioids, a collective designation for both natural opiates (opium and its derivatives) and synthetics. Although popular concern is focused on heroin, the other narcotics are also popular drugs of abuse. Some 2.6 million Americans have tried heroin at one time or another, but more than 9 million have misused other opioids, which, unlike heroin, are prescribed for medical purposes.

Early Use

Opium itself has been around for five or six thousand years, ever since the early Egyptians, Arabians and Greeks began extracting it from the seed capsules of the poppy *Papaver somniferum* as a remedy for diarrhea, even before anyone noticed that it would also relieve pain. Later, opium was taken as a sleeping aid and eventually for a mixed bag of medical complaints: snakebite, deafness, coughs, colic, epilepsy, and urinary problems.

At the start of the nineteenth century, French and German pharmacists succeeded in isolating the alkaloids of opium. Until then, solutions of opium, such as laudanum and paregoric, were the most popular forms of the drug. But with opium's soluble salts available, codeine and morphine were added to the psychoactive pharmacopoeia.

Opium use spread throughout England during the eighteenth and nineteenth centuries, and there was little recognition of its ability to create dependency. Reports of adverse effects in China prompted the English to suspect only that the Chinese were somehow peculiarly susceptible to the drug.

Awareness of dependency soon grew, however. In his classic book, *Confessions of an English Opium-Eater,* published in 1821, Thomas De Quincey described the pleasures and horrors of narcotic addiction—making it clear that the English could be just as susceptible as the Chinese. The poet Samuel Coleridge wrote: "Laudanum gave me repose, not sleep; but you, I believe, know how divine that repose is, what a spot of enchantment, a green spot of fountains and flowers and trees in the very heart of a waste of sands!''

Meanwhile, further technological developments aggravated the problem. In 1853, Alexander Wood, an Edinburgh physician, invented the hypodermic syringe. Although doctors first believed that injection might actually cure "morphinism" (as morphine addiction was called at the time), the result was to make addiction commonplace, and Wood's own wife became the first victim to overdose on injected morphine.

The heavy employment of narcotics by physicians, to whom no other pain-killers were then available, turned a good many patients into addicts. But self-medication also was popular, and the best-selling tonics, elixirs and nostrums of the day were heavily laced with opium. They were given even to children, and in 1845 Friedrich Engels reported in *The Condition of the English Working Class* that mothers "dose their children" with patent drugs to keep them quiet.

A good many nineteenth-century addicts were introduced to morphine in military hospitals, and army surgeons were credited with helping spread addiction across much of Europe. Heavy use of morphine during the Prussian-Austrian War (1866) and the Franco-Prussian War (1870–1871) sent thousands of addicts home from the battlefields. In the United States, "the army disease" spread across the country after the Civil War.

There's reason to doubt that the Civil War had as much to do with triggering drug addiction in the United States as historians once believed. Opium and morphine were already quite popular before the war began, and the postwar narcotic boom appears to have been caused at least as much by the aggressive marketing of such patent medicines as Dr. Barton's Brown Mixture and Dover's Powder.

It's hard to fault consumers of these patent drugs, even when they were aware that the nostrums contained opium or opium derivatives. Within the medical profession, there were still opium boosters who credited the drug with some astounding attributes. Dr. George Wood, an otherwise credible teacher of medicine, insisted as late as 1868 that opium expanded both the intellect and the imagination. "It seems," he declared, "to make the individual, for the time, a better and greater man."

It is hard to imagine now how the use of opium and morphine was perceived near the end of the nineteenth century, at a time when addiction was far more common than today. In 1900 (when there were only 76 million Americans), the estimated number of addicts ranged from 250,000 to 4 million, and the addicts of that time, with access to unlimited amounts of unadulterated drugs, had habits far heavier than those of today.

This was not a time of great tolerance for individual differences. Religion was strong, revivals were popular, and the temperance movement was gaining strength. The Women's Christian Temperance Union, founded in 1874, and the Anti-Saloon League, founded in 1893, were eventually able to bring about Prohibition. But they showed little interest in drugs. Indeed, opium use, if not entirely respectable, was still more socially accepted than heavy drinking.

There simply was no recognition of an American addiction problem. As A. Saper points out in the *British Journal of the Addictions,* narcotic use "was viewed as not really desirable—like not using a deodorant in today's society. Slight disapproval but no condemnation." Most addicts were from the middle and upper classes. "Pillars of the community and middle-class morality," Saper calls them, and women users outnumbered men in this population by about three to one.

Not all narcotic use escaped condemnation. It was all well and good for the moneyed and responsible to inject morphine or sip opium-laced tonics, but it was something else again for society's less favored to *smoke* opium. Opium smokers were either Chinese laborers, brought to this country in the mid-1800s to help build the railroads, or worse (in middle-class eyes)—criminals, prostitutes and other inhabitants of that netherland beyond the border of respectability. Although there had been no uproar in the United States when the first Chinese workers arrived with their pipes in the mid-1800s, smoking the drug surfaced as an issue when hard economic times hit in the mid-1870s. Unemployed workers in the West blamed their joblessness on unfair competition from cheap Chinese labor. They demanded the exclusion of Chinese workers and strengthened their case by seizing on the evils of opium smoking.

In 1877 Nevada prohibited the sale of opium for smoking, and the following year San Francisco outlawed opium dens, with city officials arguing that respectable women were "being induced to visit the dens, where they were ruined morally and otherwise."

There was no way narcotic drugs could survive the kind of puritan revival the nation was experiencing as the twentieth century began. At the urging of Bishop Charles E. Brent, President Theodore Roosevelt proposed an international conference on opium. It was held in Shanghai in 1909, with Bishop Brent presiding. The United States was represented by Dr. Hamilton Wright, a passionate advocate of narcotic controls, who had succeeded in getting federal legislation passed to bar the import of opium for smoking even before the conference opened. On returning from Shanghai he failed to get stronger measures passed. But in 1914, after The Hague International Opium Convention had recommended measures to limit the use of opium, morphine and heroin, Wright got almost all the restrictions he wanted. Congress passed the Harrison Act, which controlled production, distribution and sales of narcotics and totally banned cocaine.

The law did, however, allow narcotics to be prescribed for legitimate medical uses, and certain doctors reasonably interpreted this to mean that they could prescribe sufficient amounts of opium, morphine and heroin to maintain addicts at whatever level of drug use kept them from experiencing withdrawal. But the Treasury Department (charged with enforcing the Harrison Act, which was in form if not in fact a revenue measure) challenged the right of physicians to prescribe controlled drugs in "maintenance" doses. In 1919, the U.S. Supreme Court ruled in favor of the department, declaring that doctors could not prescribe narcotics if the purpose was simply to allow the addict to avoid discomfort "by maintaining his customary use." The result was to cut off most addicts from legitimate sources of drugs and to close down the addiction clinics that had opened afer passage of the Harrison Act. Although the court later decided a physician could give a drug-dependent person moderate amounts of narcotics to relieve the symptoms of withdrawal, few doctors then were willing to risk harassment by narcotic agents or censure by more conservative colleagues.

Today's Opioids

The first semisynthetic narcotic, diacetylmorphine, was cooked up by boiling morphine with acetic anhydride, in 1874 at St. Mary's Hospital in London. But it was nearly a quarter century before the German pharmaceutical firm Bayer marketed the drug, under the trade name Heroin, as a cough suppressant (and not, as legend has it, as a cure for morphine addiction, although a number of physicians did attempt to use it for this purpose).

Quite a variety of natural and synthetic opioids have since been developed for medical use, and many are now available on the illicit market.

Opium today is harvested from poppies grown mainly in the Middle East, the Far East and Mexico. The milky juice from unripe seed capsules is air-dried to form a brownish gummy mass and can be further dried to make opium powder. Although some opium—as in gum opium, laudanum and paregoric—is available to physicians, it is rarely used these days, and little natural opium prepared for smoking (the most common means of recreational use elsewhere in the world) reaches the United States.

Morphine, which makes up between 4 and 21 percent of raw opium, is most often seen as white crystals or prepared for medical use in tablets and injectable solutions. It has no odor, a bitter taste, and darkens with

Table 2. Opioids of Abuse

Generic Name	Trade or Brand Name	Approximate Dose in mg[1]	Usual Means of Administration	Duration of Action (hours)	Relative Abuse/ Dependency Potential	Source of Drug
Opium (salts)	Pantopon	15	Injected, oral or smoked	4–5	Moderate to high	Natural (found in the opium poppy gum)
Morphine	—	10	Injected	4–5	High	Natural
Codeine	—	120*	Oral or injected	3–4	Low	Natural
Heroin (diacetyl-morphine)	—	3	Injected, "sniffed" or smoked	3–4	High	Semisynthetic (made from morphine)
Hydromorphone	Dilaudid	2	Injected or oral	4–5	High	Semisynthetic
Hydrocodone	Hycodan	(5–10)	Oral	(4–8)[2]	Moderate	Semisynthetic
Oxycodone	Percodan	10–15	Oral or injected	4–5	Moderate	Semisynthetic
Oxymorphone	Numorphan	1–1.5	Injected	4–5	High	Semisynthetic
Levorphanol	Levo-Dromoran	1–2	Injected or oral	4–5	High	Semisynthetic
Methodone	Dolophine, etc.	10	Injected or oral	3–6[3]	High	Synthetic (made from basic laboratory chemicals)
Propoxyphene	Darvon, etc.	60–120*	Injected or oral	4–5	Low	Synthetic
Meperidine	Demerol	60–100	Injected or oral	2–4	High	Synthetic
Fentanyl	Sublimaze	.01–.05	Injected	½–1½	High	Synthetic
Pentazocine	Talwin	30–50*	Injected or oral	3–4	Low to moderate	Synthetic
Diphenoxylate	Lomotil	2.5*	Oral	2	Low	Synthetic

* Not equivalent to morphine in this dose; may not be as potent as morphine at any dose.

1. Dose equal to morphine by subcutaneous injection.

2. Parentheses indicate duration of action for oral administration only.

3. Methadone accumulates with repeated doses, so duration of action may be much longer in "chronic" users, up to 24 hours.

age. Most morphine legally brought into the United States is converted to codeine, the most commonly prescribed opioid.

Codeine is now being used with the hypnotic drug (sleeping pill) glutethimide (Doriden). The combination—known as "doors and fours" (after Doriden and Number Four, the preferred form of prescribed codeine), "four doors" or "set ups"—produces effects similar to heroin. Tolerance builds quickly, however, and some users on the West Coast, where it is most popular, have taken to calling the mixture of twice as many codeine tablets as Doridens "loads," because such heavy doses, literally handfuls of pills, are soon needed to reach the heroinlike high.

Heroin, by far the overwhelming choice of narcotic users, cannot be legally imported or manufactured in the United States. A white powder with morphine's bitter taste, it is seen on the street in colors that range from white to dark brown, because of impurities and the purposeful use of colored adulterants.

Hydromorphone (Dilaudid), a semisynthetic compound, is quite similar to heroin but at least half again as potent (five times more powerful than morphine). In spite of its short duration of action, hydromorphone is frequently given for postoperative pain and to relieve the suffering of terminal cancer patients. It causes less nausea and vomiting than morphine and less sedation. When injected intramuscularly, it produces less euphoria; but intravenous injection will result in a rush much like heroin's. Although the drug is available to physicians in injectable solutions, it appears on the street most often as tablets meant for oral use (which can be dissolved for injection) and commands the highest price ($25 to $40) of any tablet on the illicit market.

Methadone, widely used in maintenance treatment and detoxification of narcotic addicts, is itself a drug of abuse. A long-acting, highly addictive drug, it is most often available only in preparations for oral administration. Methadone moves briskly on the illicit market, usually supplied by maintenance patients who sell or trade their take-home supplies of the drug.

Meperidine (Demerol), another synthetic analgesic that can be taken orally, was developed as a morphine substitute that would create little physical dependency. Although it proved less powerful and more addictive than anticipated, it is frequently prescribed for pain by physicians and is the narcotic most often abused by health professionals.

Pentazocine (Talwin), a synthetic analgesic with some antagonist properties, has been combined with the antihistamine Pyribenzamine as a substitute for heroin. Talwin, meant for oral use, can be dissolved in water with the blue antihistamine tablets—in a mixture called "T's and blues"—to produce an injectable solution. To prevent this misuse, Talwin's manufacturers have added a narcotic antagonist to the tablets, which are effective analgesics when taken orally but now have no narcotic effects at all when combined with Pyribenzamine and injected.

Oxycodone (Percodan), like codeine, is widely prescribed as a pain-killer and has recently been found to have considerable potential for abuse. It is taken orally by users who enjoy its sedative effects and believe its relatively low potency protects them from addiction.

Effects of Narcotics

Narcotics act mostly on the central nervous and digestive systems, and currently are used for much the same medical purposes as they have been for hundreds of years—to relieve pain, control diarrhea and suppress coughing. Although a great many pain-killing drugs exist today, morphine remains the standard against which other analgesics are measured—and even the potency of other opioids is reported in comparison to morphine's.

Heroin, for example, is generally considered to be approximately three times more powerful than morphine, and its effective dose is usually given at roughly one third morphine's. However, recent tests in the United States found heroin to be only two to two-and-a-half times as potent as morphine. And in appropriate doses, no difference was found in the abilities of the two drugs to relieve pain, to alter mood or to produce side effects.

Little wonder that doctors during the past century often called morphine "G.O.M." for "God's Own Medicine." As an analgesic, there is nothing like the opioids, both in their selective ability to relieve pain without substantially dulling other senses and in their capacity to reduce *suffering* (the combined impact of both specific sensations of pain and the patient's reaction to that pain).

Yet relief from pain is only one of the remarkably diverse collection of effects that narcotics produce, including drowsiness, mood changes, some clouding of the mind and respiratory depression. Toxic doses of a narcotic can reduce a user's breathing rate, and death from morphine poisoning is almost invariably caused by respiratory arrest.

While narcotics can suppress coughing, they stimulate such other involuntary responses as nausea and vomiting. Their ability to reduce the movement of food through the intestines makes these drugs the most effective means yet discovered to treat diarrhea. They will, however, constipate users who employ them for other purposes.

In addition to their analgesic properties, narcotics produce euphoria, and it is the quality of the narcotic high that makes them such seductive and powerfully reinforcing drugs of abuse. They create a sense of warmth and well-being, peace and contentment, feelings of strength and energy. Major problems and everyday irritations fade. Anxiety and depression lessen. The world becomes more pleasant, the user "larger than life." Heroin's high, in particular, exerts a powerful hold. As the saying goes, "It's so good you don't want to try it even once."

Actually, the initial use of a narcotic can be a disappointing and unpleasant experience, often accompanied by nausea and vomiting. Rarely is euphoria achieved, although effects vary and are heavily influenced both by the expectations of the user and by the setting in which the drug is taken. Nevertheless, in spite of unsatisfactory or even distasteful introductions to narcotics, a good many users persist and, in time, achieve the immensely pleasurable effects of the drugs.

The late saxophonist Art Pepper recalled his initial experience with heroin in *Straight Life: The Story of Art Pepper:*

> I felt this peace like a kind of warmth. I could feel it start in my stomach. From the whole inside of my body I felt the tranquility. It was so relaxing. It was so gorgeous. Sheila said, "Look at yourself in the mirror! Look in the mirror!" And that's what I'd always done: I'd stood and looked at myself in the mirror and I'd talk to myself and say how rotten I was—"Why do people hate you? Why are you alone? Why are you so miserable?" I thought, "Oh, no! I don't want to do that! I don't want to spoil this feeling that's coming up in me!" I was afraid that if I looked in the mirror I would see it, my whole past life, and this wonderful feeling would end, but she kept saying, "Look at yourself! Look how beautiful you are! Look at your eyes! Look at your pupils!" I looked in the mirror and I looked like an angel. I looked at my pupils and they were pinpoints; they were tiny, little dots. It was like looking into a whole universe of joy and happiness and contentment.
>
> . . . I looked at myself and I said, "God . . . I'm beautiful. I am the whole, complete thing. There's nothing more, nothing more that I care about. . . . I don't need to worry about anything at all." I'd found God.
>
> I loved myself, everything about myself. I loved my talent. I had lost the sour taste of the filthy alcohol that made me vomit and the feelings of the bennies and the strips that put chills up and down my spine. I looked at myself in the mirror and I looked at Sheila and I looked at the few remaining lines of heroin and I took the dollar bill and horned the rest of them down. I said, "This is it. This is the only

answer for me. If this is what it takes, then this is what I'm going to do, whatever dues I have to pay . . ." And I *knew* that I would get busted and I *knew* that I would go to prison. . . .

All I can say is, at that moment I saw that I'd found peace of mind. Synthetically produced, but after what I'd been through and all the things I'd done, to trade that misery for total happiness—that was it, you know, that was it. I realized it. I realized that from that moment on I would be, if you want to use the word, a junkie. That's the word they used. That's the word they still use. That is what I became at that moment. That's what I practiced; and that's what I still am. And that's what I will die as—a junkie.

Patterns of Use

Narcotics can be taken orally, by injection or by inhalation (either smoked or sniffed). In general, they are absorbed into the bloodstream poorly and slowly when taken by mouth, although this route of administration can prolong their effects (and works well for codeine and such synthetics as methadone and meperidine). Even injected narcotics may take a while to reach the brain, because of the difficulty the natural opiates seem to have crossing the blood-brain barrier. This difficulty, however, is not shared by heroin and may be one reason for its popularity. It crosses the barrier with relative ease and speed, so that soon after injection much more heroin than morphine reaches receptors in the central nervous system.

Heroin rarely is taken orally—a decidedly inefficient route for this drug. Most users sniff it or inject it, either subcutaneously (beneath the skin) or intravenously ("mainlining" it directly into a vein). A growing number now smoke street heroin off tinfoil in a practice called "chasing the dragon."

The effects of smoking can be similar to intravenous injection in triggering heroin's orgasmlike "rush," the euphoric peak of the drug experience. The rush fades in a matter of minutes and is replaced by a prolonged period of lethargy—the "nod," which can last six to twelve hours and is marked by a sense of overall contentment and the absence of anxiety and appetite.

Some heroin users manage to take the drug cautiously enough to continue experiencing the same effects from the same size dose, and avoid tolerance for a considerable time. But the majority inevitably slide toward more regular and, eventually, compulsive use. When heroin is taken regularly, tolerance develops over time and increasingly larger doses are needed to experience the rush and euphoria. One danger is that although tolerance develops to all the drug's effects, it does not develop evenly. It is possible to have great tolerance to the drug's pleasurable effects yet built up little resistance to respiratory depression. Thus, in order to achieve the rush, a user may have to risk taking life-threatening doses.

Eventually, the compulsive heroin user experiences fewer and fewer pleasurable effects of the drug. Yet use must be continued—and even increased—to avoid the discomfort of withdrawal. The classic pattern of addiction is now in place: The user has to take the drug to satisfy cravings and to stave off withdrawal—and do so with ever increasing frequency and ever stronger doses. The addict can rightly state that he now needs the drug to feel "straight," to feel normal.

William Burroughs described the ever increasing need for narcotics in the introduction to *Naked Lunch:*

> I lived in one room in the Native Quarter of Tangier. I had not taken a bath in a year nor changed my clothes or removed them except to stick a needle every hour in the fibrous grey wooden flesh of terminal addiction. . . . I did absolutely nothing. . . . I was only roused to action when the hourglass of junk ran out. If a friend came to visit —and they rarely did since who or what was left to visit—I sat there not caring that he had entered my field of vision. . . . If he had died on the spot I would have sat there looking at my shoe waiting to go through his pockets. Wouldn't you? Because I never had enough junk —no one ever does. Thirty grains of morphine a day and it still was not enough. . . . And suddenly my habit began to jump and jump. Forty, sixty grains a day. And it still was not enough. And I could not pay.

For most heroin-dependent users, withdrawal symptoms begin around the time they are used to having their next shot of the drug. The "sickness" can begin with uncontrollable yawning, a runny nose and a cold sweat. In the classic, heavy-duty brand of withdrawal, symptoms will increase in severity over the next thirty-six to seventy-two hours. Nausea and vomiting, intestinal spasms and diarrhea are joined by muscle cramps, backaches and pains in the arms and legs. Victims alternately shiver and sweat and can neither remain still nor find a position in which they are comfortable. The withdrawing addict can suffer extreme anxiety and intense drug cravings. After seventy-two to ninety-six hours, the symptoms will start to diminish. Although they may complain of lethargy, insomnia and chills for weeks to come, most addicts get past the worst of withdrawal within a week. But the psychological aftermath—depression and drug craving—may not lift for a considerable period of time.

There is no question that physical dependency on narcotics leads to an abstinence syndrome. But there is general agreement among drug researchers and treatment experts that the classic, intense type of withdrawal hardly ever occurs today, mostly because of the minimal potency of street drugs. While experts maintain that most current heroin users rarely find withdrawal more serious than a bad bout of the flu, with the worst symptoms usually over in two or three days, some longtime heroin addicts who withdraw from the drug without medical support insist they experience a truly horrible "sickness" that can last as long as two or more weeks.

What causes withdrawal? There is some agreement among scientists studying opiate receptors in the brain that production of endorphins (the body's own morphinelike chemicals) seems to drop off when narcotics are regularly being supplied from outside the body. But what happens when this outside supply is abruptly cut off? With no heroin and little endorphin to reach their receptors and trigger "slow down" signals, a number of centers in the brain start transmitting at an accelerated rate. Communication speeds up through all their networks. The autonomic nervous system, which controls such involuntary functions as breathing and digestion, begins bombarding its outposts with garbled messages that bring on such withdrawal symptoms as nausea, cramps, diarrhea, and a runny nose.

Withdrawal symptoms vary from narcotic to narcotic, but they're never pleasant. Methadone, for example, which is a long-acting drug, has a slower-starting but longer period of withdrawal than the shorter-acting heroin. What is important to remember is that withdrawal depends on the degree of dependence—how long a person has been taking narcotics, how often he takes them and how much he uses.

Adverse Reactions

There are plenty of them—nausea, vomiting, dizziness, constipation, and diminished sexual capacity for male users, the result of the opioids' ability to suppress production of male hormones (which return to former levels within a few months after opioid use ends). But the major adverse reaction is acute intoxication or overdose, the result of a larger or purer dose than the user's tolerance can handle. Overdose may also result when opioids are taken too soon after a previous dose or when taken by a user with low blood pressure.

An overdose victim becomes lethargic, usually falling into a stupor or becoming comatose. Respiration drops sharply; blood pressure follows it down. Body temperature is low, and muscles are relaxed. There is little one can do for an overdose victim except help him keep breathing—making sure his head is straight and that there are no obstructions in his mouth or throat—and get him to a doctor or emergency room. Should the victim stop breathing, start artificial respiration and call for an ambulance or paramedic team.

Generally, there is more than enough time to get an overdose victim the care he needs—most often a narcotic antagonist, such as naloxone, that will not further depress respiration. Although victims have recovered from respiratory depression only to die of such complications as pneumonia or shock, respiratory depression itself is by far the greatest cause of overdose fatalities, often occurring with pulmonary edema (flooding of the lungs).

But there is something of a mystery about many deaths that have been routinely recorded as "narcotic overdose" over the years. Frequently, longtime heroin abusers will collapse and die within minutes or even seconds of injection. The most striking feature of these fatalities is massive and sudden pulmonary edema. Considering the ability of most addicts to survive doses far larger than they would regularly use, their considerable tolerance for the drug, and the relatively low potency of street heroin available to them, these fatalities seem unlikely to be simple instances of overdose. The pulmonary edema in these cases appears more likely to be an allergic reaction that can occur when quinine is used to cut heroin or when the victim has been drinking. Long-term users seem to be more vulnerable than short-term users to this reaction.

Long-Term Effects

Narcotics are relatively free from direct long-term physical effects other than the profound dependency they create. But they do produce a number of serious and potentially fatal indirect effects. Malnutrition and anemia are common among addicts, who are vulnerable to infection and often contract tuberculosis. Many other disorders that afflict narcotic abusers result from their use of unsterilized needles and the practice of sharing "works" (needles, syringes, etc.). Abscesses, cellulitis (inflamed swellings that spread beneath the skin), and infections occur near injection sites. Bacteria and viruses that enter the bloodstream directly may cause hepatitis, tetanus, or endocarditis (inflammation of the heart lining and valves). Impurities and adulterants in street drugs can cause kidney failure. Not long ago, several addicts were blinded by yeast spores of a fungus (*Candida albicans*) that turned up in shipments of heroin from the Middle East.

Controlled Heroin Use

There's no way use of a drug as potent and powerfully reinforcing as heroin can be anything but high-risk. Regular use almost always leads to dependency. Still, drug experts have long recognized that a certain number of users do appear to keep even heroin under control for prolonged periods of time. References to the "joy popper," the individual who uses drugs intermittently and who has never been hooked, appeared in the literature of drug abuse long before the heroin crisis of the late 1960s.

Confidence in the viability of "joy popping" or "chipping" (occasional use) was shaken, however, by a major retrospective study in 1967. Using a sample of young black men in St. Louis, researchers determined that 13 percent had tried heroin and only 3 percent had avoided addiction. Everyone who used the drug more than six times ended up an addict.

This kind of evidence, indicating little likelihood that heroin users could avoid addiction, aroused considerable concern in the U.S. government when the drug became extraordinarily popular among American troops stationed in Vietnam at the start of the 1970s. Heroin use reached rates of 100 percent in some rear-echelon units. After an army crackdown on marijuana made pot scarce, thousands of soldiers turned to heroin, which was cheap, far more potent than anything sold on the streets back stateside, and easy to come by. It was simple to conceal, could be dusted onto cigarettes or secretly sniffed.

In spite of a thirty-day detoxification and treatment program for users identified by urine screening and found to be dependent, the government anticipated a tidal wave of domestic heroin use when addicted troops returned. The Nixon administration sought ways of handling vast numbers of addicts at minimal cost. This concern prompted a federal drug abuse policy that encouraged development of methadone maintenance clinics and deemphasized other forms of treatment that could not set up shop as quickly or as cheaply.

The great Vietnam veteran heroin epidemic never materialized. Indeed, levels of heroin use in this country actually began to fall after 1972. One follow-up study of former soldiers who had received the Army's thirty-day quick cure found that only 7 percent were still using heroin one year after their return. A later study, with a sample of 571 previously addicted veterans, discovered that, although 20 percent had used heroin at some point during the three years since their return to the United States, only 12 percent of these users—a mere fourteen men—had experienced any period of addiction.

One can hardly credit this outcome to the success of the army's quick cure, and indeed almost no expert does. A clue to what probably did occur can be found in recent work with heroin "chippers." Dr. Norman E. Zinberg of Harvard's medical school has studied a group of subjects who have been able to sustain "controlled opiate use" over long periods of time, limiting their habits and avoiding addiction.

Considering the three variables that determine how much control a drug user is able to exercise—the nature of the drug itself, the user's "set" (what Zinberg describes as "the user's personality and his or her attitudes toward taking the drug"), and the physical and social "setting" of use—Zinberg maintains, "My research has emphasized the importance of the third variable." The setting, he contends, helps determine "social sanctions and social rituals that influence individuals' decisions to use a particular drug and also the way in which they use it."

What Zinberg concluded was that when his subjects constructed those "appropriate rituals and sanctions" with the help of other controlled users, when they created settings—times, places, companions—for their drug use, they built a system in which controlled use of narcotics proved possible.

Zinberg's approach indicates one possible reason why there was no domestic heroin epidemic when the soldiers returned from Vietnam. They left the setting of their drug use behind when they left Southeast Asia. They also lost easy access to the drug. Not that formerly addicted veterans paid no price for their drug involvement while overseas. A substantial number have had serious problems with alcohol. And heroin may have masked emotional problems that are now surfacing among Vietnam vets.

Despite the Vietnam experience and Zinberg's work with chippers, controlled use of opioids as potent as heroin is definitely high-risk activity. Indeed, controlled use of any narcotic is risky. It is possible, but only for a few select users or under very special circumstances. It is not something that will work for the overwhelming majority of people who experiment with narcotics. And there is no sense in trying to find out if you are one of the very few people that can control opioid use.

Danger Signs

Because the heroin and morphine high is so reinforcing and because these drugs create such profound physical dependency, *any* use is high-risk. If you use them or any of the more potent opioids, or if you inject your narcotic, you need no warning. You are involved in drug use of the most dangerous kind, and the likelihood of avoiding addiction or some other high cost is small. Even if you steer clear of the strong opioids and shun needles, you can easily come to grief. It is a mistake to believe you can't get hooked if you just snort heroin or if you take Percodan tablets.

However, if you are in the early stages of using potent opioids, or if you are relying on prescription narcotics such as Percodan or Darvon, there is a chance you can avoid addiction. There are some clear warning signs that will let you know when your risk of dependency has risen to an unacceptable level and *you* are close to, or at, compulsive use.

1. Are you increasing your use? Any increase is serious when the drug is a narcotic, because any increase either indicates or creates tolerance. It takes very strict limits on how often and how much you use to keep tolerance from starting to grow. Once it starts, tolerance grows quickly, creating physical dependency and putting you firmly onto the addiction escalator, which demands continued and increased use simply to avoid symptoms of withdrawal.

2. Do you spend much time just thinking about narcotics? You may not be using narcotics all that much, but if you spend a lot of time anticipating your next high, you've got a lot less control over your drug use than you imagine.

3. Do you romanticize opioids? If you fantasize about narcotic addiction and favor such books as De Quincey's *Confessions*, William Burrough's *Junkie*, Jim Carroll's *Basketball Diaries*, if you're fascinated with the lives of such famous addicts as Billie Holiday, you're probably into drugs a lot more than you'd care to confess.

4. Do you misuse prescription narcotics? If your doctor has prescribed codeine or Percodan or Darvon for pain and you find yourself taking more than you need, you've got a potential problem.

5. How susceptible are you to encouragement? At first, most narcotic users indulge in drug-taking with a few friends or "drug buddies" (though opioids are hardly the social or recreational drugs coke and marijuana are). If you want to get high at the slightest sign of encouragement from one of your buddies, you have little control over your drug-taking.

6. Is your work suffering? Narcotics are not drugs that enhance performance. They are not meant to be taken by people who need to be alert and efficient. They will slow you down, cloud your mind, cause you to forget things. If your work at school or on the job is starting to deteriorate, you've got a situation you'd better deal with while you can.

7. *Are you selfish with your drugs?* At first you may be all for giving a friend one of your codeine tabs or having him or her snort some of your heroin. But once you become unwilling to share your supply, you're into drugs more deeply than you probably think.

8. *Do you believe you can control your drug use?* Most narcotics users start out with some healthy fear of the drug. Once you lose that fear and start bragging about your control, it's time to stop. You are falling into a classic pattern that leads to heavier and less cautious use.

9. *Are relations with your spouse or lover deteriorating?* This can occur long before sexual interest diminishes. Opioids do nothing for sociability. In fact, you may start resenting people who come between you and your drug, who interrupt the high or the nod or disapprove of your use. If narcotics are starting to affect your relationship with someone you truly care for, you are getting all the warning you should need.

10. *Have you injected narcotics?* If you have, you're on your way to addiction—or may already be there. Injection increases the pleasurable effects of the drugs and reinforces their use. It also means you've crossed a barrier: You're likely not to want to go back to popping codeine tablets or snorting heroin.

11. *Are you scheming to get drugs?* If you are trying to con your doctor into giving you pain-killers or are forging prescriptions, you're pretty desperate and pretty dependent on drugs.

12. *Are you having trouble getting enough money for drugs?* At first, narcotics aren't very expensive—even heroin goes a long way in the hands of a novice. But costs quickly mount—whether for street drugs or prescription ones. If you've run through your savings, started borrowing money or stealing—even if it's only $20 from your father's wallet or $30 from petty cash at work—you've got a habit.

13. *Are you starting to lie?* Every addict lies about how much he's using. If you're dependent on a gram of coke a day, you'll probably tell people you do a half-dozen lines. If you're doing three bags of dope, you'll probably claim it's one. It's classic behavior for drug-dependent people. So if you're doing it, you've got a real problem.

14. *Are you constipated much of the time?* If so, your use of opioids is at a level sufficient to cause alarm. Dependency may not be far off.

15. *Are you losing interest in sex?* Opioids can help relieve sexual anxiety and allow men to sustain erections (by inhibiting ejaculation). But

over time, they reduce your ability to be aroused and result in decreased desire for sex. This is a relatively late sign of high-risk use, so if interest is flagging you've got a serious problem.

16. Are you frequently on the nod? This is a sign of regular narcotic use. If you've started dozing off at your desk or burning cigarette holes in your clothes or upholstery, you're well into a pattern of opioid use.

17. Are you mixing prescription drugs with alcohol? This is truly dangerous. What you're risking is death from respiratory depression. Yet a number of users do it to get more of a high (at less cost and without increasing tolerance). Risky by itself, the practice is another obvious danger sign.

18. Do you combine narcotics with other drugs? If you are mixing codeine with the hypnotic Doriden or have tried Talwin with Pyribenzamine to get a heroinlike high, you are well into high-risk use and could be creating a complicated and life-threatening withdrawal problem.

19. Do you feel a cold coming on a day or two after getting high? If after your last dose of narcotics your nose starts running, you feel a lack of energy, irritable and a craving for drugs, you've got the first signs of withdrawal. You have a drug habit, a small one perhaps, but a habit all the same. If you don't ride the withdrawal out and stop now, things are just going to get worse.

Narcotics addiction is a way of life. So if drugs are now your main concern and how to get drugs your main problem, then you are dependent on them—even if you don't have a heavy heroin habit. If your old friends and lovers, interests and values, are passing out of your frame of reference and your prime feeling of security comes when drugs are in your possession, then you are dependent on narcotics—even if you've only been using them for a few months.

The problem is not just that your life has changed for the worse, but that unless you stop it will keep changing—in a few years you will be leading a different life and, in many ways, be a different person.

Starting Off

As with any drug, the first step you must take to get off heroin or any of the other narcotics is to recognize you have a problem—that you're either headed toward physical dependency or already there.

This recognition is a lot easier with narcotics than with cocaine or grass or tranquilizers. Unless you're in the early stages of use, you probably feel intense drug cravings. Once you start getting sick when you're out of drugs, there's no denying you have a habit.

Of course, you can still put up a good front, still assert that things are under control, still claim you can stop anytime you want to. But if you panic when you can't locate your dealer, it's a little hard to see yourself as in control of the situation.

Users who take their narcotics by pill or tablet, or who snort heroin or smoke opium will find it easier to deny they have a problem. But eventually withdrawal symptoms will hit them and they'll have to give in, too. Not using a syringe and needle gives them some advantage—their habits will develop more slowly. But they *will* develop habits.

There is a social stigma attached to all narcotic use, though the worst of it is reserved for those who inject drugs. In a strange way this can help you come to terms with your drug dependency. There is no acceptance of narcotic use in this country, and thus there is no negative support system encouraging you to believe you don't really have a problem.

It's important to remember that you are not a bad person because you are an addict (even if you have done bad things to support your habit). There's no good or bad here. There's only healthy and unhealthy. And right now, you're in a very unhealthy situation.

Now is the time to take care of that situation, because prolonged use can only make it worse. You may be able to kick drugs by yourself. More likely, you're going to need some help in getting and staying off. And if you do need help, support, understanding, treatment, now is the time to ask for it.

There's no question about where you should start—at the doctor's office. If you have a personal physician or a family doctor who is familiar with your medical history and is aware of any special physical problems you may have, consult with him or her. But you have to be honest with the physician about your drug use. If you're not, or if you're embarrassed about seeing someone who knew you before you became involved with drugs, try to see a doctor who has some experience with narcotic dependency.

This is important because you need to know what your overall physical condition is and if drugs may have cost you something in disease, infection or malnutrition. They may have been masking signs of illness. You should also let a doctor—one who is knowledgeable about drug abuse—help you decide whether you need chemically assisted detoxification from your drug of abuse, and whether it should be done in a hospital or a residential or outpatient treatment center.

If you go for medical detoxification, you will probably be given methadone, today's "preferred" substitute drug. Still, even with methadone, you are going to feel some physical pain. Not much, and the roughest part of withdrawal will be mental, dealing with the depression that is often a part of the abstinence syndrome. It will not be a very happy time, but it needn't last that long. You can be out of the hospital, on the average, in seven days. As an outpatient, the process will take somewhat longer.

Detoxification for former heroin users who have been maintained on high doses of methadone is difficult. In the past, the patient's daily maintenance dose (often as high as 70 to 100 milligrams) was reduced by 3 to 5 milligrams a day. But withdrawal symptoms often appeared when the dose fell below 20 milligrams, and many patients continued to feel uncomfortable, irritable and tired and experienced insomnia, pain, diarrhea and premature ejaculations for months after detoxification ended. Today, many medical researchers believe methadone detoxification should be extended for as long as four to six months.

A clue to what may complicate detoxification of methadone maintenance patients was recently uncovered by two studies of former patients that found lower endorphin levels persisting for six to twelve months after methadone use had ended. If little of the body's own pain-and-discomfort-relieving chemical is reaching their receptors, it's understandable that former methadone users might feel lousy much of the time.

There is great interest now in a nonnarcotic drug for detoxification of narcotics addicts. Not only might such a drug help in detoxification of methadone patients, but it would also meet the needs of narcotic users who are reluctant to take methadone to detoxify. (Some addicts fear that because of methadone's potency, they will wind up with heavier habits than they started with.) In addition, a nonnarcotic would make it possible to start antagonist therapy immediately after detoxification (eliminating the present need to wait until the patient is free from all residual methadone effects). Clonidine, a drug now used to treat hypertension, has shown some ability to relieve symptoms of narcotic withdrawal and is being studied as a possible replacement for methadone.

Because physicians are reluctant to substitute a stronger drug with more abuse potential for a weaker one with less potential, methadone is rarely used in detoxification from pentazocine (Talwin) or propoxyphene (Darvon). Pentazocine users get gradually diminished doses of pentazocine itself, while users of propoxyphene are usually detoxified with propoxyphene napsylate (Darvon-N).

Detoxification, by itself, is not treatment. It is not going to help you make the kinds of changes in your life you must make to stay free from drugs. And treatment is something you should be thinking about before you choose how you're going to handle withdrawal. You may choose to withdraw in a residential treatment center. Deciding whether or not you need treatment and choosing which kind of treatment to consider is a decision you should make with a doctor or drug abuse counselor.

You can get some idea of your treatment needs and how they can be met from the following drug involvement test, which should be used with the personal resources test in Chapter 2.

Drug Involvement Test

Answer each question as honestly as you can, but don't trust yourself too much. Remember, honest self-assessment is not your strong suit. Ask someone close to you—your husband or wife, friend or lover—to check and correct your answers.

	YES	NO
1. Do you inject heroin or any other opioid?	—	—
2. Do you use opioids daily?	—	—
3. Do you use opioids at least three times a week? (Answer Yes even if you have responded positively to the previous question.)	—	—
4. Is heroin your drug of choice?	—	—
5. Do you use at least $100 worth of opioids a week?	—	—
6. Do you use any injected drug, any sedative, or alcohol in combination with an opioid?	—	—
7. Has there been any significant increase in your use of opioids during the past three months?	—	—
8. Have you ever tried to quit?	—	—
9. Have you tried to quit three or more times?	—	—
10. Have you used opioids constantly during the past year with no period of nonuse lasting a month or longer?	—	—

A Yes answer to Question 1 or 2 or a total of five or more Yes answers indicates *profound* drug involvement. Three or four Yes answers indicate *serious* involvement and less than three *moderate* involvement.

If your drug involvement is profound—no matter what your personal resources—you have to consider some rigorous treatment options. The same options should be considered if your involvement is serious (particularly if you need medical detoxification), unless your personal resources are remarkably strong. You can think about less demanding alternatives if you have only moderate drug involvement and your resources are either strong or at the strong end of the limited range.

Treatment Alternatives

When drug abuse treatment was getting organized in this country, there was a preoccupation with treatment for only one form of abuse—narcotic addiction. This reflected a political necessity to respond to the crisis of heroin addiction that was developing during the 1960s. Public officials all recognized that treatment was necessary—even if few thought it was possible. While there was evidence that a number of hard-core addicts did "burn-out" and give up narcotics later in life (for no obvious reason and with no medical assistance), most of the treatment plans then available—simple detoxification, long-term hospitalization and traditional psychotherapy—had proven generally ineffective.

Complicating the treatment problem was the nature of the addict population. Not only were many antisocial, but most were emotionally, educationally or vocationally underdeveloped as well. Rehabilitation for these drug abusers was an awesome task. If they were to stand any chance of remaining abstinent, then social, emotional, educational and vocational deficits all had to be remedied.

The many needs that treatment for narcotic abuse has had to address and the freedom to try nontraditional methods has meant that a great many quite different alternatives have been developed. But it is not as difficult as it might seem to find one that will work for you. Your own instinct (and a sound one) will be to opt for what is minimally intrusive, makes fewest demands and will least disrupt your life. If what you first try doesn't seem to be working, you can always try something more rigorous. Once you are involved in almost any kind of treatment, you should be able to count on your counselors to help decide what is best for you. That is why it is so important, when choosing a program, to select one that screens admissions carefully and will refer clients to more appropriate agencies at any time the need becomes apparent.

All of the treatment forms to be discussed here (with the exception of methadone maintenance) are covered at greater length in Chapter 2. What follows are the points you should consider when deciding which might be most useful to you.

Methadone Maintenance

Drug maintenance is nothing new in the United States. Narcotic clinics were opened in several major cities after passage of the Harrison Act (although all were shut down by 1925) to provide "maintenance doses" of morphine to addicts, enough of the drug to prevent symptoms of withdrawal. Maintenance with heroin has existed for some time in Great Britain. Although the British experience is generally regarded there as unsuccessful and new maintenance patients are now given methadone, there is still periodic advocacy for heroin maintenance programs in the United States.

Methadone maintenance was developed during the early 1960s by Drs. Vincent P. Dole and Marie E. Nyswander, who became convinced that basic changes in the metabolism of narcotic addicts created a "drug hunger" that persisted long after withdrawal ended and could be relieved only by opioids. They sought a drug that would satisfy this hunger and create a "narcotic blockade," to prevent patients from feeling the effects of even a large dose of another narcotic. The drug they found, methadone, was a synthetic narcotic that had been developed during the later stages of World War II by German chemists seeking a way to replenish Germany's dwindling supply of morphine. It was well suited for the purposes Dole and Nyswander intended. It could control a physical dependency without producing either euphoria or withdrawal symptoms; it was cross-tolerant with other narcotics, long-lasting, inexpensive to produce, and free from significant long-term effects. Also, it could be taken orally, thus preventing patients from experiencing the rush of injected narcotics and the health complications associated with self-injection.

Today methadone maintenance is widely available in hospital outpatient programs and both public and private clinics. Treatment basically consists of a daily oral dose of methadone dissolved in orange juice or some other flavored drink. Admission to methadone programs is limited by federal regulations to users who are over sixteen and have been *addicted* for at least one year.

There is some disagreement about the optimum dosage for maintenance. "High-dose" advocates believe in gradually increasing the amount of the drug until the patient receives enough to prevent even substantial amounts of another narcotic from having an effect. "Low-dose" advocates aren't concerned with Dole's "narcotic blockade" and use a relatively small amount of methadone, just enough to control the craving for heroin and avoid the symptoms of withdrawal. At maintenance levels, methadone does not produce euphoria, although most users experience a mellow, warm feeling known as the "methadone glow." Side effects include drowsiness, sweating, constipation, some loss of sexual interest and capacity to achieve orgasm.

Federal guidelines require methadone clinics to check periodically on the possible use of other drugs by patients through screening of urine samples. The right to take home supplies of methadone is restricted to patients with no evidence of other drug use and who have demonstrated commitment by regular attendance.

There is a great variety among methadone clinics, and this is most apparent in the supportive services that all are required to provide. Some offer counseling that matches in quality the best outpatient drug-free clinics. Although the mental health model is usually followed, and one-to-one therapy is considered more significant than groups, many counselors employed in methadone clinics are trained former abusers, some of whom are themselves methadone patients. Educational and vocational counseling are also available, and family counseling may be offered as well.

In spite of urine screening, nonnarcotic drugs (most often cocaine, amphetamines and sedative-hypnotics) are often used by methadone patients. However, the incidence of other drug use is lowest in clinics with strong counseling programs. Alcoholism is an even greater problem. Some studies have found as many as 25 percent of a clinic's patients abusing alcohol and increases in alcohol use among clinic populations at even higher percentages.

How long does methadone maintenance last? It was designed to be lifelong, for Dole and Nyswander anticipated that victims of narcotic addiction would use methadone much as victims of diabetes use insulin. But today there is a growing belief, even among methadone clinic staff members, that eventual abstinence should be the goal for methadone patients. However, it is a goal that is not frequently achieved. A number of methadone patients do choose to be detoxified from the drug after a period of maintenance, and detoxification is done cautiously. Often dosage is reduced by as little as 3 percent a week. Nevertheless, the post-withdrawal success of these patients has not been entirely encouraging.

How well does methadone maintenance work for patients who do not attempt to withdraw? Effectiveness of methadone programs is generally measured by how long patients continue to participate, by their employment or other productive activity and by degree of criminal involvement. Early studies of patients in New York City clinics found 75 percent had remained in treatment for three or more years, with sizable increases in employment and reductions in arrests. A later, large-scale study of clinics throughout the country found 46 percent of the patients remained in treatment for as long as one year and indicated far less improvement in employment and avoidance of criminal activity.

Methadone maintenance—or treatment with LAAM, a longer-acting relative of the drug—is not an alternative that should be considered by anyone to whom other modalities offer a reasonable chance of achieving abstinence. It ought never to be a first choice, and probably should be reserved until after *several* treatment failures. It is best regarded as a last resort.

However, if you are convinced that you have no choice other than methadone maintenance, you should pick your clinic carefully. If there is a hospital program available to you, check it out before considering any others. Look for strong support services, counselors you feel comfortable with, and group therapy. Pay attention to the "feeling" of the place. Many clinics are depressing places and do not provide a setting appropriate to a goal of eventual abstinence. If a clinic always seems to have a crowd hanging out, or if you suspect that drug dealing goes on around it, find a better-run, more responsible one.

Drug-Free Treatment

Residential treatment (described in more detail in Chapter 2) can be demanding. But if your drug involvement is profound or serious and your personal resources are weak or very limited, then long-term residential treatment in a *therapeutic community* (TC) is likely to be your best bet. Here, you will find, in addition to treatment, the kinds of educational and vocational services that can help you start your new life.

TC treatment is based on the self-help concept—the individual taking responsibility for his cure—and leans heavily on the use of mutual support groups. This approach was borrowed from Alcoholics Anonymous and was adapted at Synanon for narcotic addicts, but it has proven effective for dealing with all kinds of compulsive behavior. The emphasis on self-help prepares you for the day you leave the program. The structured environment of the TC, with its twenty-four-hour-a-day supervision and the complete break with the past that it demands, will help you to overcome your old conditioning and aid you in resisting the drug-taking cues to which narcotic users are extremely vulnerable.

What should you look for when choosing a TC? Begin by selecting a well-established institution that is approved or licensed by your state's drug abuse agency, one that has experienced paraprofessional counselors and avoids physical and other extreme forms of coercion. The program you pick should be able to evaluate carefully the needs of applicants, provide alternate forms of treatment or make referrals to other types of programs. Most important are your feelings about the program itself. You have to like the place and you *must* trust the staff.

Although most TCs are publicly supported, many accept private, fee-paying residents, and there are special residential programs (both public and private) for adolescents. There are also private hospitals and clinics that provide therapeutic community treatment along with other forms of intervention. Even though traditional hospital care has not proven an effective way of dealing with narcotic dependency, a number of hospitals now offer a great variety of innovative treatment methods.

For narcotic users, the importance of a clean break makes some form of residential intervention desirable at the outset, even for those who do not require so intrusive a form of treatment over the long haul. This is one reason you should consider hospital detoxification or withdrawal in a residential treatment setting. However, although the need for short-term residential treatment is now well recognized, there are currently few programs that provide this alternative.

Outpatient, drug-free (OPDF) treatment is what you are most likely to need if your drug involvement is only moderate and your personal resources are strong. You may try an outpatient program even if your involvement is serious, and this form of treatment generally will work well for older users who have been able to hold down jobs and meet family responsibilities in spite of their drug use. As with residential programs, outpatient clinics that use the mutual-support, self-help group are likely to be most effective. In choosing a program, you should look for one that has been around for a while or is part of an established agency with experience in the treatment of drug dependency. You want a program that offers a regular schedule of evening groups and opportunities for more intensive participation on weekends. You will also want one that encourages the participation of those who care about you (husbands, wives, lovers, parents, employers) and offers regular groups for these significant people in your life.

Outpatient programs come in more than one variety. In addition to the self-help model, there are many that bear a closer resemblance to traditional mental health programs; the emphasis is placed on one-to-one counseling rather than on group therapy. These programs also often offer opportunities for family participation.

Antagonist therapy uses nonaddictive drugs to block the effects of narcotics. A former addict taking naltrexone, for example, will not be able to get high no matter how much heroin he shoots. The therapy is still experimental, but it is offered by a number of private clinics and individual physicians, as well as at several publicly supported outpatient or methadone programs. This is an alternative you might want to consider after short-term residential treatment or in addition to a regular schedule of outpatient group therapy.

Individual Efforts

Getting off drugs is really up to you, for the process demands changes that no one can make for you. Treatment helps. It offers guidance, encouragement and ways to monitor your progress. The more demanding residential programs establish a framework within which to accomplish change, and the less demanding the treatment you choose, the more structure you must provide for yourself.

Start with the immediate problem of quitting—withdrawal. If you are a heavy user, and certainly if you inject narcotics, you should not consider withdrawing on your own. You need medical supervision (probably a hospital detoxification program). But if your doctor agrees that you are capable of kicking by yourself, there are ways to go about it sensibly.

You'll find a scenario for individual withdrawal from any drug in the "individual efforts" section of Chapter 3, on cocaine. When you are withdrawing from narcotics, the basics are the same. You need to take some time off from work or school (use a vacation period if you can). You need isolation (not only from drug buddies and dealers, but even from well-meaning friends and relatives). You need someone to take care of you, and the spouse, lover or friend who undertakes this chore must be prepared for just how bad things can get. When you break with drugs, you should break clean; you don't want to romanticize drug use by treating yourself to a farewell blowout, one final high. You will have to throw out all the drugs, paraphernalia, books and memorabilia of your drug-taking days—anything that might serve as a drug-taking cue. Don't set specific goals; think about quitting only one day at a time.

Those are the general rules. When withdrawing from narcotics, there are additional considerations:

1. Anticipate some pain. You've got to expect physical discomfort. But don't let your imagination get out of hand. Expectation can aggravate withdrawal, and anticipating the worst is one way to ensure it. Assume nothing more dreadful than a bad case of flu, with diarrhea, vomiting, chills, fever and muscle aches.

2. Get away. Distance counts more for the withdrawing narcotic user than for other drug users, because a more powerfully conditioned response is involved. You are highly vulnerable to drug-taking cues, and your own home is full of little reminders. You'll be best off getting out of town, borrowing or renting a place in the country. While you don't want a remote location (should there be a medical emergency), you do want to put real distance between you and the context of your drug use.

3. Prepare your partner for just how bad things could get. It will be messy and difficult. There are not only the shopping, cooking and house-keeping to do, there's preserving your isolation too—answering the phone, dealing with worried friends or relatives, and turning them away gently. He or she will have to clean up after you—and may need to clean you too. You will be no joy to be near, for you'll have little desire to move or wash or get out of bed (and probably no inclination to share it). Your partner is also there in case withdrawal goes badly or you need medical attention for some other reason. He or she should be aware that your drug use may have masked symptoms of disease that will appear as you withdraw.

4. Use medication carefully. Your doctor is likely to prescribe some nonopioid analgesic to help you handle pain. You may also have tran-quilizers and nonbarbiturate sleeping pills. You'll probably be tempted to load up on whatever you've got to avoid depression, and it's important to resist that temptation. The prescribed drugs are for when you really need them.

5. Let it all out. Don't bottle up your feelings. You will be sick, angry, miserable and depressed. This is no time to show how tough you are. It is a chance to start uncovering some of the true feelings you are going to have to recognize and deal with in the months to come.

6. Remember the bad times. That's the rule for any kind of with-drawal, but particularly important for narcotic users. You can begin to break your heavy conditioning by concentrating on the times you got ripped off or came close to overdose. Forget the highs and recall what it was like when you couldn't score. Face up to how many people you have let down or disappointed, the friends you cheated or hurt, the relation-ships that fell apart because of your drug use.

7. This is your time. Even if you are lucky enough not to experience much physical discomfort, you may feel just awful and have so little energy that walking up a flight of stairs will be a major effort. This is not the time to show how strong a person you are or to act stoic. Indulge yourself. Admit you're feeling awful. Give in to tears if you feel like crying. Don't talk to your partner if you don't feel like it (though you should prepare him or her beforehand for this). This is your time. You are sick and you should feel entitled to do whatever makes you feel better —be it just lying in bed or watching TV all day.

8. Save analysis for later. Although thinking of the lying and cheating you've engaged in may strengthen your resolve to get off drugs, don't start feeling guilty or analyzing your behavior of the past few months. You're going to feel bad enough just coming off drugs. Give yourself a break. Don't reprimand yourself. That's no help at all.

Withdrawal doesn't last all that long, and having come through it, you deserve to be proud. But don't get cocky about your strength. The real battle begins when you have to go back to everyday life. At first, you will be running into drug-taking cues almost everywhere. It will surprise you how many people, places and situations will trigger drug cravings or elicit even more intense responses. A classic example of just how potent these stimuli can be is the former addict who found that withdrawal symptoms recurred when he returned to the neighborhood where he used to score.

While the need to drop your former drug buddies, to avoid them and the settings of your drug use, is obvious, it isn't always easy. What if your spouse or lover is a user? What if you have been getting off at or near school or work? What if you scored drugs in your own neighborhood?

Certain changes you can make. Others you cannot. If your spouse or lover is a user, or if some other member of your family or a close friend uses, then you've got to do whatever you can to get them to quit too and to start treatment with you. To get away from familiar drug scenes, you might think about moving, finding a new apartment. Changing your job, too, can help you break with the past. But there are limits to what you can change, and some cueing situations you may have to live with. The point is to minimize your exposure as much as possible and to find alternative activities and associations, new interests and friends.

You're not going to be all that eager to launch yourself into anything new, though. The emptiness you are likely to feel will tend to immobilize you, and it must be actively resisted. Physical exercise is a way to begin. Something strenuous, like body building, can help accelerate the changes in body chemistry that will relieve your sluggishness and some of your depression. It will add to your new awareness of your body and help build self-esteem, as well as improve muscle tone.

You will be tight and wound up much of the time and find it difficult to relax. But there are ways to handle this. Learning how to relax deep muscles is one way, and biofeedback is a technique you might consider. Meditation is another route to relaxation and a means of dealing with depression as well.

A good many former narcotic users have found that the easiest route to new interests and activities has been spiritual, becoming more involved in their church or in some other religious organization. A point to remember is that drug use tends to make you a fairly insular individual, reduces your exposures to new ideas and information, limits your experience. You may well have some catching up to do, and now is the time to do it. It is a time to pick up on old interests, learn new things, engage in lots of different activities and meet new people.

Staying Off

Once you are off narcotics, truly off, involved in new activities and new social networks, finished with treatment, and have a stretch of drug freedom under your belt, you should think about how to sustain abstinence. If your former life was drug-centered, with no family responsibilities and no job you cared about, you might think seriously about relocating, breaking away completely from the settings and situations to which you still will have some vulnerability. One recent study in the Southwest found former drug abusers who relocated were three times more successful remaining abstinent than those who stayed in the same city.

But relocation isn't an option for everyone. Certainly it is not something you should consider if you have substantial personal resources and strong family or professional ties. Yet you may well need some support in your new life. Today, many treatment programs offer aftercare groups that provide this kind of structure. There are also several organizations for former drug users that use the self-help model started by Alcoholics Anonymous. Narcotics Anonymous was established specifically for former opioid abusers, and some local AA chapters will accept former drug users as members.

All these organizations employ the mutual support, self-help group. They hold regular meetings and provide a network of understanding peers, who have shared your experience and have the same vulnerability you do. They can step in and lend a hand when life gets hard to handle or you feel your commitment to abstinence is shaky. Members help each other recover from relapse. (You may slip at some point, but don't think this negates all the work you've done to stay clean, and a strong support group can keep you from sliding all the way back down.) These organizations offer a safety net, opportunities to talk over problems no nonuser can understand, such as the drug cravings that may recur years after you have quit.

Recognizing your vulnerability is important. It means you really must continue to stay away from your old haunts and drug buddies and avoid situations that prompt strong drug-taking cues. Don't test yourself by handling drugs or paraphernalia. Instead of proving your progress, you may be orchestrating your own fall. And alcohol poses a great threat to former narcotic users. Watch your drinking carefully. You know your own history of substance abuse. If alcohol starts to become a problem, then you clearly need a self-help group like AA.

You probably will have a lot of unfinished business when you've ended treatment. This is the time to seek help for the emotional problems that may have been uncovered while you were getting off drugs and to understand the behavior that led to compulsive drug use. It is a time to deal with difficulties you may suddenly find in relationships with friends or colleagues or with your husband, wife or lover. Remember, they have been used to a much different person, harder to get along with in some ways (less dependable, less honest) but much easier in others (more pliant and readily manipulated). As you have become more responsible for yourself, you have probably become more aggressive as well.

In addition to these new pressures, there may well be problems in your relationship with your partner (spouse or lover) that you have put off confronting. The relationship may be loaded with guilt and anger because of your drug use. Now is the time to come to grips with these problems, too, and it might be wise to consider professional help in resolving them.

Notes for the Narcotics User's Partner

If you are tied to a narcotic user, as spouse or lover, you've got to recognize the possibility of becoming involved yourself. Male users, in particular, will often attempt to share their drug habit with their wives or lovers, and if both partners are using, then it becomes very difficult—if not impossible—to keep drug use from escalating rapidly.

If you aren't involved with drugs yourself and your partner is, you may have to take some of the responsibility for his (or her) habit. If you've been tolerating it, accommodating it, then you have become party to it. If you haven't made your feelings known, then it's time you did so, and that means refusing to support (financially, emotionally, or in any other way) his use of narcotics. You can put pressure on him to quit, if you are willing to follow through and believe it will work. If you threaten to leave him or expose his drug use, then that's what you must do if he doesn't stop.

If he agrees to quit, he'll need plenty of support. Helping him through withdrawal, with all its physical and emotional strains, is only the beginning. After withdrawal, the two of you will need to sit down and sort lots of things out.

If he has asked for your help, then he must understand that he cannot place many restrictions on it. He can't say, "Help me," then limit the kinds of help he is willing to accept. He should realize that you have been making a good many of the decisions the two of you should probably have shared. You've been doing this because his drug use made him less aware and less dependable. If you continue making these decisions (and you probably should), he's likely to start resenting it. But there's no way you can help him to overcome the lethargy and depression that usually follow withdrawal without either some heavy-handed manipulation or outright bossiness. He should understand that now is the time to swallow his resentments and go along. It's up to you to recognize when to cut back, to ease off and start sharing more decisions as he accepts more responsibility for himself and his behavior.

Obviously, the more pressure you can take off yourself, the better, and a good treatment program can take off quite a bit. Treatment will work best—and so will your relationship—if you, too, become involved. While you can't expect a treatment program to deal with long-standing or root problems in your relationship, you should expect some help with the day-to-day difficulties of dealing with a husband, wife or lover who is getting straight.

This is going to be a very demanding time. Since so many addicts go back to drugs, you may have to make some hard decisions. You're going to have to decide how to deal with a slip, and you may have to confront the possibility of failure. What will you do if he goes back to drugs after you have given him all the help and support you can? Can you go through it all again, or is it time to end the relationship or marriage?

5

AMPHETAMINES

Amphetamine and amphetaminelike stimulants are drugs of immense abuse potential. Their ability to raise energy levels, to reduce appetite and the need for sleep, to produce feelings of clearheadedness, power and euphoria makes them attractive to a variety of users—housewives who want a lift, high-powered professionals who feel they need extra energy to keep up with the competition, truck drivers who must stay awake to complete an all-night run, students cramming for exams, and hard-living men and women who crave the thrill of life in the fast lane.

But there are high risks, for not only can these drugs do serious physical and psychological harm but sustained use produces a rapidly rising tolerance. Escalating dosage and unlimited use during "runs" create in many users a profound dependency—a true addiction.

Stimulant use has dropped sharply during the past decade, the result of rigid government controls and a greater awareness on the part of doctors of the dangers these drugs pose. Nevertheless, a substantial stimulant-dependent population still exists, although users find it increasingly difficult to wangle legal prescriptions and count more and more on bootleg (illegally imported or diverted) and bathtub drugs from the illicit market.

Early Use/Present Trends

Amphetamine was first synthesized in 1887, but it lay around the laboratory for years before its medical properties were recognized. Indeed, it wasn't until 1927 that doctors learned its value as a decongestant and stimulant and as an aid in treating narcolepsy, a condition marked by incidents of instant slumber that physicians call "sleep attacks."

Misuse of amphetamines started early. By the 1930s, amphetamine sulfate (Benzedrine) was being squeezed out of inhalers then available without a prescription. Popularity of the drugs increased dramatically during World War II, when soldiers—British, American, German and Japanese—were routinely issued amphetamines to overcome fatigue and lift flagging spirits. Kamikaze pilots are said to have taken amphetamines before starting off on their suicide missions, and it was the marketing of war-surplus supplies of the drug in Japan that touched off that country's huge postwar amphetamine crisis.

In the postwar United States, prescription and production of amphetamines grew to immense proportions. The drugs were prescribed not only for rare cases of narcolepsy but also for depression and weight loss— more often to help women shed a few spare and unattractive pounds than for true obesity. Doctors also innocently prescribed the drugs as a way of perking up patients, giving them some extra energy to get through the day. While amphetamines had been popular for decades in certain segments of society—among artists, criminals and the convention-flouting rich—the 1950s saw these users joined by housewives and business executives, who took an "up" in the morning to get going and a "down" at night to go to sleep.

In addition, amphetamines and amphetaminelike stimulants (most often Ritalin) were given to hyperactive children. Although these drugs do increase the attention span of such youngsters and will calm rather than excite them, stimulants were prescribed so indiscriminately—sometimes on the recommendation of school officials—that misuse became common. Not until the late 1960s and early 1970s did the practice begin to come under control, and only after exposure by outraged patients, drug abuse experts and social critics.

In the 1960s, although awareness of the abuse potential of amphetamines and other stimulants was growing, the drugs continued to be widely prescribed, and a number of celebrated "Dr. Feelgoods" maintained patients on them, some administering daily amphetamine-spiked vitamin injections. At the same time, a good many young members of the counterculture were turning from marijuana and hallucinogens to stimulants

—"popping" amphetamines and snorting or shooting the more potent methamphetamine, "speed." By the end of the 1960s, huge amounts of stimulants could be found in New York's East Village and San Francisco's Haight-Ashbury district. In just a few short years, a substantial number of flower children had become "speed freaks"—drug-dependent, isolated and uncommunicative, frightened and violent.

The epidemic of stimulant use peaked in 1971, when some 12 billion doses of amphetamines were manufactured by U.S. pharmaceutical companies—enough to supply sixty tablets or capsules to every man, woman and child in the country. Physicians became far more cautious about dispensing the drugs. Federal legislation severely limited production and distribution. Pharmacists became more careful about filling prescriptions, and some even refused to stock amphetamines.

Abuse of the drugs did not stop. Some Dr. Feelgoods went on prescribing and dispensing amphetamines well into the 1970s, and there was a growing market in "bootleg" stimulants (most of which were American-manufactured drugs shipped abroad and smuggled back). Yet use declined. Word spread through the drug-using community that "speed kills," and the message (if not entirely true), was heeded. As government controls tightened, some users who still craved an energizing high switched to cocaine, which was becoming more available.

Today, amphetamines are rarely prescribed. They are usually employed as diet aids only as a last resort—and not at all in New York State, where any use for weight control is now prohibited. They are almost never prescribed for depression. But the most telling statistic is the drop in U.S. amphetamine production—from that 12 billion dose high to well below a billion.

Recently, however, there has been a marked increase in reported amphetamine use among adolescents. But what this most likely reflects is the presence of a good many look-alike drugs on the illicit market. Made of nonprescription stimulants with no amphetamine content, these drugs are produced in capsules and tablets that resemble real amphetamines in shape, color and size; they even have the appropriate code numbers and company trademarks. The look-alikes share the illicit market with bootleg amphetamines—the real stuff, now usually manufactured abroad. And there are bathtub amphetamines as well, made in illicit labs for distribution to the street market.

Today's Stimulants

To the big three stimulants of abuse—amphetamine sulfate (Benzedrine), dextroamphetamine (Dexedrine), and methamphetamine (Desoxyn or Methedrine)—pharmacologists have added a number of amphetamine-like substances over the years and increased the variety of stimulants available by combining ingredients and mixing them with other drugs. For example, dextroamphetamine is combined with amphetamine in Biphetamine and with the depressant amobarbital in Dexamyl.

Amphetamine, dextroamphetamine and methamphetamine act in similar ways and produce almost identical effects, but differ in potency. However, amphetamine users will usually favor one over the others. The amphetamines are available in tablets and time-release capsules (as are the amphetamine/depressant combinations), although methamphetamine is traded on the illicit market mostly as a powder that can be snorted or made into an injectable solution.

Methylphenidate (Ritalin) and phenmetrazine (Preludin) are included with the amphetamines in the federal government's Schedule II classification of drugs, a grouping of the most stringently controlled substances available for medical use. Until recently, Ritalin was the drug most often presecribed for hyperactive children; Cylert is now commonly recommended for this purpose. Preludin was usually given to aid in weight loss (although it became a favored drug of abuse in Sweden, where widespread use during the 1970s reached crisis proportions).

Doctors who prescribe stimulants today tend to favor benzphetamine (Didrex), chlorphentermine (Pre-Sate), phendimetrazine (Plegine) and phentermine (Ionamin). These drugs are much less potent than the amphetamines and amphetaminelike substances and are less tightly regulated. They are also considered to have less abuse potential, although stimulant abusers who must settle for what they can get have been known to take large numbers of Didrex tablets daily.

Effects of Stimulants

All stimulants work in much the same way, with effects on the central nervous and cardiovascular systems similar to cocaine's. All produce euphoria, relieve fatigue, suppress appetite and reduce the need for sleep. Users feel alert, full of energy and have an overall sense of well-being. The world looks a bit better to them and they feel sharper, more powerful, more in control of themselves and able to tackle any project or any problem. Indeed, the euphoria produced by amphetamines includes exhilaration and feelings of boundless strength and intellectual acuity. Users often believe they achieve profound insights, solve baffling riddles, and bring true brilliance to their work.

Depending upon the route of administration, stimulants can produce a rush or "flash." When methamphetamine is snorted, for instance, the user first feels a tingling sensation in the head. Taken intravenously, the drugs hit hardest, with an abrupt rush that jars all body systems and has been compared with both a splash of water and an orgasm. The effects of the drugs follow within minutes, and sometimes seconds, of an injection.

Patterns of Use

Just about all amphetamine misuse starts for one of the following reasons: to overcome fatigue; to sustain, increase or improve performance; or to complete a particularly difficult or time-consuming chore or piece of work. And there are a few close-to-classic types of users. There is the ambitious businessman who starts taking amphetamines to remain alert throughout twelve-hour workdays, who wants to appear lucid and quick-thinking to his clients and bosses, and will stay up half the night to prepare a presentation for the next day's meeting. He will almost certainly get his drugs prescribed by a sympathetic physician.

Housewives, too, abuse stimulants and many start with drugs prescribed for weight loss. These women often find their daily routine—cleaning, shopping, taking the children to school, preparing meals—as grueling as the executive's. To get going in the morning and keep moving through the day, many come to count on stimulants.

Then there are students who need to write papers in a day or two or to cram for final exams. And truck drivers to whom time is money, and who must keep going, often without sleep, to make deliveries on schedule. Students and truck drivers, who generally live in a world more tolerant of pill-popping than that of executives or housewives, often come by their drugs illicitly—buying them from campus dealers or at roadside restaurants. Athletes are also given to stimulant misuse, although cocaine now seems to be their drug of choice. But while cocaine can only be obtained illicitly, athletes have often received stimulants from team doctors or friendly physicians. Indeed, the locker-room environment almost encourages drug use; athletes are routinely given injections so they can play without feeling the pain of injuries.

While stimulants initially prove attractive to these users because of the ways they affect performance, there have always been other users lured solely by the drugs' "kicks." It was this energized euphoria that prompted widespread use in the counterculture during the late 1960s and early 1970s; these young users delighted in intense "speed raps," the insights the drugs seemed to produce, the dynamism it gave them when they wrote or painted or played music.

No matter what the type of user, it is easy to move from casual, occasional drug-taking to high-risk use and drug dependency. A good many housewives, executives and students slide from periodic use of low-dose oral amphetamines to more frequent use, eventually increasing their drug intake to three or four times a day and upping their dosage. Consumption increases not only because the effects of the drugs are so reinforcing but because tolerance to those effects builds very quickly.

Tolerance builds so quickly, in fact, that some users wind up taking staggering amounts—up to 300 or 400 milligrams daily. The bottom-line user almost always favors methamphetamine (also the favorite of the narcotic user, who sometimes mixes it with heroin in a "speedball"), and though he or she may snort it at first, the ultimate route of administration is intravenous injection. This was how most "speed freaks" of the 1960s took the drug and the way some Dr. Feelgoods ministered to the likes of Andy Warhol's superstar crowd.

In their book on Edie Sedgwick, *Edie: An American Biography,* Jean Stein and George Plimpton quoted Joel Schumacher's account of one of these Dr. Feelgoods:

A friend of mine—well, an ex-friend of mine—told me about this terrific doctor where you'd get these vitamin shots—Dr. Charles Roberts. I used to run into Edie there. I went one night, got this shot, and it was the most wonderful shot in the world. I had the answer: I mean, it gives you that rush. There were vitamins in it, and a very strong lacing of Methedrine. I'd never heard of Methedrine or speed. They never told me what was in the shot anyway. It was a slow evolution. I went there first and got a shot. I went a week later and got another one. And maybe one week later I was feeling kind of down, and I went twice a week. Eventually I was going there every day, and then I was going two or three times a day. Then I went four times a day. Then I started shooting up myself.

Dr. Roberts was the perfect father image. His office, down on Forty-eighth Street on the East Side, was very reputable-looking, with attractive nurses, and he himself looked like a doctor in a movie. He was always telling me of his wonderful experiments with LSD, delivering babies, curing alcoholics . . . and he was going to open up a health farm and spa where all this was going to go on . . . and natu-

Table 3. Amphetamines and Similar Stimulants of Abuse

Drug (Generic Name)	Representative Brand Name(s)	Duration of Effects	Maximum Safe Dose per Day[1]	Relative Abuse Potential
Amphetamines				
Amphetamine	Benzedrine	4 hours[2]	30 mg/day	High
Dextroamphetamine	Dexedrine	4 hours	15 mg/day	High
Methamphetamine	Desoxyn, Methedrine	4 hours	15 mg/day	High
Amphetaminelike Drugs				
Phenmetrazine	Preludin	4–6 hours	75 mg/day	High
Methylphenidate	Ritalin	4–6 hours	60 mg/day	Moderate to high
Related Stimulants				
Benzphetamine	Didrex	4–6 hours	150 mg/day	Moderate
Chlorphentermine	Pre-Sate	8–10 hours	65 mg/day	Moderate
Phendimetrazine	Plegine	4–6 hours	210 mg/day	Moderate
Phentermine	Ionamin	8–10 hours	30 mg/day	Low
Pemoline	Cylert	10–12 hours	112.5 mg/day	Low

1. In divided doses—for individuals with no medical conditions that would preclude the use of drugs in this class (such as high blood pressure).

2. Time-release forms of many of these drugs are also available. In these cases, a single dose is usually compounded so that the dose is released over an 8- to 12-hour period.

rally he was stoned all the time, too. He wasn't a viper. I just think he was so crazy, he truly thought he was going to help the world. He wasn't out to kill anyone. We were the ones going in and getting the shots. I mean, anyone can set up a booth on the side of the road reading: I'M GIVING ARSENIC SHOTS HERE, but *you* have to stop and take them.

Over the years that he was riding high, tons of people went to see Dr. Roberts. But there was a little crowd of favorites. When you were a favorite, it meant that you were allowed special privileges. Even if the waiting room was filled with twenty people, you got right in. When you were addicted, being able to get right in was very important. You got bigger shots; you got shot up more than anybody else, and you became more of an addict. It was wonderful to be part of this special group. Edie fit right in. The minute she hit there, she became a special Dr. Roberts person.

I'll give you a description of what it was like to go to Dr. Roberts. The time is two-thirty in the afternoon. I'm going back for my second shot of the day. I open the door. There are twenty-five people in the waiting room: businessmen, beautiful teenagers on the floor with long hair playing guitars, pregnant women with babies in their arms, designers, actors, models, record people, freaks, non-freaks . . . waiting. Everyone is waiting for a shot, so the tension in the office is beyond belief.

Lucky you, being a special Dr. Roberts person who can slip right in without waiting. Naturally, there's a terribly resentful, tense moment as you rush by because you're going to get your shot.

Intravenous injection produces the strongest and sharpest amphetamine rush, lasting only a few minutes, though the euphoria endures for several hours (far longer than the euphoria of cocaine). Interestingly, there is reason to believe that impurities in street methamphetamine are responsible for the powerful impact of this rush, since commercial preparations of the drug apparently do not produce anything so intense when injected.

Whatever the type of user or method of ingestion, amphetamine use is usually followed by depression, difficulty sleeping and nervousness. Attempting to medicate these reactions with sedatives, depressants and alcohol, users often fall into the classic "upper-downer" cycle. In addition, amphetamine users can be much like cocaine users when it comes to dealing with the crash that inevitably follows the high. They too seek to escape the resulting depression by sustaining euphoria through drug-taking sprees or "runs" (protracted use that lasts several days). This is particularly true of shooters. As tolerance builds they may inject huge doses—as high as a gram every hour or two—in an attempt to get a rush and reach a satisfactory high. When the run finally ends and the crash comes, users are exhausted, disorganized, wound-up. They may need sedatives to get to sleep, but then stay asleep for forty-eight hours and longer.

Adverse Reactions

Adverse reactions to amphetamines outnumber desired effects by a considerable margin. In doses larger than a user's sensitivity or tolerance to the drug can handle—and this may be as little as 2 milligrams, although it is generally in the 30- to 60-milligram range—there are a host of unpleasant effects: dizziness, headaches, nausea, wheezing, muscle and chest and back pains. Users sometimes feel confused. Their hands shake. They may become flushed, sweat a lot and feel as though their hearts are beating doubletime. Often they feel as if they can't breathe. At higher doses, vomiting or abdominal cramps may develop.

After a run, chronic users are often on the very edge of stability. The depression deepens and the irritability grows. They can feel lethargic for weeks, sleep for extended periods, and even though they may be off the drug during this period, they still are prey to panic reactions, heightened anxiety and fear of losing control. Some users become so unstable that they fly into rages, become violent and even commit suicide.

At near-toxic levels, amphetamine brings out various kinds of bizarre behavior. Users pick and poke at things, including their skin. They become engrossed in meaningless and often repetitive tasks, like taking apart and reassembling bits of machinery or lining up all the books in the house. They may lose themselves, drawing an endless series of mazes. A slight nudge and they are over the edge. Amphetamine-induced psychosis, which characteristically takes a paranoid form, can be hard to differentiate from schizophrenia. Compulsive behavior becomes more pronounced. The victim may withdraw or speak in seemingly meaningless sentences. Mood changes are frequent, as suspiciousness grows into full paranoia and users become convinced they are targets of nameless enemies bent on doing them harm. They experience pseudohallucinations identical with those of cocaine-induced psychosis—the same imagined sights and sounds, even the tactile delusion of bugs crawling on or under the skin. The evidence of this delusion—scratches and lacerations on the arms—is so common that doctors look for it to help determine whether patients are true schizophrenics or victims of amphetamine- or cocaine-induced psychosis. This psychotic reaction to amphetamine, although much like cocaine's, lasts longer, sometimes as long as a week if not treated with antipsychotics or tranquilizers, and the hallucinations end before the paranoid delusions do.

In addition to psychosis, there are more life-threatening toxic reactions to amphetamine. Acute toxic reaction, which can be induced by doses of less than 100 milligrams, raises blood pressure, heart rate, breathing rate and temperature. Seizures much like epileptic attacks can occur and may result in serious or permanent damage if medical attention is delayed. Death, although not common, can result from convulsions or stroke.

Long-Term Effects

Stimulants can do quite a job on the body and mind. Long-term use frequently results in physical deterioration because of improper rest and diet. In some cases, amphetamine users come close to starving themselves. Lack of food and sleep lowers the body's resistance and leaves the abuser prey to sores, infections and illness.

The strain amphetamines put on the cardiovascular system can lead to all kinds of trouble—hypertension (high blood pressure), irregular heart rhythm and stroke. Injury to small blood vessels serving the eye can damage the retina. And there is the possibility of brain damage, particularly to users who inject the drug. Shooters can also suffer infections at the injection site, septicemia (blood poisoning), endocarditis (inflammation of heart membrane), hepatitis and other "needle" diseases.

When amphetamine use was at its height, much was made of the way "speed freaks" seemed to "burn out" (something quite different from the apparent spontaneous remission of addiction among older heroin addicts who are said to have burned out). This referred to the mental impairment and memory loss many heavy methamphetamine users seemed to suffer. Although researchers found that in most cases the victims, in time, regained whatever mental capabilities had been lost, this outcome is by no means guaranteed. The heavy use of methamphetamine can cause small blood vessels serving the brain to deteriorate and rupture, resulting in permanent damage.

Are amphetamines and other stimulants addicting? For years, expert opinion held that they produced no physical dependency but clearly created psychological dependency. Now there is less certainty about physical dependency. While these drugs may not create the kind of classic physical dependency seen in narcotics addicts, regular use does produce tolerance and can lead to psychological dependence, drug craving, compulsive and irrational drug-taking and such withdrawal symptoms as lethargy, depression, irritability and muscle aches. All of which would seem to make the issue of true physical dependency moot. Put another way, amphetamines may not lead to the kind of addiction associated with narcotics, but you can certainly—and easily—get hooked on them.

Danger Signs

If you're taking stimulants once in a while, they may seem fairly harmless. And there are indeed many occasional users who can avoid becoming dependent on them. But it is easy to slide from low-risk use of these drugs to high-risk use.

Here are some warning signs of amphetamine and stimulant abuse. If any of these signals sound true for you, then you may be moving toward high-risk drug use. Or you may already be there.

1. Are you using stimulants for purposes other than occasionally increasing your ability to perform a specific task? Amphetamines can enhance performance—if used sparingly—and allow you to work for prolonged periods with great concentration. But they are not "recreational" drugs. If you find yourself taking stimulants on your day off, when you don't have a project or task to complete, or if you are getting together with friends to do speed, you may be becoming dependent on the drug. Any use other than for periodic enhancement of performance can soon become high-risk.

2. Do you spend a lot of time just thinking about amphetamines? You may not be using them much, but if you spend time thinking about when you're next going to take them, you may have much less control over your drug use than you imagine.

3. Do you romanticize amphetamine use? It's hard to imagine how anyone can get caught up in romanticizing drugs that have so many adverse effects. So if you are fascinated by accounts of the speed-freak days of a decade ago, you may be extremely susceptible to stimulants.

4. Do you regret things you have said or done while under the influence of amphetamines? Many drugs loosen inhibitions, and amphetamines also make users more talkative. If you're falling into the "next day" syndrome—wishing you hadn't divulged certain information or talked about certain things the night before—you are probably taking too much amphetamine and taking it for the wrong reasons. It's time to reevaluate your use of these drugs.

5. *Do you need to take amphetamines or other stimulants to get going in the morning?* This is one of the clearest signs of abuse. Once you feel you need the drugs' extra "lift" to start your day, you are psychologically dependent on them. Use can only accelerate and tolerance will build quickly.

6. *Are amphetamines really improving your performance?* This may be a hard question to answer objectively because stimulants can play tricks on you. The great term paper you've written while on speed may read like gibberish a few days later. Amphetamines can enhance production when taken sparingly, but regular use leads to physical and mental fatigue (partly due just to lack of sleep) and confusion. If your work is suffering and your performance is off, you are definitely taking too much speed.

7. *Are amphetamines affecting your sex life?* Stimulants can prolong sexual activity, and some users find the drugs add pleasure to their sexual experiences. But sustained stimulant use can play havoc with your sex life. An orgasm delayed soon becomes an orgasm denied, with one or both partners unable to climax. In men, amphetamines can help maintain erections, but can also make an erection difficult or impossible to achieve. If any of this is happening, you are well into high-risk use.

8. *Do friends find you have become a "different person"?* You probably have. Amphetamines induce mood swings that come close to the manic-depressive pattern. You are bound to become touchy and irritable much of the time, and this new personality of yours is probably going to put off a good many friends and create problems for you at work.

9. *Have you become secretive and suspicious?* These are also some less endearing characteristics of the high-risk amphetamine user. Paranoid tendencies develop with regular use, and they are a serious danger sign.

10. *Do you have trouble keeping your temper?* You can be losing control of more than just drug use. Moodiness and irritability, common among amphetamine users, can lead to displays of anger, violent rages, and incidents of real violence. These are more than just warnings of dangerous drug use, they are signs of dangerous behavior.

11. *Do you spend much time worrying about getting enough amphetamines?* Even a moderate-size habit is hard to supply. Doctors are reluctant to prescribe amphetamines (or any abusable stimulant). Little real amphetamine is available on the street (and much of what is available

comes from basement labs). Buying prescriptions or forging them is what a good many users must resort to.

12. Do you take stimulants two or more days in a row? If you do, you are working up to psychological dependency or have already achieved it.

13. Are you eating normally in spite of amphetamine use? Tolerance to the different effects of amphetamine develops at different rates. Whether or not you become tolerant to the drug's ability to suppress appetite, you may still find yourself needing larger and larger doses to experience euphoria or to avoid feeling depressed and irritable. The only way to limit tolerance is to do what physicians who prescribe amphetamines do. They periodically cut off their patients, imposing a so-called drug holiday, until neurochemical balance is restored. But the chances of so joyless a "holiday" being self-imposed are remote. Once tolerance develops, you're usually on a clear run to compulsive use.

14. Are you into sprees and runs? If the answer is yes, you're a high-risk user.

15. Have you experienced toxic or near-toxic reactions? If you have experienced these bizarre and dangerous effects of amphetamine use, the message should be clear. Stop taking the drug. You not only have a drug abuse problem, you are risking your mental and physical health.

16. Are you injecting amphetamines? This is one of the clearest signs of abuse of any drug. Tolerance will build quickly, dependence will develop, and you will find it almost impossible to go back to pills.

17. Are you using other drugs to bring you down? When you start taking stimulants you can probably handle the depression and malaise that set in when these drugs wear off. But the more you take, the heavier the depression gets. You may also start getting shaky, feel somewhat paranoid, and have trouble falling asleep even when you're exhausted. Many users turn to depressants, alcohol and even heroin to take the edge off the amphetamine high and get to sleep. If you're doing this, you're not only taking more speed than is good for you, you're risking becoming dependent on two drugs.

Starting Off

There are a few basic things to keep in mind when you start to get off stimulants. You've got to admit that you have a drug problem, that you cannot control your use of stimulants. This isn't always easy. Because there is no great public perception of stimulant abuse now, you may think: "If society doesn't seem bothered by amphetamines, why should

I be?'' You may feel that since the taking of pills for all sorts of maladies is condoned and even encouraged, what's the harm in taking those that help you get by. And now that cocaine—which is also a stimulant—has become so widely used and accepted, you may ask: "If everyone's doing coke, why can't I do speed?" What you must remember is that continued uncontrolled use of stimulants will play havoc with your mind and body. You must recognize the reality of your drug problem—and try not to justify it.

Remember, too, that getting off amphetamines and staying off them can be very difficult. At the very least you're bound to feel depressed at first. You may be able to kick your habit by yourself and may be lucky enough to encounter few problems doing it. But if you can't do it alone, if you need help, encouragement, support and care, then ask for them. Amphetamines may have made you feel that you could tackle any problem solo. This is one problem you probably will be unable to solve by yourself.

You are not the first person who ever got hooked on amphetamines— and you're not likely to be the last. It's important to keep in mind that there is no moral right or wrong where drug abuse is concerned. There is only healthy or unhealthy. You needn't feel guilty about turning into a "drug addict" and disappointing your partner, parents, children and friends. You have a problem that needs to be dealt with—that's all. If you've wronged people, there will be plenty of time to apologize and make it up to them. For the present, you've just got to think about getting yourself clean and back in shape.

Your first move should be to your doctor, particularly if he or she prescribed stimulants for you in the past. If you have no doctor of your own or don't want to reveal your heavy drug use to a personal or family physician, then you should look for one who understands drug dependency and prescribes psychoactives cautiously. If your use of amphetamines has been intense and long-term, you may be in pretty bad physical shape. Even if you managed to avoid disease or infection, there's a good chance you are malnourished or anemic and need a high-protein diet and vitamin supplements. The physician will probably also want to see if you have damaged your heart or other organs in any way.

Withdrawal from amphetamines is of real concern, and you should talk this over carefully with the doctor you choose. While withdrawal is usually brief and has few physical signs or symptoms, it can be a terrifying experience. The impact is essentially psychological. Rebound from amphetamines is marked by changes in sleep patterns (including increased periods of REM—"rapid eye movement"—sleep). Users experience restless nights and vivid (frequently frightening) dreams, as well as fatigue and depression. The depression can become so severe, the despair so intense, that users have attempted suicide.

While withdrawal can end after a single prolonged period of sleep, it may drag on for weeks, even months. The depression will last, along with disturbed sleep, lethargy and sometimes mild tremors or "shakes" and muscle aches. Some users carry into withdrawal some of the paranoid tendencies of their drug-taking days and remain suspicious and hostile for a prolonged period after drug use ends.

Because the depression of withdrawal can be so severe and involves the risk of suicide, many doctors will want you closely watched as you come off the drug. This may require hospitalization or a period of residential treatment. How you choose to go about withdrawing will depend upon the size of your habit and the stability of your living arrangements and other resources. If you have been using daily for a month or more, have experienced delusions or pseudohallucinations, and have run into real trouble in your life—fighting with friends or employers and missing work—then a hospital or some other controlled environment probably is where you should start getting off the drug.

Treatment Alternatives

Whether or not you need treatment and what kind of treatment would serve you best depend upon your personal resources and the extent of your drug involvement. To get some idea of treatment need and options, use the drug involvement test that follows (together with the personal resources test in Chapter 2.)

Drug Involvement Test

Answer each question as honestly as you can, but don't trust yourself too much. Remember, honest self-assessment is not your strong suit. Ask someone close to you—your husband or wife, friend or lover—to check and correct your answers.

	YES	NO
1. Do you inject stimulants?	—	—
2. Do you take at least 100 milligrams on any day of use?	—	—
3. Do you use stimulants daily?	—	—
4. Do you use them at least three times a week?	—	—

      (Answer Yes even if you have responded positively
      to the previous question.)

YES   NO

5. Do you take at least 50 milligrams on any day of use?   __   __
   (Answer Yes even if you have responded positively
   to question 2.)
6. Is your stimulant of choice an amphetamine?   __   __
7. Do you use any injected drug, any opioid, sedative,
   or tranquilizer in combination with a stimulant or to
   compensate for stimulant effects?   __   __
8. Do you use stimulants in runs that last for more than
   forty-eight hours?   __   __
9. Do you use them in runs that last more than twenty-
   four hours?   __   __
   (Answer Yes even if you have responded positively
   to the previous question.)
10. Has your use of stimulants increased significantly
    during the past three months?   __   __

A Yes answer to Questions 1 or 2 or a total of more than five Yes answers indicates *profound* drug involvement. Three to five Yes answers indicate *serious* involvement and less than three *moderate* involvement.

If your involvement is serious or profound, you are going to need some form of treatment, no matter how strong your personal resources. On the other hand, with personal resources less than strong, you are also likely to need treatment, no matter how modest your drug involvement.

While the general rule is to seek treatment that provides all the support you need while being minimally intrusive, there are users who require interventions that force them to rearrange their lives dramatically. The treatment approaches covered here are described more fully in Chapter 2. A major consideration before choosing any treatment program is the care with which candidates for admission are screened and the willingness of admission counselors to refer clients to more appropriate programs.

Residential treatment is an alternative you should weigh carefully if your resources are far from strong. If you don't have a job you care about or have lost your job and have no family responsibilities, then long-term treatment in a therapeutic community might well be the best bet for you, especially if your drug involvement is serious or profound. It is a way of strengthening your resources while dealing with your drug dependency in the kind of structured environment where you stand the best chance to succeed.

Some less demanding form of residential treatment might well be considered during the difficult weeks when you start off amphetamines, even if your resources are strong or on the strong side of the limited range. If your personal relationships have survived the suspiciousness, hostility and basically nasty behavior of your drug-taking days, you might want to spare your spouse or partner the most trying days of your recovery by completing withdrawal in a residential treatment center and putting in as much time there as you can spare without unduly disrupting your life.

The points to consider before choosing a therapeutic community or other residential program are covered in Chapter 2 and in the "treatment alternatives" sections of the chapters on cocaine and narcotics.

Outpatient, drug-free (OPDF) treatment is a reasonable route to take if your personal resources are fairly strong, although you may want to start out with a period of residential treatment (unfortunately, this may not be easy to find, for short-term residential therapy is not available in most areas). The place to start is with a strong outpatient program that makes real demands on you—one or more sessions a week and some weekend involvement as well—that uses the mutual support, self-help group that most good TCs and Alcoholics Anonymous use, and that includes the participation of family and other important people in your life. Outpatient programs that rely on a more traditional mental health approach with the emphasis on individual counseling can also be useful. (What to look for in choosing an outpatient program is also discussed in more depth in Chapter 2 and in the "treatment alternatives" sections of the chapters on cocaine and narcotics.)

When seeking treatment, you should be wary of programs, physicians or private therapists who are quick to suggest other drugs to help you cope with stress, depression or the discomfort of abstinence. What you are trying to do is get off drugs, not get involved with new ones. While sedatives may help you sleep during the weeks after you quit stimulant use, they offer no long-term solution to insomnia. Antipsychotic drugs— like Thorazine, Stelazine or Haldol—are useful in controlling stimulant-induced psychosis, but they are not going to do you much good, or even be very pleasant to take, once the psychotic episode ends. Antidepressants, while they can certainly perk up your mood, provide real help only for former amphetamine users whose depression has a biological basis.

Basically, be wary of any program that promises a quick cure for your ills. You may be able to get off amphetamines pretty quickly. But making the changes that will help you break your drug-taking conditioning can't be done overnight.

Individual Efforts

Getting off drugs is up to you. That's true no matter what drug you are taking. Treatment helps and is most often essential if you are to deal successfully with your drug use. It can offer guidance and encouragement, provide a system of support and aid you in making the changes necessary for a drug-free life. It can provide a safety net when things get tough and abstinence is threatened. But in the end, getting off drugs is your job—and there's a lot you can do on your own.

The scenarios for individual withdrawal from most drugs are pretty much the same; again, refer to the "individual efforts" sections of Chapter 2 and the chapters on cocaine and narcotics. And if your doctor has not recommended either hospitalization or withdrawal in a residential treatment setting, then he or she thinks you can safely start off amphetamines by yourself. The basics, then, are: Take some time off work or school and pretty much isolate yourself (from dealers, any drug buddies and even well-meaning friends and relatives). You need someone to take care of you and you have to prepare whoever takes on this task (spouse, lover or friend) for all the unpleasantness that's likely to occur—depression, lethargy and sleeplessness. You should make a clean break from amphetamines, with no final good-bye high. Toss out all the paraphernalia and drug-taking reminders you have around. And don't set any elaborate goals. Think about quitting one day at a time.

There are a number of things that can help you through this period. Remember that many other people have gone through what you are attempting. Keep in mind the bad times, the toxic reactions and the depression that followed your highs; this is important because drug users tend to block out the bad times and reminisce about how great it all was.

Give in to your feelings. Amphetamines, like other psychoactive drugs, can lift your mood and thus let you ride over depression, sadness and anxiety. It's quite possible these and other feelings will now come flowing out, and if they do, the best thing is to indulge them. If you feel like crying, then go ahead and cry. In fact, it's a good idea to think of this first period of withdrawal from amphetamines as your time. Do whatever you please and whatever makes you feel better, whether it's just sleeping for a few days or watching TV. As you get your strength back, activity will be very helpful, but for now indulge yourself.

Reward yourself for getting it together as well as you have and taking the initial step. Treat yourself to a great dinner, a movie or whatever pleases you most and your mood and energy allow.

The most important consideration, when you are withdrawing from amphetamines, is the severity of the depression you are likely to experience. Be prepared for it. But don't anticipate the worst, because withdrawal tends to be just about what you expect it to be. Still, you've got to take precautions. While it's useful to get away to a place in the country or some other new setting when you are coming off cocaine or narcotics, this is not a reasonable idea when you are withdrawing from amphetamines. You may need to get medical attention quickly should your depression prove more than you can handle. Your doctor, even if he or she doesn't recommend hospitalization, may still want to see you frequently during this period.

You are not going to feel too great even after withdrawal ends. Some depression may persist. You're likely to feel empty and lethargic, unwilling to start getting your life together. Nothing is more important than activity. Exercise is a good way to begin, and sustained exercise that increases the body's demand for oxygen can help raise mood levels. Diet, too, can be important. New interests and associations will help. While you may not have a network of drug buddies (amphetamines aren't very social drugs) to replace, you will have to break out of your shell, overcome your tendency toward isolation and self-involvement.

Staying Off

Even when you have gotten your new life moving along well and you feel relatively comfortable with your abstinence, problems can crop up. Some former amphetamine users report craving an "up" to get going months and even years after stopping use. Whether this represents a physiological craving or an emotional response to a given situation doesn't matter much. What's important is that it can lead to renewed drug use.

You may also be tempted to dismiss drug-taking as some kind of aberrant incident that you now have put behind you. This is dangerous thinking. You are still vulnerable to the cues that once triggered the drug-taking response. It's important to remember that you may be vulnerable for a very long time (all drug-dependent people are), and you might need the security of a support system to remain drug-free.

A number of treatment programs and several national organizations (listed in the Appendix of this book) provide self-help groups that can give you this kind of support. Most have developed methods like those used by Alcoholics Anonymous (described in detail in Chapter 7 on alcohol), and Pills Anonymous was created specifically for former users of drugs like amphetamines. These organizations hold regular meetings and make use of a mutual support network—people who understand what you have been through and are now dealing with, who share your vulnerability and who can offer you support when your commitment to abstinence is threatened.

Don't discount the importance of all this. These groups can help anchor you. And a network of peers is of great help when you falter or slip. Relapse is common among amphetamine users, but it need not be tragic if there are people who can help you put it in perspective and can provide support to keep you from falling all the way back into regular use.

In addition, you now may have to deal with some of the emotional problems that were uncovered as you got off drugs, some of the problems that made you so vulnerable to abusing drugs. Now is a good time to seek a therapist's help. You also will probably want to work at salvaging those relationships that are important to you and that may have suffered considerably during your drug-taking days. If your spouse or lover stuck with you through the bad times, he or she may be carrying around a lot of hostile feelings. Now is the time to bring this anger and resentment out in the open, to make repairs in the relationship. You may need professional help to do this. If so, it's probably a good idea to seek out some form of couples therapy.

Notes for the Amphetamine User's Partner

If your partner, spouse or lover has been using amphetamines with any regularity over a prolonged period of time, you have probably been putting up with a lot. Amphetamine users are just about the hardest of all drug users to live with. It is almost impossible to keep up with their mood swings. They are often depressed, irritable and very touchy; they have trouble controlling their temper and can sometimes turn violent. At times, their behavior is simply bizarre. So your relationship is unlikely to have survived without some real damage.

If he (or she) is going to quit, that's good news. The bad news is he isn't going to be any easier to live with for a while. If he goes through withdrawal at home, then you've got to be aware of how extreme his depression can become and be ready to get medical help should it seem to reach a suicidal level. Even when withdrawal ends, his mood level may not rise all that much. Then it's up to you—if you want to see this through—to do all you can to get him moving again. Suggest new activities and interests. You can start by encouraging him to have a new concern for his body; talk about getting back into shape through exercise and diet. This all may take some heavy-handed manipulation—remind him of things he used to enjoy and coax him into trying some of the things that please you. But the major obstacle to overcome will be his conviction that nothing he does is going to make him feel any better.

You can also play an important role by urging him to get the treatment he needs to get off drugs or the support he needs to stay off. This will make life easier for both of you. Your own participation in the treatment program he chooses will show you practical ways to help him and aid you in dealing with the anger and resentment you are bound to feel.

And you *are* bound to feel them. Living with a drug user is hard. You will probably feel shut out of his life, and you can't help but resent that your love hasn't been enough to get him off drugs. But if you decide to help your spouse or lover get off drugs, letting your anger and hurt show won't help at all. He will probably feel miserable enough. Once he has made it through—not just past withdrawal but all the way to a new way of living and thinking about himself—*then* it is time to deal with your feelings. If you then think professional help can be of assistance to the two of you, he should be willing to go along with you.

Only you can decide when his drug use becomes too much for you to deal with. Not everyone can take on the repeated rejection heaped on by a drug-using partner. Not everyone can deal with repeated promises and failures to quit. And not everyone can take on the burden of helping see someone all the way through, from drug dependency to abstinence. If you feel you have to bail out of the relationship, don't take on a load of guilt. You've probably done all you could to help your spouse or lover. And there's nothing wrong with starting to think and care about yourself.

6

DEPRESSANTS

When social critics talk of America's "drugged society," they are more likely to have in mind the popularity of prescribed depressants than the illicit use of cocaine and heroin or marijuana. Depressants, more accurately called sedative-hypnotics, range from barbiturates and barbiturate-like drugs to tranquilizers, and are the most frequently prescribed substances in the United States. If one adds to this the number of these drugs traded on the street and alcohol (which rightly belongs to this drug class), depressant use in America is truly enormous.

Nevertheless, the prescription of all depressants has actually dropped off since 1975. Even earlier, the medical and nonmedical use of barbiturates had declined, while medical and nonmedical use of tranquilizers is now well below the mid-1970s peak levels. Still, one out of nine Americans will take some kind of tranquilizer this year, while the nonmedical use of Quaaludes (methaqualone) rose abruptly at the end of the past decade. (The recent decision by the Lemmon Company to halt production of Quaalude means there is now *no legal manufacturer* in the United States of this very popular drug.)

Not only are the depressants widely used and abused, they are also extremely dangerous. In addition to psychological and physical dependency, depressant users run a grave risk of overdose. Often, they simply lose track of how many pills they have taken or use the pills with alcohol, increasing the depressant effects of both substances. Regular users run even higher risks, because tolerance does not increase evenly, and while it may take much larger doses to get high, little more may be needed to overdose. And withdrawal from depressants can be truly life-threatening. While the narcotic abstinence syndrome can be a fearsome ordeal, it is most unlikely to prove fatal. You can, however, easily die withdrawing from depressants.

Depressant Use

Although chloral hydrate, paraldehyde and various bromide drugs were being used before barbiturates appeared, it was only with the introduction of barbital in 1903 that physicians were able to employ the full range of depressant effects: sedation, relief from anxiety, sleep and even anesthesia. Since then more than twenty-five hundred barbiturates have been developed, although only about fifty made it onto the market.

The ability of barbiturates to cause psychological and physical dependency was recognized early, leading to the search for a safer depressant. The results were not only barbituratelike depressants but also tranquilizers, the first of which, meprobamate, appeared in the early 1950s. Better known by its brand name Miltown, meprobamate was hailed as a relatively safe depressant, and its introduction was cheered by physicians who prescribed it heavily. They soon realized, however, that Miltown too could be habit-forming.

Much better, thought physicians, were the benzodiazepine tranquilizers. The first of these, chlordiazepoxide (Librium), was developed in the late 1950s. Valium followed soon after, and for the past twenty-five years these drugs have enjoyed enormous popularity. In fact, they are now the most frequently prescribed psychoactive drugs. Although not as dangerous as other depressants, regular use can produce both physical and psychological dependency.

The *barbiturates* come in four durations of action—long, intermediate, short and ultrashort. In general, only the short-acting and intermediate-acting drugs, like secobarbital (Seconal), amobarbital (Amytal) and pentobarbital (Nembutal), have much appeal for the nonmedical user.

Barbituratelike depressants were developed as substitutes less likely to be abused than barbiturates and with fewer side effects. However, the more effective replacements, like glutethimide (Doriden) and ethchlorvynol (Placidyl), have proven no less dangerous and have their own downside. Since it is more difficult to rid the system of these drugs than of barbiturates, overdose is more likely to be fatal.

Table 4. Depressants of Abuse

Generic Name	Trade or Brand Name	Duration of Action[1]	Relative Abuse Potential
Barbiturates			
Secobarbital	Seconal	Short[2]	High
Amobarbital	Amytal	Intermediate	High
Secobarbital and amobarbital	Tuinal	Short–intermediate	High
Pentobarbital	Nembutal	Short	High
Butalbital	Sandoptal (in Fiorinal)	Short–intermediate	Moderate
Talbutal	Lotusate	Short	Moderate
Butabarbital	Butisol	Intermediate	Moderate
Phenobarbital	Luminal	Long	Low
Barbituratelike Substances			
Glutethimide	Doriden	Intermediate	Moderate–high[3]
Methyprylon	Noludar	Short	Moderate
Methaqualone	Quaalude	Short	High
Ethchlorvynol	Placidyl	Short	Low–moderate
Ethinamate	Valmid	Short	Low
Benzodiazepines			
Diazepam	Valium	Intermediate	Low[4]
Chlordiazepoxide	Librium	Long	Low
Lorazepam	Ativan	Short	Low
Oxazepam	Serax	Long	Low
Flurazepam	Dalmane	Short	Low
Triazolam	Halcion	Very short	Low
Other Depressants			
Chloral hydrate	Noctec	Short	Low
Chloral betaine	Beta-Chlor	Short	Low
Meprobamate	Miltown, Equanil	Intermediate	Low
Paraldehyde		Short	Low

1. Short: 4 hours or less; intermediate: 4–6 hours; long: 6 or more hours.
2. Generally the shorter-acting depressants produce a more intense physical withdrawal.
3. High abuse potential when used with codeine compounds ("loads," etc.).
4. All benzodiazepines have the potential for producing physical and psychological dependence when used in high doses or for long periods of time.

Methaqualone (Quaalude, Sopor) was introduced in the United States in 1965 as another replacement for barbiturates. Of all the barbituratelike drugs, methaqualone has achieved the greatest popularity as a drug of abuse, while revealing the capacity to create severe dependencies. In late 1983, production by its U.S. manufacturer was discontinued.

Benzodiazepine tranquilizers (Librium, Valium, Ativan) are prescribed primarily to relieve anxiety and muscle spasms, for sedation or to prevent convulsions. They have a much greater margin of safety than other depressants. Nevertheless, regular use can produce both physical and psychological dependency.

Chloral hydrate, the oldest of the hypnotic drugs, is still frequently prescribed for insomnia. Because its effects start to diminish so quickly, however, it is not a useful antianxiety agent. Nor is it today a common drug of abuse.

Effects

Although the depressants operate in the central nervous system in different ways, their impact is pretty much the same. They slow down neurochemical activity, with results that may vary from drug to drug. Yet, depending upon dosage, just about any depressant might be called a tranquilizer, a sedative, a hypnotic (when it induces sleep) or even an anesthetic. The progression of depressant effects starts with relief from anxiety. Next, inhibitions are suppressed, prompting behavior of the sort best observed in alcohol intoxication. Then, sedation occurs. At high doses, sleep results, and even general anesthesia may be achieved if large enough amounts of certain drugs are used. Overdose—which can result not only from taking too potent a dose but from combining depressants (which are cross-tolerant) or using depressants with alcohol (which may increase the effects of both)—can lead to coma and death, most often from respiratory depression.

Relief of inhibitions (technically called "disinhibition") results from suppression of the self-control mechanisms in the cortex and the release of impulses from the lower and older (in evolutionary terms) part of the brain. This effect produces the euphoria common to all depressants, alcohol included; it is quite different from the euphoric effects of narcotics, however, which involve no loss of self-control or impairment of judgment. Disinhibition can cause mood swings that are often rapid and wide, and it is not uncommon to see a user go from calmness to agitation, joy to sorrow, and passivity to belligerence.

It is sometimes hard to recognize that disinhibition is the result of depressant action, for it so often involves behavior that more resembles stimulant effects. Yet, all depressants can induce disinhibition, and this is a primary motive for abuse of these drugs. A good many users take depressants to relieve anxiety in social situations, and disinhibition can be heightened or limited by a user's mental "set" or by the setting in which use occurs.

Indeed, the relief of inhibitions brings the socially insecure out of their shells and can turn them into jovial, talkative partygoers. In addition, this effect can overcome cultural or self-imposed restraints on sexual activity. However, once the cortex is no longer able to monitor behavior, feelings of aggression and hostility often get out of control and may result in violence. This is why alcohol is so often a factor in criminal assaults and homicides. Not that alcohol is the drug most likely to let aggression get out of hand. It is most often involved in criminal violence because its use is so widespread. Barbiturates are even more likely to produce behavior that ends violently—and because of its strong disinhibiting effects, seco-barbital (Seconal) is the barbiturate most likely to cause this kind of behavior.

Sedation, marked by diminished responsiveness to stimuli and reduced levels of spontaneous physical and mental activity, does not always follow rapidly on the heels of disinhibition. Indeed, many drug users choose specific depressants (especially the short-acting and intermediate-acting barbiturates) because of the amount of time they allow between the suppression of inhibitions and the onset of sedation.

Sleep can be induced by depressants, but not all *kinds* of sleep may be possible once dosage rises above a certain level. At higher doses, most depressants will suppress REM (rapid eye movement) sleep, the periods during which dreaming occurs and which may well be essential for emotional health. Without REM sleep, users do not feel rested when they awaken. Depressants also gradually reduce the amount of time spent in the deepest stage of sleep. Because of these disruptions in normal sleep patterns, depressants often can cause insomnia. Furthermore, when the drugs are discontinued after prolonged periods of use, the former user, having been deprived of REM-sleep for so long, will experience excessive dreaming and have frequent nightmares.

Anesthesia can be induced by depressants, but this is not a recognized medical use for these drugs—although the ultrashort-acting barbiturates are often employed for this purpose in combination with other substances. Generally, the anesthetic effects of depressants are observed only in cases of attempted suicide.

Dependencies, both physical and psychological, are created by just about every depressant drug and by all those likely to be abused. Withdrawal is severe and *the most life-threatening* of all drug abstinence syndromes.

Patterns of Use

Because depressants have a variety of effects, they are taken for several nonmedical purposes, and there are classic patterns of depressant abuse—just as there are classic patterns of amphetamine abuse.

Depressants are often used, and initially may be legitimately prescribed, to relieve acute distress or profound anxiety. The widow who is given "something to get her through the funeral" is a popular example in life as well as fiction. More common, perhaps, is the individual for whom depressants are prescribed to relieve tension and stress when a marriage breaks up or a job is lost. While the drugs may initially help during a particularly troubled time, medical use of depressants to alleviate psychic distress frequently backfires. Patients allowed to avoid coming to grips with the causes of their distress will often continue using depressants and eventually seek more powerful ones. In such a case, the physician who prescribes the drugs may actually be a party to developing dependency. Even more abhorrent is the doctor with little patience for a patient's tale of woe who, unable to find anything physically wrong, prescribes a depressant (most likely a tranquilizer) to make his client *feel* better.

Depressants are also taken to achieve euphoria. For some users, this is an idiosyncratic reaction, a reversal of the drug's normal effects caused by peculiarities of the user's body chemistry. More often it is the result of disinhibition. Because tolerance to the various effects of depressants grows at different rates, disinhibition is achieved more readily than sedation as drug use continues over any substantial period of time. Seekers of this depressant "high" (what drug experts call the "stimulated" state of "disinhibition euphoria") can consume large quantities of depressants and often go on sprees. These users greatly resemble drinkers who, after belting down a few, loosen up, grow noisy, become extremely sociable and say and do things they otherwise would not. Although such users may regret their actions the next day, this response is exactly what they are after, for it frees them from social—and often sexual—insecurity.

Methaqualone has a not-undeserved reputation for enhancing sex, but it is no aphrodisiac. It does not increase sexual prowess or appetite any more than other depressants do. It may, however, relieve inhibitions while inducing a sedation that is somewhat milder than many other depressants provide.

Depressants are frequently taken with other drugs, particularly stimulants. While some users enjoy the high the combination can produce, more take the depressants to cushion the effects of amphetamines or cocaine and help cope with the depression that follows as the stimulant wears off. Typically, the result of this "upper-downer" cycle is the creation of dual dependency. Even more dangerous is the mixture of different kinds of depressants and the combination of depressants with alcohol. Less popular but no less dangerous is the mixing of depressants and opiates, as in "four doors," a mixture of Doriden and codeine that mimics the effects of heroin. In addition, some methadone maintenance patients take Valium or Placidyl, claiming the drugs "boost" the effects of their medication.

The hard-core "barb freak" is relatively rare these days. Those who are still able to obtain barbiturates seem to be seeking more than euphoria or the depressant high. They crave total intoxication, just as the true alcoholic does. These barbiturate users generally wind up so physically dependent that withdrawal is life-threatening. They are likely to take the drug intravenously—which makes them an exception among depressant users, who almost always stick to pills. Injection is dangerous not only because it exposes users to all the "needle diseases"—hepatitis, abscesses, etc.—but also to the greater danger of respiratory arrest.

Then there is the user who doesn't fit any of the regular stereotypes. He or she, typically, takes Valium to deal with the stress of a career or pops pills to cope with the everyday demands of life, to get to sleep or simply to unwind. Such users are, in part, the products of a society with considerable tolerance for drug use, a nation that accepts the notion of taking something to feel better. This attitude toward drug-taking has been reinforced by many physicians and encouraged by pharmaceutical companies.

Barbara Gordon described her dependency on Valium in *I'm Dancing As Fast As I Can:*

> Valium [was] as much a part of my morning ritual as putting on lipstick. . . . How many times, how many, many times have I taken these pills, popped them like aspirin, like vitamins, thinking only that the anxiety would go away, thinking only that they would help me? Whatever the menace is, the danger, the peril, I should be able to fight it without pills. . . . Impulsively I threw the vial on the floor and watched the yellow pills make a circle on the rug.
>
> I had never considered giving up Valium before. . . . I knew it wouldn't be easy. I had just seen films about heroin withdrawal. . . . But I wasn't a junkie; I was going off medicine, not drugs, I thought. . . . Valium wasn't heroin; it couldn't be such a rough withdrawal.

Valium is an interesting drug. It isn't an upper or a downer. It's a leveler. It evens things out silently, quietly. No rush, no thrill, no charge. It's called the safe and sane drug; millions of prescriptions are written for Valium every year. . . . So obviously I was in good company. It had certainly helped my anxiety attacks in the past, but it didn't always work anymore, no matter how many I took. I had started taking Valium for a back problem, beginning with four milligrams a day. Now I was up to thirty and couldn't get out of the house without taking them. I was taking them *before* an anxiety attack. . . .

I didn't know why Valium worked when it did, or why it didn't. Nor did I know that withdrawal from Valium can cause . . . serious complications. . . . Months later, I would see other addicts—and believe me—tranquilizer takers can become addicts—being withdrawn from Valium five milligrams a week over a long course of treatment. I was taking thirty milligrams a day and I went off it cold. . . . I blew my head open.

Of the 20 million Americans who will be using benzodiazepines (Valium, Librium and Ativan) this year, nearly half will use only a moderate amount, and more than three-quarters will stop within four months. For about 15 percent, however, tranquilizer use will be sustained. Most of these users are older Americans with physical disabilities that require this kind of medication. But a good number—most of them women—will predictably be abusing the drugs in time, needing and taking increasingly larger doses and combining tranquilizers with other drugs or with alcohol.

In spite of the growing unwillingness of many physicians to prescribe tranquilizers, few abusers have much difficulty getting the prescriptions or pills they want and little reason to turn to the illicit market. Other depressant abusers, however, have a harder time meeting their drug needs. Barbiturates have become harder to find on the street. Federal limits on domestic production have been lowered each year, few smugglers find it worthwhile to carry the drugs, and they are none too easy to whip up in basement labs. What is sold illicitly as barbiturates these days proves to be something else about half the time, usually either methaqualone or over-the-counter antihistamines.

While Quaaludes were being legally manufactured in the United States, they were far more commonly offered on the street than barbiturates and even less likely to be genuine. Even then only a small percentage of pills sold as Quaaludes actually were. Frequently, street drugs called Quaaludes are lower-dose tablets or capsules of methaqualone (often produced in basement labs with the impurities that prove it). Antihistamines are sometimes substituted, as are high doses of benzodiazepines, with sometimes as much as fifteen times the normal strength of these tranquilizers. Since American production of Quaaludes has ceased, there will be even more counterfeit drugs on the street.

Adverse Reactions

Depressants have a host of minor side effects, including impairment of judgment and muscle control, confusion, and loss of concentration and reflexes. Users may become irritable or belligerent, quarrelsome or morose. They may be unable to control their laughter or their tears. Heavy-duty users frequently take on slovenly ways.

Methaqualone has its own set of special side effects. Among them are fatigue and dizziness, menstrual irregularity, skin troubles (rashes, blotches and eruptions), and a loss of muscle control so severe that users may become grotesquely awkward. Paresthesia (tingling and numbness in patches of skin) occurs often, indicating the possibility of nerve damage near the skin surface that may persist for months or even years.

Hangovers are common to all depressants, with the same "morning-after" effects of alcohol. Cutting down on depressants produces a rebound effect that can include anxiety, insomnia, loss of appetite, headaches, stomach cramps, tremors or "shakes," and even nausea and vomiting. Once you are physically dependent, rebound effects will progress to full-blown withdrawal.

Withdrawal itself is deadly serious. Abrupt deprivation of depressants for the heavily dependent user provokes the most dangerous of all abstinence syndromes (see the "starting off" section). But there are other major dangers of depressant use, including behavioral toxicity, the damage you can do to yourself because of your lack of judgment, muscle control, or even balance. Driving, swimming, operating machinery (including simple kitchen appliances) can be risky, and so can climbing stairs and getting into the bathtub (falls and fractures are common) or smoking in bed.

Barbiturates and certain other depressants—but not the benzodiazepines—can provoke the liver to behave in strange and life-threatening ways. Some drugs may be speeded out of the system, while levels of others are raised, and toxic wastes can be produced that will do severe liver damage. Depressant-induced changes in metabolism also can lead to vitamin and hormone deficiencies and lower calcium levels.

An acute overdose of a depressant usually will lower blood pressure and breathing rates so much that failure to get proper medical attention can result in death through respiratory failure or shock. But even timely medical aid may not prevent a fatal outcome, for there is no antidote for overdose, no equivalent to the narcotic antagonists that will control opioid overdose.

Death has also resulted from the effects of toxic depressant doses below lethal levels. When the "gagging" reflex is suppressed, victims have choked to death on their own vomit—as Jimi Hendrix is alleged to have done.

Because it is so difficult to get such drugs as Doriden and Quaaludes out of the bloodstream, overdoses of these drugs are particularly dangerous. In addition, Doriden has its own toxic impact on the central nervous system; it raises the heart rate instead of lowering it, increases body temperature and produces convulsions. Quaaludes, too, at toxic levels will cause convulsions that can prove lethal.

Long-Term Effects

It's hard to separate long-term effects from other adverse reactions to depressants. While the liver malfunctions that depressants induce can severely upset body chemistry, few effects are necessarily permanent, except for the nerve damage that may result from elevated levels of porphyrin, a chemical whose production is greatly increased by depressants' stimulation of certain liver enzymes. Longtime users, however, generally suffer from a number of medical problems, including ulcerations, infections and nutritional deficiencies (the results of poor hygiene and diet) and damage caused by falls and other accidents. Those users who inject depressants are exposed to all the "needle diseases"— hepatitis, abscesses, inflammation of the membrane around the heart, and so on.

Danger Signs

Almost any nonmedical use of depressants is risky. The drugs have too much potential for abuse—psychological and physical dependence easily results from regular use, you can accidentally harm yourself, withdrawal is life-threatening, and there is real chance for overdose. So if you are starting to look forward to your next high, think about the drugs a lot and even tend to romanticize them, you are putting yourself in jeopardy. There are also some clear indications that your depressant use is out of control—an overdose, for example, or an act of violence committed while under the influence of the drugs. But you can manage to overlook a good many clues that are almost as obvious once you acquire the kind of selective vision that comes with a growing depressant habit. What can't be overlooked can often be minimized. So recognizing the following danger signs for what they are is important:

1. Have you been raising your dosage of prescribed depressant on your own initiative? If you've been deciding your depressant needs for yourself, without consulting your doctor, and particularly if it has been a while (a month or more) since your physician had a chance to reevaluate your use of a sedative, hypnotic or tranquilizer, then you're on the edge of abuse.

2. Have you suddenly become accident-prone? If you've been having lots of minor mishaps—spilling and dropping things, knocking objects over—or if you've had a serious fall or automobile accident since you began using depressants, there's a good chance the drugs are getting to you. You'd be wise to quit before you learn any more about behavioral toxicity.

3. Are you becoming a slob? If you put off straightening up the house, have a sink full of dirty dishes, and no longer bother to make your bed, those are warning signs of dangerous depressant use. Letting your personal appearance slide, forgetting to wash your hair or change your clothes, makes it even clearer. You can't simply dismiss these changes; almost all depressant users fall into this pattern.

4. Do your friends find you harder to get along with? Depressants can bring out the beast in you, make you surly and belligerent. Disinhibition prompts wide mood swings. Elation can be followed rapidly by depression, and thoughts of suicide often occur during depressant sprees. If you've been experiencing plenty of quick mood changes and feel as though you are becoming a lot of different people, it's time to quit.

5. Do you often need a stimulant to feel right? Regular users of depressants can come to depend upon amphetamines or other stimulants to get "up" for work or other ordinary activity. Balancing your depressants with stimulants and falling into the "upper-downer" cycle means you are building two drug dependencies instead of one.

6. If you skip a dose, do you get tremors or "shakes"? This is the rebound effect. As you build tolerance, you may also experience anxiety or panic attacks, stomach cramps, nausea or vomiting when your depressant dose is overdue. These are strong signals. They say you've got to stop before physical dependency becomes even stronger.

7. *Have you ever blacked out?* Brief periods of amnesia aren't all that rare among depressant users. If you've awakened with bumps, bruises or cuts you can't remember getting, you shouldn't need much more warning.

8. *Are you getting prescriptions from more than one doctor?* Once you've built a good-size tolerance, it can be difficult to meet your growing drug needs, even if your depressant of choice isn't one doctors are reluctant to prescribe (for example, barbiturates). A number of users find they must consult several different doctors to get all they need—and this, of course, is a clear sign of deep trouble.

Starting Off

When you are ready to get off depressants, see a doctor. For other drugs, medical attention at this point is important; for depressants, it is *imperative*. While the danger and the discomfort of withdrawal from most psychoactives are often exaggerated, it's hard to make too much of the risks involved in withdrawal from depressants. *Don't* try to get off without help and *don't* quit cold. The only place to isolate yourself is in a hospital or other residential facility that can care for you.

Withdrawal starts slowly and symptoms may not reach peak levels for several days. With barbiturates, withdrawal can begin about twelve hours after you have stopped using and can work up to a maximum impact in one to three days, usually ending before the week is out. Withdrawal from meprobamate (Miltown, Equanil) and methaqualone follows a similar schedule, while withdrawal from longer-acting depressants like the benzodiazepine tranquilizers starts more slowly and doesn't reach full force until the fifth to eighth day.

The first signs of depressant withdrawal include anxiety, insomnia and nightmares, loss of appetite, nausea and sometimes vomiting. You may have uncontrollable tremors and twitching movements. Your muscles may seem weakened, and your blood pressure can drop suddenly, making you dizzy when you start to stand up. These minor symptoms can last as long as two weeks. On the second or third day, however, the heavy-duty symptoms show up—extremely high temperatures and convulsions that resemble epileptic seizures. These are not only scary, they are truly life-threatening. If untreated, these symptoms can prove fatal. Death as a result of respiratory or cardiovascular collapse is far from rare.

During withdrawal, anxiety levels keep rising, and a good many depressant users develop psychotic symptoms at this point. The psychosis of depressant withdrawal is not all that different from the DTs (delirium tremens) of alcohol withdrawal. You can become disoriented—unsure of where you are, confused about time. Agitation increases and you may experience delusions and hallucinations.

Clearly, depressant withdrawal is not something you want to take on by yourself, and no doctor will suggest you do it unless your depressant use has been truly modest. Nor will many physicians recommend you quit cold. As Dr. David Smith of the Haight-Ashbury Free Medical Clinic and his coauthors point out in *NIDA's Handbook on Drug Abuse,* "Abruptly discontinuing sedative-hypnotics in an individual who is physically dependent upon them is poor medical practice and has resulted in death, as well as malpractice suits."

Hospital detoxification is generally the rule for the dependent depressant user. You'll be withdrawn by taking progressively lower doses of either your chosen depressant or a long-acting barbiturate, usually phenobarbital. When your own drug is used—and this is usually the case in withdrawal from benzodiazepine tranquilizers—you are started with a dose large enough to produce mild intoxication. Dosage can then be reduced about 10 percent each day, a reduction that will not produce withdrawal symptoms. With this rate of reduction, however, the intense —often disturbing—dreaming that follows prolonged deprivation of REM sleep will usually occur. For this reason, some physicians prefer to reduce dosage more slowly over a longer period of time.

When phenobarbital is substituted for your chosen depressant, it may take several days to find the right stabilizing dose, your starting point for detoxification. After that, doses are reduced by 30 milligrams a day, and you are watched carefully for any signs of either intoxification or withdrawal.

Two to three weeks may be all it takes to complete detoxification. Sometimes the process lasts longer. When it's done, you have gotten over the highest hurdle you'll encounter, but you are still a long way from drug freedom.

Treatment Alternatives

Chances are your doctor will recommend further treatment after detoxification, and you are likely to need it. The following drug involvement test (when used with the personal resources test in Chapter 2) can give you a good idea of what kind of treatment (if any) might be most appropriate for you.

Drug Involvement Test

Answer each question as honestly as you can, but don't trust yourself too much. Remember, honest self-assessment is not your strong suit. Ask someone close to you—your husband or wife, friend or lover—to check and correct your answers.

	YES	NO
1. Do you inject depressants?	—	—
2. Do you take at least ten pills on any day of use?	—	—
3. Do you use barbiturates or barbituratelike depressants?	—	—
4. Do you use depressants daily?	—	—
5. Do you use them more than three times a week? (Answer Yes even if you have replied affirmatively to the previous question.)	—	—
6. Do you take at least five pills on any day of use?	—	—
7. Do you use cocaine or any other stimulant to compensate for depressant effects?	—	—
8. Do you use any injected drug, any opioid, or alcohol in combination with depressants?	—	—
9. Do you take depressants for euphoria or sedation or to avoid symptoms of withdrawal?	—	—
10. Has your use of depressants increased significantly during the past three months?	—	—

A Yes answer to Question 1 or 2 or a total of more than five Yes answers indicates *profound* drug involvement. Three to five Yes answers indicate *serious* involvement, and less than three *moderate* involvement.

If your drug involvement is moderate, your drug of choice a benzodiazepine or meprobamate tranquilizer, if you have developed no physical tolerance and your doctor does not hospitalize you for detoxification, you may well need no treatment. You should, of course, consult your doctor about this and would be wise to discuss it further with a therapist he or she recommends.

If your drug involvement is serious or profound, you may be self-medicating some physical or emotional disorder. Your doctor should be able to determine this more easily once you have been detoxified. If the condition you have been treating with depressants is an organic depression, then he or she can prescribe a more appropriate psychoactive to deal with this condition. However, you should be wary of rushing into psychotherapy to resolve the emotional problems that may be at the root of your drug abuse. You may well need therapy, but you are not likely to benefit much from it this early in the getting-off-drugs process.

With serious or profound drug involvement and resources that are considerably less than strong, *residential treatment* may be the route to go. While the general rule is to opt for treatment alternatives that are least intrusive and will least disrupt your life, you may not have all that much in the way of responsibilities and relationships to be disrupted. If you are out of work or dissatisfied with your job and have few family responsibilities, you should think seriously about long-term treatment in a therapeutic community. (Descriptions of residential treatment and criteria for selecting an appropriate program can be found in Chapter 2 under "treatment alternatives.")

If your personal resources are strong or on the strong side of the limited range, then you probably should consider *outpatient, drug-free (OPDF) treatment* (also covered in Chapter 2).

Individual Efforts

Although treatment can be of great help to you, success or failure in getting off drugs primarily depends upon what you can do for yourself, and the critical time for mounting your individual efforts is after withdrawal is over and your system is depressant-free. Depressant users are not much different from users of other drugs when it comes to the post-detoxification letdown. Your system is clean but you are likely to suffer insomnia and feel emptiness from the loss of your major source of satisfaction and relief. You may be anxious and irritable, possibly depressed. You need alternative activities and new friends, not only to replace drugs and keep you clear of the settings and situations that cued a drug-taking response for you, but also to overcome the lethargy, anxieties, and joyless emptiness that now threaten your abstinence.

Physical exercise is a good way to begin, a means of releasing pent-up energy that anxiety produces and a way to raise mood levels. It is also your best bet to beat insomnia, for hard and exhausting physical exercise is a natural sleep aid and has definite tranquilizing effects as well.

There are specific exercise techniques for relaxation. You can learn these and master ways to relax deep muscles at exercise centers or from physical therapists. Biofeedback is a fine way to learn muscle control and to boost your self-confidence at the same time. Yoga and meditation can help, too. These disciplines also will open you to the kind of spiritual interests that are particularly helpful to many recovering drug abusers.

For some former depressant users, making new friends or social contacts may prove a problem. If you were using depressants to overcome anxiety in social situations, you may find that meeting lots of new people exposes you to some powerful drug-taking cues. This isn't a situation you want to rush into. Work up to it gradually, building your resistance and self-confidence—possibly through a "cue-exposure" strategy that lets you master progressively more challenging situations.

While you should seek new outlets, you will want to be cautious about taking on new challenges and pushing yourself into anxiety-provoking situations. Rushing out to make up the college credits you may still need or taking on some new and demanding piece of work may be better projects farther down the road than they will be at first. For openers, you might try more failure-proof activities, such as attending lectures or concerts and becoming involved in church or political projects or volunteer work. (A more detailed description of what individuals can do for themselves can be found in the "individual efforts" section of Chapter 2).

Staying Off

Getting clean and becoming comfortable with abstinence say a lot about your level of commitment and the support you may have found in treatment or gotten at home. But how do you guard against relapse?

One way is to keep doing as you have been—a day at a time, just one more day without drugs. Another is to seek help for emotional problems that may have surfaced during treatment.

And don't neglect the obvious safeguards, such as not letting yourself get too cocky about being drug-free, avoiding the settings and situations that once cued your drug use, and dropping your old drug buddies. Above all, recognize the danger that alcohol poses to all former depressant users. It is risk number one. You are no more likely to control alcohol use than you are to control use of any other depressant. The bottom line is simple; you can't drink.

You may be tempted to think of your drug-taking days as a strange episode, foreign to your real life. This is dangerous. It's important to remember that you are still vulnerable, even if you feel comfortable with your abstinence and your life is coming together pretty well.

Many former users need a support system to help them remain drug-free, and you might want to consider this path. Pills Anonymous was created for users of depressants and stimulants, and Alcoholics Anonymous may also help. These groups hold regular meetings that make use of the mutual support, self-help group. They provide you with a network of people who have been where you've been and know where you are. They share your problems, your vulnerability and probably even your slips. And because of this, they can help you when your commitment wavers or when you do lapse back into drug use. Their support can make the difference between a relapse from which you recover and a long slide all the way back to dependency.

Notes for the Depressant User's Partner

If you have stuck by your spouse or lover during his (or her) drug use, you have been carrying a heavy load. You have probably been cleaning up and picking up after him—not only his dirty clothes, but the responsibilities he shirks and the obligations he ignores. If this is true, then you have to face the fact that you have, in many ways, been making it possible for him to use drugs. You are an "enabler" or "facilitator." Because of you, his socks get washed and his bills get paid. He is shielded from the consequences of his drug use.

Don't feel guilty about this. You didn't create the situation, and your response has been a reasonable one—and a loving one. Nevertheless, you may want to consider some other ways of responding to the situation. (For groups that provide help to relatives and friends of drug abusers see the "notes" section of Chapter 2 and the Appendix.)

If you are going to start putting pressure on him, that's fine. But don't try the dramatic step of tossing out all his drugs. Even when he decides to stop using, he will have to ease off depressants. Withdrawal from depressants is far too serious for users to attempt instant abstinence.

Suppose he does decide to quit and even is willing to enter a treatment program. Make sure he chooses one that encourages your participation too. You are both going to need some help. Such a program gives you the chance to learn how best to support him during this period. It also lets you get your own support and reinforcement from others in the same boat.

Helping him to find new interests and friends is one way to aid him. If you have friends of your own (and separate sets of friends are not uncommon for user-nonuser couples), you might start there, by sharing your social network with him.

Specifics for the partner of a recovering depressant user include keeping an eye out for the possibility of alcohol abuse. Drinking is a trap for many former drug users. For anyone who has been dependent upon a depressant, it has special attractions and special dangers—alcohol is, after all, simply another depressant and is available without prescription.

Once his treatment ends, you should encourage him to seek help to deal with whatever emotional problems may have been uncovered during the getting-off process. You also may need outside help for your relationship. It has undergone significant strain, accommodating first to his drug use and then to his treatment. Now that he has decided to become drug-free, a new balance of responsibilities and new kinds of sharing may be necessary if the relationship is to survive.

7

ALCOHOL

By any measure—the number of users, abusers and fatalities, the costs
to society in crime, violence, accidents, family breakdown, medical and
psychiatric care, and loss of productivity—alcohol has more impact on
America than any other drug. About 70 percent of all adults in the United
States drink, and alcohol is the drug most frequently abused by adolescents. Estimates of the number of alcoholics in this country vary widely,
from 1 to 5 million, and there are 4 to 10 million "problem drinkers."
Alcohol is involved in roughly half of the nation's crime. Almost three
fourths of all homicides are committed by individuals under the influence
of alcohol, as are one third of all suicides and two thirds of all suicide
attempts, three fourths of all assaults and half of all rapes.

Society has been trying to minimize the danger of alcohol since 1700
B.C., when the Code of Hammurabi attempted to regulate drinking houses
in Babylon. The Romans tried during the first century A.D. by cutting
back grape production. Arbors were plowed under and replanted with
grain to reduce the amount of wine available for the Roman market.
Three centuries later, historian Ammianus Marcellinus tells of sterner
measures. For their excesses, heavy drinkers were led about town by a
cord strung through their nostrils. Although religion has been able to
reduce alcohol use and even to impose abstinence (when it is a tenet of
the dominant religion in a culture), legislation has been less successful.
Prohibition failed to stop drinking in the United States during the early

part of the century and more recently in India. In fact, just about all Prohibition accomplished was to strengthen organized crime, which smuggled, produced and supplied booze to a still thirsty nation.

Chemically, the alcohol we drink (ethyl alcohol or ethanol) belongs not only to the depressant drug category but to a specific family of depressants that includes chloral hydrate. It has been produced from earliest times by fermenting sap, honey, fruits, grains or tubers. Fermentation yields a beverage that is 14 to 16 percent alcohol. Stronger spirits are made by distilling fermented products, as brandy is distilled from wine. Today, most alcohol comes in one of three forms:

- beer or ale, normally 2 to 5 percent alcohol, although brews with as much as 6 percent are available
- wine, normally 9 to 14 percent alcohol, except for those, such as sherry and port, that are "fortified" with brandy and have an alcohol content as high as 20 percent
- distilled spirits, such as brandy, whiskey, rum and gin, that usually run between 35 and 50 percent alcohol

Effects of Alcohol

It's easiest to think of alcohol as an intermediate-acting depressant with some special characteristics. One is its calories, which are generally "empty"—lacking vitamins, minerals or protein food value (except for small amounts in beer). Another is its bulk. Pharmacologists tend to think of alcohol as a "sloppy" chemical, because so much is needed to produce an effect. Indeed, it is the great volume users must consume that makes alcohol so toxic and does such damage to the liver, pancreas, heart and brain.

In many ways, however, alcohol behaves much as other depressants do. Small amounts will relieve anxiety and larger amounts produce disinhibition, along with loss of judgment and coordination and the revelation of emotions normally concealed or repressed—feelings of hostility, aggression, sorrow or remorse. The impact of disinhibition is affected by both the user's mental "set" and the setting in which use occurs. Behavioral toxicity—the result of impaired judgment and physical incapacities—is common and includes auto accidents (half of all fatal accidents involve drivers who have been drinking), as well as boating accidents, fires, falls and drownings.

The main difference between alcohol and other depressants is the variety of effects it has on the body. It produces vasodilation—the relaxation of blood vessels—which in turn may cause changes in heart rate, falling blood pressure, flushed skin, feelings of warmth and loss of body heat. Small doses of alcohol can increase breathing rates. Larger doses produce a more predictable depressant response, slowing respiration. Although malnutrition is common among heavy drinkers, who often get as much as half their calories from alcohol, small amounts will improve appetite. Production of stomach acid is increased by lower concentrations of alcohol in beer and wine, while the higher concentrations in distilled spirits irritate the stomach lining, so drinking is a risky indulgence for persons with peptic ulcers. The dryness in your mouth after an evening of moderate to heavy drinking is caused by alcohol's diuretic effect. Production of urine increases, and the body loses fluid no matter how much liquid has been consumed.

Alcohol creates both psychological and physical dependencies. Like users of other depressants, longtime drinkers will need to drink more to achieve levels of disinhibition reached earlier with smaller doses, although the increase in effective dosage tends to be modest. As high-risk drinking progresses and liver damage results, this tolerance may be reversed. Less alcohol is needed to relieve inhibitions, and drinking progresses rapidly to intoxication. Before prolonged alcohol use begins to cause liver damage, however, the liver builds some tolerance of its own, producing more of the enzymes needed to handle its heavy alcohol traffic. There is, in addition, a kind of behavioral tolerance to alcohol. Many drinkers learn to handle its sedating and disinhibiting effects.

Adverse Reactions

The major adverse reactions to alcohol are the ways the drug affects behavior. These include crimes, acts of violence and self-destruction, the accidents drinkers are involved in and the injuries they do to themselves.

The most common adverse reaction is the hangover, which is not that different from what other depressant users experience the morning after drug-taking and includes such rebound effects as fatigue, headache, dizziness, nausea and vomiting. Dehydration and extreme thirst occur with the alcohol hangover, which also can involve sleep disturbance. You are likely to sleep heavily for the first four hours after a night of drinking, then wake and sleep fitfully until morning.

Alcohol overdose also follows the depressant pattern. However, there is very little safety margin between an anesthetic dose and a lethal one. Fortunately, it takes an enormous amount of alcohol for the average user to achieve anesthesia, and even acute intoxication does not often produce this result. Nevertheless, a large enough amount can do the trick, and death from respiratory depression or shock, although rare, does occur.

Long-Term Effects

It is the chronic effects of alcohol, often aggravated by malnutrition, that pose the most serious problems for high-risk users. Prolonged drinking plus B vitamin deficiencies lead to a number of severe neurological and mental disorders. Brain tissue is destroyed; the aging process accelerates. The obvious results are flawed judgment, forgetfulness and an inability to concentrate. After years of deterioration, the alcoholic may demonstrate impaired motor functions as well—slurred speech and a drunken gait even when sober. While some of the neurological effects of alcohol, such as double vision, are reversible, others, like gaps in short-term memory, are not.

The liver takes a beating from prolonged alcohol use. Even though the organ is tough and keeps bouncing back, liver damage is almost inevitable for the problem drinker. Most drinkers recover with little permanent damage from "fatty liver syndrome," which is usually the first liver disorder they experience. But recovery from alcoholic hepatitis is far from automatic. Even when inflammation of the liver is relieved some scarring usually occurs.

Periodic inflammation of the liver destroys cells, which are replaced by scar tissue, and limits the organ's ability to function—to produce enzymes and remove body waste. The massive scarring of cirrhosis actually deforms the liver. Death can occur when blood is unable to pass through the organ and internal bleeding results. Victims may also die of anemia or of the inability of their blood to clot.

The pancreas, too, takes punishment, and chronic pancreatitis may result from heavy alcohol use, depriving the body of digestive enzymes and of insulin. Victims become malnourished and develop diabetes. Irritation of the stomach lining may lead to peptic ulcers or cause the lining to hemorrhage or rupture. Swollen and bleeding gums are common among alcoholics, who are also likely to have swollen glands (caused by the thickening of saliva) that give them a mumpslike look.

Because alcoholics consume so many calories with little nutritional content, they tend to be overweight. They are likely to suffer dysfunctions of the immune system and become more vulnerable to infection. Atrophy of the testicles among male alcoholics, although unusual, does occur and can result in permanent impotence.

Alcohol contributes heavily to the death rates of heart disease and cancer. Heavy drinkers are prime candidates for heart attacks. Many have irregular heart rhythms or damaged heart muscles. Because of thiamine deficiency, some develop *beriberi* which, if untreated, causes the body to retain fluid; the heart is enlarged and heart failure results from the dilation of blood vessels throughout the body. Prolonged consumption of alcohol also appears to encourage the growth of tumors. Drinking plays a significant role in liver cancer and increases the risk, particularly among smokers, of cancer of the mouth, larynx and esophagus.

Drinking during pregnancy raises the risk of birth defects. As many as two newborns in every thousand may suffer from what doctors call fetal alcohol syndrome (FAS), which causes retardation, abnormalities of the heart, lungs and sexual organs, defects of the joints or facial disfigurement. The most serious defects are found in children of mothers who drink most heavily. The risk of FAS can be reduced by abstinence that starts as late as the second trimester of pregnancy.

Alcoholism

Alcohol abuse has always been considered somewhat different from other forms of drug abuse. Because so many users are able to control their drinking, the inability of others to do so has often been ascribed to a genetic predisposition toward compulsive use. In many ways this belief in a physical or psychological basis for alcoholism parallels the notion of the "addictive personality." Such recent research as Dr. George Vaillant's study, *The Natural History of Alcoholism,* has revealed more similarities than differences between alcohol and other drug abuse. It now appears that alcoholism occurs through conditioning and the development of psychological and physical dependencies, as other compulsive drug use does.

Although alcohol is a high-risk substance, most drinkers can sustain relatively low-risk use. This probably has less to do with the nature of alcohol than with the early exposure of most users to a great variety of drinking behavior. Dr. Norman Zinberg of the Harvard medical school, makes much of the "informal rituals" that help control drug use. He points out that the rituals involved in controlling use of alcohol are picked up almost casually by young people, who have a great many role models to demonstrate the advantages and pitfalls of various kinds of drinking behavior. Vaillant, too, stresses the importance of role models. He notes the high rates of alcoholism in his study among men from Irish families that gave tacit approval to male drunkenness but did not drink within the home. By contrast, study subjects from Italian families that disapproved of drunkenness but drank at family meals were seven times less likely to become dependent upon alcohol.

What makes one an alcoholic, according to Vaillant, is not always being able to control when you start drinking or when you stop. A number of easily recognized danger signs let you know when heavy drinking crosses the line. It's generally agreed, for example, that five or more drinks a day are excessive. You're also likely to be in trouble when you start drinking alone, sneaking drinks, giving yourself an extra refill or stopping for a "quick one" on the way home. If you drink in the morning, feel guilty about your drinking, or have had a blackout, these are all clear warning signals. So are the negative effects drinking has on your job or your relationships. If you're difficult to get along with, often hostile and resentful, you're heading for even deeper troubles.

A portrait of an alcohol-dependent woman was presented by John M. Neale, Thomas F. Oltmanns and Gerald C. Davison in their book, *Case Studies in Abnormal Psychology.*

After giving her a complete physical examination, Cathy Henry's physician determined that many of her problems were psychological. To be sure, she had reason to be concerned over her medical status because she had been having trouble sleeping for several months, suffered from almost continual diarrhea, felt very fatigued most of the time, and had allowed her once trim body to become flabby and poorly conditioned. One key question that the physician had asked during the examination, however, led him to be concerned about her personal life. "Have you been drinking much alcohol lately?" he had queried, as casually as possible. "No!" she had exclaimed a bit too loudly. She then had burst into tears and recounted the following story.

Twenty-eight years of age, quite attractive, married for 7 years to a successful business executive, and the mother of two children in elementary school, Cathy Henry had watched her drinking patterns change over the previous several years. She had been a social drinker since her college days, but her consumption increased and changed in nature during her first years of marriage. Initially it was the martinis that she would mix for her husband and herself to greet him each evening when he came home from his job in the city after traveling for 1 hour on the commuter railroad. It helps him unwind, she would think to herself, but soon she realized that it was she who looked forward to the drinks. Then there were the parties they would go to or have in their spacious suburban home. She was not particularly fond of the people she met at these gatherings; in fact, when she was honest with herself, she had to admit that she found them aversive. Dick's friends and their wives led lives that were different from the way she thought she would be living. Yes, she did enjoy the affluence, the nice clothes, the obligatory Mercedes, the private school for the children, the vacations, and all the rest. But she longed for more.

She began to look forward to the numbing effects of that first drink. And then the further numbing of the second. Wasn't booze the social lubricant par excellence? What could be wrong with it if you saw it everywhere you turned? Dick's business lunches, after all, always included a Manhattan or martini before and usually a bottle of wine during the meal. And her lunches with one or two women she had managed to befriend usually followed the same pattern. No, that was not the problem. It was the drink she took by herself before making the early evening batch of martinis to enjoy with her husband before dinner and the drink she poured for herself downstairs in the kitchen while Dick was in the bedroom getting dressed for a party she was not looking forward to. And more and more often it was the second drink she somehow found herself pouring, now secretly, after she had gotten dressed and Dick was picking up the babysitter. Most recently it was the doubts she felt about being sober enough to be the perfect hostess as she sipped a drink while making the canapes on Saturday afternoons in preparation for the dinner party in her home that evening, while her husband was at the supermarket with the children for some last-minute shopping.

Different as well was the kind of drink she found herself imbibing. If a dry martini is good, then a very dry one is better. And if there is Tanqueray in the liquor cabinet, why mask its exquisite taste with anything more than a twist of lemon? And why dilute such good liquor with ice cubes if the green bottle can be kept in the back of the refrigerator, next to the long-stemmed goblet that so nicely accommodated a jigger of gin, and later two jiggers and, finally, as much as she felt like pouring without using a measuring glass.

So she awakened one morning and realized that even before she got herself out of bed, she was thinking of that first drink. She also wondered whether she would be able to wait until her husband left for work and her children left for school. And if she had to do the driving for the carpool that day, would she have a few gulps of gin before she left with them to pick up the other children, or would she wait until her return? It seemed to her now that she wanted that first drink not so much to feel better but to avoid feeling worse for not having the drink.

Additional information about her drinking convinced the physician that Cathy might be addicted to alcohol. Clearly her consumption had steadily increased over the past year, the best estimate being at least 15 ounces of 90-proof gin every day. Her drinking almost always began in the morning and continued more or less unabated until she went to bed. If she was out of the house during the day, she often found excuses not to drive. She would drink alcohol in any form available to her, whether it was a fine wine at a restaurant during lunch with a friend or a beer purchased while shopping for groceries and consumed in her car before leaving the supermarket parking lot for an unsteady and dangerous drive home. Especially alarming to both her and her husband was her reaction to being deprived of alcohol for several days during a camping trip. She had dreaded the time away from her cache of liquor (she had a few bottles hidden in her dresser drawers), and the first day had been sheer hell: hands shaking, a feeling of pressure in her head, and an overall feeling that something dreadful was about to happen. Her constant preoccupation was with how and where she was going to get a drink. By the time they returned home several days later, she was a physical and emotional wreck. She had not slept more than a few hours the entire trip and had been abusive to her family during the drive home. Any pretense about not being a problem drinker vanished as she bolted from the car on their arrival home to dash into the house for several gulps of gin right from the bottle.

One final aspect of her predicament worried the doctor. Not surprisingly, Cathy's marriage had been deteriorating as her drinking worsened. Intimacy was gone. Her secretiveness and shame about her drinking, coupled with extreme anger whenever her husband made a comment or suggested she get some help, created a distance between the partners. Dick Henry also resented his wife's increasing unreliability in looking after the children and their home. It was becoming the norm in recent months that he would arrive after work to find the children roaming the neighborhood unsupervised, dinner unprepared, and the house looking as unkempt as his wife did, propped up on pillows in her room, on the night table next to her a glass filled with gin as she looked idly through magazines or watched whatever mindless program was on television at the time. Sex was infrequent, since Cathy was usually so anesthetized that she made an uninteresting partner in bed, to say the least.

Drinking had become the center of her life. She had denied this for some time, but it no longer seemed possible to continue the charade. Her life was going out of control.

Starting Off

Although DTs (delirium tremens) have long been a basis for humor, jokes about drunks who see pink elephants are far from funny. Alcohol is an addicting drug, and withdrawal from alcohol can be just as severe and life-threatening as withdrawal from any other depressant.

If you have a relatively short alcoholic history and are coming off a binge, withdrawal may last only a couple of days and involve only minor symptoms—agitation and anxiety, tremors or "shakes," rapid heartbeat, heavy sweating, and rising temperature, along with nausea and some vomiting. It won't be pleasant, but you won't feel as though you are going to die—and you are unlikely to actually do so.

When longtime alcoholics withdraw, however, symptoms are more severe and withdrawal lasts a week or more. It may start slowly, but major symptoms follow minor ones. Temperature keeps rising. Victims become disoriented and confused, even delirious. They may suffer toxic psychosis, with delusions and hallucinations. Extreme temperature and agitation can lead to convulsions, and when victims are malnourished or in poor health, they can die as a result of shock or respiratory collapse. For longtime alcoholics, mortality may result from mismanaged withdrawal as often as from overdose, and the street-corner drunk who tells you how badly he "needs" a drink probably knows what he is talking about.

No one with a serious drinking history can simply quit cold. You need medical help, and a doctor should decide the best way for you to go about starting off. For a true alcholic, who has been drinking regularly for a period of years, hospital detoxification will probably be recommended. Along with plenty of fluids, vitamins and rest, you'll be given a long-acting sedative, such as phenobarbital, to control withdrawal symptoms and let you ease your way to abstinence. For patients who are already suffering from withdrawal symptoms, a shorter-acting sedative, such as Nembutal or chloral hydrate, may be used at first. To control toxic psychosis that can accompany withdrawal, doctors may administer antipsychotics—Thorazine, Stelazine or Haldol.

Treatment Alternatives

If you haven't already had one, a complete medical examination should follow detoxification. You need to find out just how much damage drinking has done and what medical treatment you may need. Although you should also discuss treatment for alcohol dependency with your physician, keep in mind that traditional medical practice offers little to the recovering alcoholic.

The following drug involvement test for alcohol (when used with the personal resources test in Chapter 2) will give you some indication of your treatment needs:

Alcohol Involvement Test

Answer each question as honestly as you can, but don't trust yourself too much. Remember, honest self-assessment is not your strong suit. Ask someone close to you—your husband or wife, friend or lover—to check and correct your answers.

	YES	NO
1. Do you ever lose consciousness or experience amnesia as a result of drinking?	—	—
2. Have you ever suffered delirium tremens (psychosis with hallucinations)?	—	—
3. Do you indulge in binges?	—	—
4. Do you drink on five or more days each week?	—	—
5. Do you drink distilled spirits more often than wine or beer?	—	—
6. On days when you drink, do you consume: 10 or more ounces of distilled spirits a quart or more of wine, or seven or more (12-ounce) glasses of beer?	—	—
7. Do you sometimes get belligerent or violent when drinking?	—	—
8. Do you experience any physical symptoms, anxiety or depression when you stop drinking?	—	—
9. Do you use any opioids, depressants or stimulants with alcohol?	—	—
10. Do you frequently drink when you are alone?	—	—

A Yes answer to Question 1 or 2 or a total of more than five Yes answers indicates *profound* involvement. Three to five Yes answers indicate *serious* involvement, and less than three *moderate* involvement.

If your involvement is profound and your personal resources are less than strong, you may well benefit from continued hospital care after detoxification or from residential treatment in a clinic or residential alcohol program. This may not provide the long-term answer to your treatment needs, but it can give you the kind of controlled environment you may need to launch your rehabilitation.

Although doctors have tended to call alcoholism a "progressive and *incurable* disease," many alcoholics have been able to stop drinking, and the most effective alternative available both for treatment and for subsequent support—for staying off—is Alcoholics Anonymous. There are, in addition to AA, both residential and outpatient programs for recovering alcoholics that have demonstrated considerable treatment success. Unfortunately, programs that treat both alcohol and drug dependency are rare. However, both residential and outpatient programs for alcohol are similar in many ways to those for other drug abuse.

Researchers have found that the type of treatment provided by a program matters far less than how comfortable a resident or participant feels there and how trusting a relationship he or she has with therapists or counselors. Success also depends heavily upon how long participants remain in treatment.

While traditional psychotherapy has not proven very useful in the treatment of alcoholism, both residential and outpatient centers for alcoholics employ many of the nontraditional approaches used by drug abuse programs. Self-help groups and group therapy that is closer to the conventional mental health model are both available, and many programs involve family members and lovers and friends in treatment. In addition, some clinics and programs also provide chemical support for abstinence, using the deterrent drug disulfiram (Antabuse). Although this drug has no direct effects of its own, it will alter the metabolism of any alcohol subsequently consumed, causing headaches, nausea and vomiting.

Alcoholics Anonymous

Anybody can join AA, and there are AA meetings almost everywhere. In major cities, you can find one in just about every neighborhood (there are some thirty thousand in the United States and Canada) and at almost any hour of the day; from early morning until late at night. A telephone call is all it usually takes to connect, for AA has volunteer-staffed referral centers in most areas. The sole requirement for membership is the "desire to stop drinking." There are no dues, although collections are taken to pay for refreshments.

Anonymity is basic to the program. Members don't give their names at open meetings—following the example of Bill W., who started the organization in 1935. But they do not keep their membership a secret from those they feel need AA's help, for an obligation of membership is to reach out to other alcoholics to bring them into the fold.

Alcoholics Anonymous is less a national organization than an association of thousands of autonomous chapters (although regional units coordinate communications, referral services and literature). The existence of so many and so many different kinds of meetings means that you should have no trouble locating one nearby and one where you will feel socially comfortable as well. There are gay AA meetings and AA meetings for agnostics, meetings that accept abusers of other drugs, and meetings that do not. The difficulty so many drug abusers find in other support programs—the problem of establishing peer group relationships with members whose life experience, education and attitudes may be markedly different from their own—rarely occurs within AA. Chances are you may not even have to find an AA group. One may find you. If your alcohol troubles are becoming apparent, you might well be approached by a colleague or neighbor whose membership in AA you had never known.

There are various forms of meetings held by AA groups. Anyone can attend an "open" meeting, which may feature a designated speaker (it's an honor to be asked) and include "sharing"—volunteered statements of experience from participants. "Closed" meetings are for self-help groups and may focus on problems or suspected problems of members. "Step" meetings are seminars that focus on each of the "Twelve Steps" that embody the principles of AA. "Beginners" meetings tend to be less structured and more free-flowing than most AA sessions and are usually run by an "old-timer," a member with at least eight years' experience.

The organization's approach is strictly self-help—with the emphasis on mutual support and individual responsibility—and it was the AA treatment model upon which therapeutic communities were based. No professional or paraprofessional counselors run AA therapy groups, which use none of the dynamics of the encounter to break through barriers to self-disclosure. The expectation is that members will open up, acknowledge their sickness and accept the need to change. Still, each new member has a "sponsor," a guide or counselor who shows him the ropes. There's a lot to learn, and new members are expected to start strong. The general rule is "ninety meetings in ninety days," and you'll spend a good deal of time on the Twelve Steps.

These begin with the need to recognize what you are, to "deal with denial" as they say in AA, give up your myths and delusions and honestly admit, "I am powerless over alcohol." Your membership is a commitment to "recovery" not "cure," for the organization perceives alcoholism as a lifelong condition. Its conviction that alcoholics can never safely drink again is consistent with what we now know about the inability of all compulsive drug users to return successfully to controlled drug use.

Many of the Twelve Steps address the need to make changes in your life—to take inventory of your strengths and weaknesses, to make amends to those you have harmed, and to proselytize and help others. Other steps emphasize the spiritual side of the program, the need for belief in some "higher power," the need for help in changing, and the importance of prayer and meditation.

While the spirituality of AA may put off skeptics and some former drinkers, it is a vital aspect of the program and contributes significantly to its success. Some sort of faith, a source of hope, seems essential to the recovery process. It provides a counterweight to the acceptance of "powerlessness" over alcohol. But AA also provides substantial practical support in a network of other former users, men and women to whom you can reach out when troubled or whom you can call when you feel the cravings for a drink, who will stand by you should you suffer a relapse and will get you back on track.

There is a general belief among AA members that their program, and other Twelve Step programs like Narcotic Anonymous and Pills Anonymous are not only the right route to freedom from addiction but also a better way to live. Members become more than just recovering alcoholics or drug abusers, they become better people—more loving husbands and wives, more competent professionals, more loyal friends.

Individual Efforts

In many ways, alcoholics are no different from other drug abusers, and you will find that much of the material on individual efforts in Chapter 2 and the preceding drug chapters applies to you. You too must beware of cues and settings that trigger a drinking response. You too need new outlets and associations. You too must keep busy, find new activities and make new friends. You can find many of these through and within AA itself.

Notes for Partners and Parents

If you are the partner of an alcoholic and an alcoholic yourself, you can choose either to make his (or her) recovery just about impossible or to join him in treatment. Getting off alcohol together, using the treatment and subsequent support of AA, isn't easy, but is less difficult for you two than for couples dependent upon many other drugs. There is a network and support system in place that you can count on.

If you are not an alcoholic yourself and not much of a drinker, then you should become involved in Al-Anon, an organization linked to AA, which uses self-help groups and the Twelve Steps to help family members, friends and even colleagues or employers of alcoholics. The program offers more than just advice on how to handle your alcoholic spouse, lover, friend or employee. It provides a way to work out some of your own problems and deal with your own feelings. While membership in Al-Anon—or Alateen, a similar organization for the adolescent children of alcoholics—will be useful after a spouse, lover or parent has joined AA, it might be even more important to start attending or even to sign up while he or she is still drinking.

Parents should realize that lots of alcohol abuse takes place during adolescence. Not all of it necessarily leads to alcoholism, but it shouldn't be discounted just because drinking is a familiar form of drug abuse, less frightening than the use of marijuana or cocaine. Make rules about drinking for your kids, set limits. Make clear when it is permitted, with whom and where. Remember, however, that your greatest impact on their alcohol use is as role model rather than as rule-maker. How you use alcohol is significant. If your kids see you come home "needing" a drink or see you drunk and out of control, they are getting powerful negative messages about why and how to drink.

Control of alcohol appears to be learned behavior, and it seems best learned at home. Letting youngsters see you drink without drunkenness and allowing older adolescents beer and wine at mealtime or for special family events are probably the best ways to protect them from future alcohol abuse.

8

MARIJUANA

After alcohol, marijuana is by miles the nation's next favorite drug of abuse. Although use has dropped a bit in recent years, there are still about 20 million current users. The popularity of the drug seems based on a number of factors—availability, social reinforcement, an attractive disinhibiting high—but most of all, on the perception of marijuana as a relatively low-risk substance that has been smoked by large numbers of users with no apparent ill effects.

Like cocaine, marijuana seems to have a better name than it deserves. While the great majority of smokers appear to suffer little for their pleasure, grass is a demonstrably high-risk drug for certain users—pregnant women, nursing mothers, anyone with heart trouble or respiratory problems, epileptics, and *adolescents*. What's more, the recognition of likely long-term effects of marijuana—and their danger to *all* users—has been quite recent. It is clear that the drug does produce tolerance, and sustained use can lead to psychological dependency. Even physical dependency, though lightweight, is counted a possibility by a good many drug researchers. This is a powerfully reinforcing drug, and it is hardly surprising that many of the experimenters who try it become regular users. While marijuana is far from a sure and certain path to more profound drug use, it is still what experts call a "gateway drug." Chances are that you will use it before moving on to anything more potent.

Public perception of marijuana has shifted back and forth over the

181

rs, and most of what has been popularly believed about the drug has
subsequently proven to be untrue. Marijuana was not the public menace
it was made out to be during the 1930s, nor was it the direct route to
heroin addiction many Americans believed it to be in the 1960s. Neither
is it as benign a substance as a good many pot apologists still maintain
it is.

Use in the United States

Marijuana is an old drug. There is some evidence that the Chinese
knew about it as early as the third century B.C., and cultivated the hemp
plant *(Cannabis sativa),* the source of marijuana and hashish, for its
medicinal properties. In ancient India, hemp was initially grown for religious purposes, although eventually—and perhaps inevitably—recreational use followed.

In the United States, marijuana didn't get off to a big start. Unlike
opium, morphine and cocaine, pot had no golden early days of upper-
class use and medical endorsement during the nineteenth century. Before
World War I, it was smoked almost exclusively by immigrants from
Mexico, and use spread from the Mexican border along the Gulf Coast.
When immigration increased after that war, so did the use of marijuana,
which now had a foothold in the black community and attracted a certain
number of white users as well. However, to the solid citizens of the
Southwest, there developed during the 1920s an unshakable association
of marijuana with Mexicans and crime.

During these years, marijuana was finding its way into new parts of
the country. Boatloads shipped to New Orleans moved upriver to St.
Louis and on to the cities of the East Coast. In New Orleans, black dock
workers and a good many musicians took to the drug. Years later, Louis
Armstrong remembered his introduction to "Mary Warner." As he put
it, "Honey, you sure was good and I enjoyed you 'heep much.' But the
price got a little too high to pay, law wise. At first you was a misde-
meanor. But as the years rolled by you lost your misdo and got meanor
and meanor."

A number of local ordinances were passed to control marijuana use
between 1914 and 1931, but enforcement was relatively lax in most
places, for police were more concerned with alcohol traffic during the
years of Prohibition. Still, a 1929 report from the U.S. Surgeon General
gave credence to the popular notion of marijuana as a drug that led almost
inevitably to crime and insanity.

The Depression helped focus public attention on marijuana. In California and throughout the Southwest, conflicts grew between Mexican farm workers and growers whose farms they tilled and between Mexicans and other workers in Western cities. Marijuana became a major issue, a means of inflaming anti-Mexican sentiment.

Law enforcement officials in the Southwest demanded legislation to control marijuana, while local police chiefs in such cities as Denver and New Orleans contributed to the clamor by blaming rising crime rates on use of the drug. The pivot man in Washington, the official whose support was essential to congressional action, was the head of the new Federal Bureau of Narcotics (FBN), Harry J. Anslinger.

Anslinger has since been given credit for single-handedly creating the myth of "the killer weed" and campaigning for federal restrictions because of his ambition—to give him a competitive edge in his rivalry with the FBI's J. Edgar Hoover. But Anslinger clearly resisted the considerable pressure on him from Southwestern police officials and their representatives in Washington. His bureau reported in 1932 that the role of marijuana in rising crime rates might well be exaggerated, and he pushed hard for a uniform state drug code—which included an optional marijuana provision—rather than lobbying for a federal law.

By 1936, however, Anslinger yielded and joined the chorus of those advocating federal legislation, even though most states had passed marijuana measures of their own by then. And once converted, Anslinger acted with impressive fervor. The FBN's annual report began carrying a "marijuana crimes" section—a catalogue of grisly murders and assaults. The press happily picked up on these and other tales of blood and violence, including the oft-cited story of an otherwise exemplary and God-fearing young man who, after smoking a single joint, grabbed an ax and did away with his entire family—father, mother, sister and two brothers.

As Patrick Anderson puts it in *High in America,* "Never in history have so many mothers been ax-murdered, so many virgins lured into white slavery, so many siblings decapitated, as in the heyday of Anslinger's antimarijuana campaign. The spirit of the era was most perfectly captured in the 1936 movie classic *Reefer Madness,* in which casual marijuana use was shown to lead swiftly to murder, rape, prostitution, addiction, madness, and death."

In 1937, Anslinger published his *Marihuana: Assassin of Youth,* pushing the proposition that marijuana was the stem if not the root of most evils. "How many murders, suicides, robberies, criminal assaults, hold-ups, burglaries, and deeds of maniacal intensity [marijuana] causes each year, especially among the young, can only be conjectured," he declared. Anslinger's testimony in support of the proposed antimarijuana bill was similarly hyperbolic. Congress heard almost nothing but how dangerous the drug was. Just about the only exception was a warning from the American Medical Association's legislative counsel, Dr. W. C. Woodward, who pointed out that no scientific evidence linked marijuana to crime or violence and suggested some medical use for the drug might yet be discovered. But Woodward carried little weight with the legislators, and the Marijuana Tax Act was passed in August 1937 after hardly any debate.

Strangely, once armed with the new law, Anslinger's bureau did surprisingly little to enforce it. Those FBN agents who proved overly aggressive in their pursuit of marijuana users were told to redirect their energies toward heroin dealers. The bureau's antimarijuana publicity campaign ended abruptly—and public concern wound down just as quickly as it had been stirred up.

The public heard little about marijuana for the next twenty-five years, although use continued among blacks and Mexican-Americans, among musicians and "beats." When pot resurfaced in mid-1960s, it was as the "gateway drug," not for individual users, but for a whole generation of Americans—the young members of the counterculture, many of whom were questioning and protesting not only the war in Vietnam and racism, but all the standards and values of their parents' culture.

"Marijuana, like rock music and long hair," Patrick Anderson writes, "became another symbol of rebellion for the young. It was illegal, it produced a nice high, and it drove parents up the wall: Who could ask for more?"

Pot smoking was also an instrument of bonding for the young. It was something young blacks shared with young whites during the civil rights movement, and Anderson believes the habit moved, along with the times and changing concerns, from the civil rights movement to the antiwar movement. A significant aspect of the counterculture became the supply lines along which grass—not so easily obtainable in the early 1960s—crossed the country.

Marijuana soon ceased to be a rarity, and use expanded with availability. In 1962, only 1 percent of the nation's youth (ages twelve to seventeen) and just 4 percent of young adults had ever tried the drug. Five years later, 7 percent of the youth and 13 percent of the young adults had sampled pot. The numbers kept rising until, in 1979, one third of all youngsters and two thirds of all young adults had at least tried marijuana, and half of those experimenters were current users. (The number of arrests for marijuana offenses increased dramatically, too, from fewer than 20,000 in 1965 to nearly 450,000 in 1976.)

Since 1979, however, the popularity of pot has slipped some. Current use among youth slid from nearly 17 percent to slightly more than 11 percent between 1979 and 1982, while among young adults current use dropped from more than 35 percent to less than 28 percent. Interestingly, the move to "decriminalize" pot, which had extended to twelve states, ground to a halt during this same period. Attitudes about marijuana, particularly among high school students, seem to be changing as well, with greater awareness of possible hazards and considerably less approval of use.

Effects of Marijuana

Made from the crushed leaves, twigs, seeds and sometimes even flowering tops of cannabis, marijuana is not a simple drug. It contains hundreds of different chemicals, including sixty-one cannabinoids that are unique to hemp. Hashish, a concentrated resin made from cannabis leaves and flowers, and hashish oil, an alcoholic extract of cannabis, have the same components and produce the same effects and reactions. More potent than pot, they have higher concentrations of THC (delta-9-tetrahydrocannabinol), the active ingredient in all three drugs.

Like alcohol, marijuana has depressant properties, and its high—usually, but far from invariably, marked by relaxation and a sense of well-being—is caused by the same kind of disinhibition alcohol induces. But pot has some tricks of its own, characteristics of a mild hallucinogen, which not only alter mood and feelings but affect perceptions as well. You see things differently when you are high, and the hallucinogenic properties of marijuana are responsible for the "dreamy" state that prompts fantasies and makes users highly suggestible. While pot-induced hallucinations are rare at normal doses, most users find their sense of time is warped, as is their perception of distance and dimension.

Not everyone finds marijuana a delight. Dysphoric responses (the opposite of euphoric ones) are common, most often among inexperienced users who are frightened and confused by distorted perceptions. A sizable number of new users don't feel very much of anything when they first try grass, and many later explain how, over time, they "learned to get high."

In addition to these subjective effects, marijuana will raise heart rate and increase appetite. The drug has some anticonvulsant properties and the ability to dilate (expand) small blood vessels. Although neither marijuana nor THC is regularly used for medical purposes, there has been some study and limited use of both to control the nausea of cancer patients undergoing chemotherapy and to treat glaucoma, since THC will relieve pressure within the eye by dilating conjunctival blood vessels.

Patterns of Use

Although marijuana and hashish can be taken orally—hashish fudge and cookies have a prominent place in the folklore of drugs—most U.S. users prefer to smoke the drugs. This is a far more rapid route of administration. Effects can be felt within seconds and are four times more potent than when pot follows the digestive route. Effects peak in ten to thirty minutes, and blood levels of THC fall rapidly, dropping to between 5 and 10 percent of initial levels within an hour. Still, the subjective effects of the drug—the disinhibition and sensory distortions—linger on for another hour or two. And there are less readily recognized effects, such as impaired memory, concentration, coordination and judgment, that last even longer.

Once in the body, THC takes its time getting out. A fat-soluble substance, it is absorbed by fatty tissues (although little appears to be retained in the brain and reproductive organs), and even when released it may be reabsorbed in the intestines and recycled. A week after you have smoked a joint, one fourth to one third of its THC will still be retained, and traces may remain in the body for much longer.

A point to be considered by today's marijuana users is the increased potency—the higher proportion of THC—in the marijuana they can buy. As late as the early 1970s, it was rare to find pot with a THC level much above 0.5 percent. Today, with large amounts of high-quality marijuana being grown in the United States—a major, if illicit, source of domestic agricultural income—THC levels range between 3 and 5 percent. The concentration may be even higher for exotic imports and such high-priced varieties as *sinsemilla,* which can have THC levels up to 11 percent. Within the past five years alone, the strength of street samples has increased about fivefold. In addition, the paraphernalia available today—from "bongs" that concentrate smoke to home apparatuses that purify pot by raising the THC levels and even extract hash oil—permits stronger doses and greater risk of untoward effects. Nevertheless, researchers engaged in long-term studies of marijuana use have noted few reports of more extreme or longer-lasting highs from heavy users.

Most marijuana smokers use the drug the way most drinkers use alcohol—to enhance sociability. Unlike alcohol, however, pot does little to spark conversation. Speech becomes difficult as the time lag (and the perception of the lag) between thought and articulation stretches. Non sequiturs give way to incoherence, and while there may be a greater sense of intimacy, communication deteriorates.

Disinhibition allows some users, normally anxious in social situations, to relax and enjoy themselves. For socially insecure adolescents, this is a powerful motive, as is peer group membership that may be contingent upon marijuana use. In high school studies, most heavy users give "relaxation" as one of their main reasons for smoking, and many claim pot helps them overcome boredom.

Marijuana also helps a good many people cope with sexual anxieties. While medical opinion is divided on whether the drug increases desire, disinhibition makes it easier to overcome cultural restraints or self-imposed taboos. The suggestibility of marijuana users is also a factor that counts here, as are perceptual distortions that increase awareness of tactile sensations and create a sense of prolonged sexual activity. The high correlation between marijuana use and sexual activity, however, appears less a function of any aphrodisiac qualities in pot than the likelihood that youngsters who come early to marijuana will become sexually active early as well. But if their marijuana use increases and persists, they may find their interest in sex diminishing.

In two studies conducted in 1969 and 1978 among seniors at a large northeastern university, only minor differences between users and nonusers were discovered. The one exception was sexual activity—drug users tended to be considerably more active than nonusers (a difference that showed up among heterosexuals but not among homosexuals.)

The results of the two studies were quite similar, although between 1969 and 1978 the number of seniors who drank at least once a week had dropped from 44 percent to 38 percent, while the number who smoked marijuana that frequently had risen from 16 percent to 26 percent. The slight differences in academic performance between users and nonusers discovered in 1969 had narrowed by 1978. Virtually no significant differences were found in grades, participation in college activities, or career plans, causing the authors to suggest that "drug use had merged even further with 'normal' college life."

While the studies seem to show that large numbers of marijuana users can perform just as successfully as nonusers, they do not provide grounds for believing that *all* users can. Absent from the studies, because they were absent from the university, were those drug-using students who had failed to make it to their senior year. Equally unrepresented were the large number of high school marijuana users who didn't get to college at all.

Adverse Reactions

Marijuana has a number of side effects, such as sudden hunger, slight tremors, and a drop in body temperature. Some users may also suffer headaches and nausea. But the more pronounced and dangerous reactions, aside from any drug dependency, are those that limit or diminish intellectual or physical performance, for marijuana impairs short-term memory, concentration, judgment and coordination. Users become sluggish and have difficulty forming concepts, understanding what they read, tracking moving objects, sitting erect and controlling movement of their hands.

These effects may persist for more than four hours after smoking, long past the point at which most users believe their performance might be impaired. Because marijuana interferes with so many basic activities in so many ways, the behavioral toxicity of the drug is its most lethal aspect. Marijuana causes a substantial number of automobile fatalities and accidental drownings. It is also responsible for a growing number of industrial accidents and may well be as devastating as alcohol in causing falls, fires and other potentially tragic mishaps around the house.

Marijuana has some scary short-term, toxic psychological effects, too. Many users become fearful and confused, others suspicious or aggressive. Paranoid reactions are frequent, and many users have experienced "panic attacks." Although usually brief, anxiety builds quickly during these attacks, and victims become fearful of losing control. They may feel an intense need to get home or to some other safe place; sometimes they will just get into bed and hide under the covers. They can become highly agitated but will usually respond to being "talked down" by someone they know and trust. Doctors prefer not to medicate victims of panic attacks but may prescribe a benzodiazepine tranquilizer in some cases.

Reports of panic attacks are less frequent now than they once were (earlier studies found that a quarter or more of all users had experienced panic reactions at some time). Generally, it is younger and less experienced users who panic, though some older former users cite these attacks as the reason they gave up the drug. Younger users, too, are most likely to suffer toxic psychosis as a result of marijuana use. Not a common reaction, the psychosis, which can last for several days, generally involves paranoia and other kinds of delusions. Victims may behave in wild and unpredictable ways. Hallucinations appear, although true visual hallucinations are usually seen only when very high doses or concentrations of THC have been involved. Rarely is medication prescribed, although doctors may use antipsychotics should they be necessary.

Flashback is another trick marijuana plays on its users. Intoxication can recur, with distorted perceptions, some time after the drug has been used. Most drug researchers credit these flashbacks to "involuntary recall,'' triggered by anxiety, other drug use or anything else that might jog the memory and cause it to replay the drug experience.

Long-Term Effects

No issue more sharply divides today's drug libertarians from their opponents than the long-term dangers—real or imagined—of regular marijuana use. Although a significant number of Americans now use the drug, there have been no large-scale epidemiological studies (of the kind that established a link between tobacco and cancer) that might produce irrefutable evidence of risk from marijuana. There have, however, been a good many clinical reports, laboratory studies, animal experiments and some research with human subjects. The resulting findings are less than consistent in some areas and less than convincing in others. Nevertheless, there is sufficient information available today for intelligent marijuana users to draw their own conclusions about several of the risks of their drug-taking.

A danger is no less real because it remains unproven. The standards of scientific evidence are often more rigid than should be necessary to convince reasonable men and women to be wary. To judge that marijuana is probably responsible for a long-term effect, you needn't be convinced *beyond a reasonable doubt*. You're wiser letting the *preponderance of evidence* indicate what is likely.

With this in mind, let's look at what can be said about marijuana's long-term effects on the brain, the heart, the lungs, the reproductive system and the immune system.

Brain. There is little evidence that marijuana produces any permanent change in brain structure or does any damage to brain cells. While changes in the brain's electrical activity induced by marijuana have been shown to persist after use of the drug has been discontinued, these changes do not appear harmful.

Heart. Marijuana increases heart rate, making the heart work harder, and may also alter blood pressure for some users. While the added stress is not sufficient to pose a threat to a normal user, it is a real danger to those with hypertension (chronic high blood pressure), hardening of the arteries, heart disease or irregular heart rhythm.

Lungs. There is no doubt that smoking marijuana reduces the lungs' ability to supply the body with oxygen and rid it of carbon dioxide. After only six to eight weeks of use, there is measurable obstruction of air passages. Heavy smoking, particularly of hashish, has been shown to produce chronic bronchitis, shortness of breath and significant loss of lung capacity. Pot also appears to lower the lungs' resistance to infection. In laboratory tests, lung-dwelling macrophages (white corpuscles that attack invading microorganisms) became less effective when exposed to marijuana smoke.

The evidence of marijuana causing or abetting lung cancer, while less than overwhelming, is still convincing. Marijuana smoke is quite similar to tobacco smoke, and contains a higher concentration of carcinogens in its tars than tobacco does. While pot smokers generally smoke far less than tobacco users do, they smoke more destructively—attempting to draw smoke as deeply into their lungs as possible. Marijuana smoke has accelerated the growth of cancers on both animal and human lung tissue in laboratories, and its tars (in heavy concentrations) have produced tumors in laboratory animals. While this is not enough evidence for scientists to resolve the question, it should be sufficient for most marijuana users to accept that lung cancer is one of the risks they run.

Reproductive System. Most researchers accept the fact that marijuana inhibits production of male hormones—but to a lesser degree than either alcohol or opioids do. Reduction in sperm production has also been noted in users, as have increases in the number of abnormal sperm cells. In spite of these effects, however, both sperm production and the amount of abnormality remain close to normal levels. For women, there is evidence (mostly from animal studies) that marijuana may suppress ovulation, but the findings are not sufficient to make this more than a possible risk.

Immune System. While THC has been shown in laboratory animals to have a mild and short-lived effect on the immune system, reducing its capacity to protect the body from infection, studies with human subjects have thus far failed to produce consistent results. While the possibility of risk exists, there really isn't enough information on which to base a thoughtful assumption.

Birth Defects. Animal studies have demonstrated clearly that high doses of marijuana can cause severe abnormalities in embryos, retard fetal development and increase the likelihood of spontaneous abortion. Yet, although marijuana use is widespread among women in their childbearing years, no consistent pattern of birth defects equivalent to fetal alcohol syndrome has yet emerged. The only threats to offspring of marijuana-using mothers that have been noted are symptoms of depressant with-drawal, mainly convulsions, that many infants seem to be born with. However, since THC does cross the placental barrier and can be retained in fatty tissue of the fetus, there may well be effects too subtle to have been noted thus far. It is not known, for example, what the reduction in production of male hormones, which seems to have little effect on adults, has on the developing male fetus. In the absence of hard evidence on either side, there is too much uncertainty for a thoughtful expectant mother to run the risks that are plainly possible with marijuana use.

Behavior. Since the late 1960s, a good many clinicians and drug abuse counselors have used the term "amotivational syndrome" to describe the apathy, lack of ambition, ineffectiveness and diminished performance on the job or in the classroom that many heavy marijuana users display. The existence of such a syndrome has been challenged by some drug re-searchers, who point to studies (such as the university senior study cited earlier) that show relatively little difference in performance between users and nonusers. They ask if "amotivated" users might not be smok-ing marijuana simply *because* they are so ineffective and unsuccessful.

There is, however, no question of marijuana's *capacity* to affect per-formance. It can impair short-term memory, communication skills, read-ing comprehension, and the ability to concentrate—and do all these for a good long while after a joint has been smoked. Where the impact of these disabling effects on performance shows most clearly is in studies of reg-ular users in high schools—perhaps because these users are least likely to have developed controls over their drug use and are thus most likely to smoke pot at inappropriate times or in unreasonable ways.

In high school, there are usually clear differences between grass users and nonusers. Users tend to have lower expectations of themselves and most often behave accordingly, getting lower grades and making fewer long-term plans. They also generally have lower self-esteem and less ego strength than their nonusing classmates, though this may be a cause of their drug use rather than a result. "Kids tend to turn to marijuana during adolescence," says Dr. Stephen Pittel, who has been studying drug ef-fects and treatment for almost two decades, "because they haven't de-veloped the internal resources to deal with adolescence." Heavy use, of course, prevents some of them from *ever* developing these resources, for it can result, says Pittel, "in a developmental moratorium."

Not all regular or heavy high school users necessarily start because they lack emotional resources. These youngsters are also prey to social coercion, peer pressure and the natural anxieties that all adolescents experience. Whatever the reason for their use, the one clear danger is what Dr. Mitchell S. Rosenthal of Phoenix House describes as "the way marijuana impedes the process of maturation. At a time when youngsters should be developing long-range goals," he says, "their time-frame is shrinking. When they most need to learn how to deal responsibly with others, they become more self-involved, more infantile. Instead of expanding, their world is contracting. Rather than cope with pressures, they escape them. They do not cope, and they do not learn how to cope. They do not grow up, and some may never grow up."

Danger Signs

The signs that say you are starting to smoke too much grass are not much different from those that warn of other excessive drug use. But they may be easier to ignore, because pot is so prevalent and has had a reputation as a basically harmless substance. Still, if you recognize any of the following signs, it may be time for you to quit:

1. Do you spend a lot of time thinking about grass? Even if you're not using much, grass is playing a bigger role than you think.

2. Are you romanticizing marijuana use? If you are fascinated by the exoticism of marijuana and hashish, if you're up on all the different kinds of grass available, if you treasure your copies of Baudelaire's hashish fantasies, marijuana is more important to you than you might think.

3. Can you turn down a joint? If you can't, you are on your way to becoming a heavy smoker.

4. Can you hold on to a stash of grass? If you can't, if you're starting to smoke whatever you have, you probably are smoking too much.

5. Are you smoking more or stronger pot and feeling the same high? Then you're building tolerance, working up to real dependency and trouble controlling your use.

6. Are you usually stoned at concerts and the movies? If you need marijuana to add that "extra something" to what's happening on the stage or on the screen and have to smoke a joint or two to enjoy a dance, a walk in the park or a day at the beach, then you are not enhancing experiences anymore, you're losing touch with reality.

7. Would you rather stay home and smoke than go out with your friends? It can happen. When marijuana ceases to be something you enjoy with friends, and instead begins to replace your friends, then you are close to compulsive use.

8. Do you sometimes lose track of conversations or forget something you just finished reading? Short-term memory loss is a common effect of marijuana. When you start experiencing it while you think you're straight, then you don't need much more of a warning to quit.

9. *Do you often smoke while driving or on the job?* It may relieve boredom or make the time pass, but what you are doing is making high-risk use a habit.

Starting Off

Once you've decided to get off grass, just stop taking it. Marijuana is about the only drug that you may safely be able to start getting off without checking first with your doctor. Withdrawal is not much of a problem for most users, and a good many physicians are not convinced there even is a marijuana abstinence syndrome. Still, regular users often experience a short period of distress when they quit. They become irritable, anxious and have trouble sleeping. Sweating and upset stomach are other symptoms, but these are generally not severe; loss of appetite can cause you to shed some weight. What's going to be harder to handle will be the drug cravings, the depression and the sense of loss you are going to feel.

Treatment Alternatives

A good many marijuana users are able to get off the drug without any treatment at all. But the following test for drug involvement (when used with the personal resources test in Chapter 2) will give you some idea of your own treatment needs:

Drug Involvement Test

Answer each question as honestly as you can, but don't trust yourself too much. Remember, honest self-assessment is not your strong suit. Ask someone close to you—your husband or wife, friend or lover—to check and correct your answers.

	YES	NO
1. Do you use hashish or hash oil?	—	—
2. Do you use a bong or similar piece of paraphernalia?	—	—
3. Do you use marijuana or hashish daily?	—	—
4. Do you use three or more days a week?	—	—
(Answer Yes even if you have replied affirmatively to the previous question.)		

5. Do you smoke five or more times on any day of use?   — —
6. Do you smoke more than twice on any day of use?   — —
   (Answer Yes even if you have replied affirmatively
   to the previous question.)
7. Do you sometimes smoke alone?   — —
8. Do you experience psychedelic reactions when you
   smoke?   — —
9. Do you sometimes experience panic attacks or have
   paranoid reactions, feel confused after smoking or have
   difficulty concentrating?   — —
10. Do you have adverse physical reactions (nausea or
    headaches) or become aggressive or belligerent
    or have you been involved in an accident as a
    result of marijuana use?   — —

Count only your Yes answers. A total of more than five indicates *profound* drug involvement, three to five *serious* involvement, and less than three *moderate* involvement.

For adults, profound or even serious use, when personal resources are weak or on the weak end of the limited range, calls for some kind of treatment. Even with more in the way of personal resources, you may stand a better chance to succeed by opting for treatment. As a rule, residential alternatives—and certainly the heavier residential interventions like therapeutic communities—are not necessary if marijuana is your sole drug of abuse. But if marijuana is only one of the drugs you use, then you should consider residential treatment. Long-term treatment in a therapeutic community may even be appropriate if your drug use is profound and your resources weak.

In general, however, a less intrusive option, such as an outpatient program, can provide all you need to break even a substantial marijuana habit. Descriptions of both residential and outpatient, drug-free (OPDF) treatment are found in Chapter 2 and in the chapters on cocaine and heroin.

For adolescents there is a wide range of alternatives: school programs, drop-in or "rap" centers, day programs and a growing number of special residential programs. The self-assessment test will not provide an accurate guide to adolescent treatment needs, however, and you'd be better off getting in touch with a school or drug program counselor to see what kind of treatment will be most effective.

Treatment choices for adolescents are usually made by parents, and you shouldn't rush your kid to the nearest program available. Be sure the program you try first does a careful preadmission screening, offers several kinds of treatment or, if not, refers clients it cannot serve to more appropriate programs. You also want to be sure that the program your child enters works out individual recovery plans, involves parents and other family members in the treatment process, and either provides regular education (if it is a residential or day program) or coordinates its schedule with school activities.

An effective outpatient model for youngsters whose drug involvement is only moderate is the IMPACT (Intervention Moves Parents and Children Together) program developed by Phoenix House. Youngsters in IMPACT meet in two-hour groups of the mutual support, self-help type, at least twice a week. Parents attend educational seminars that deal with values, attitudes, approaches to discipline and ways to take and hold positions. The program, which also brings parents and children together in groups, is aimed at strengthening the family's ability to handle its own drug problems. Although the IMPACT model is new, a growing number of treatment programs throughout the country now recognize the need for close family involvement in the treatment of adolescents.

Individual Efforts

Your first individual effort will be to stop, and you may be surprised how easy that can be. If you do feel some withdrawal symptoms, they shouldn't slow you down much. But you will *miss* marijuana and *want* it. Distraction is the best antidote. New activities and new associations are just as important for you as for any other drug abuser (individual efforts are discussed in more detail in Chapter 2 and the preceding chapters on other drugs). You also must avoid, if you can, the settings and situations that cued your drug-taking behavior. If you smoked pot in school or where you worked, you may not be able to make a clean break with that part of your past, but you should be able to work out ways to minimize contact with old pot buddies and to avoid spots where you used to smoke.

The best way to minimize contact is to find new activities and organize your day around these. Some of the activities you choose can give you almost as much of a high as pot—only naturally. Long-distance running isn't the only form of exercise that lifts mood levels. There are swimming and cycling, and just about anything that puts a heavy oxygen demand on your body. Competitive sports can help, too, as can strenuous adventures like rock climbing or canoeing. You can get a lift from more sedentary pursuits as well, from creative activities like art and music, or spiritual activities like yoga or meditation. The important thing is to keep busy and find new things to do and make new friends. You really have to

look at giving up drug use as giving up a part of your life—your old life
—and finding new interests to take the place of what's gone.

Staying Off

Some youngsters and some adults who have had heavy marijuana
habits may need support long after they have gotten off. Youth programs
often have aftercare services that allow kids to maintain contact and get
the help they need even after treatment has ended. For adults, a Twelve-
Step program, such as Alcoholics Anonymous or Pills Anonymous (see
Chapter 7), can provide that kind of long-term support. For both youngsters and adults, the big danger to continued abstinence is not returning
to marijuana so much as starting to use and abuse alcohol.

Notes for the Marijuana User's Parents

How do parents deal with marijuana? If you're lucky or wise, you
already know where you stand on marijuana—and so do your children.
It isn't very useful to start deciding how you feel about your child's
smoking pot once that is what he (or she) is doing. And it may not comfort
you much to know that the way kids handle drugs often reflects how they
have seen drugs (of all kinds) and alcohol used at home.

But even youngsters with the best of all possible parent role models
can get themselves in trouble with marijuana. What should you do when
you find out? If you catch him smoking or if he comes home stoned, let
it ride; there's no sense confronting a kid when he is high. But when you
do confront him, stay calm—you can't blow him away. You've got to
hear him out. Listen to his reasons, and try to understand them. Sometimes, you can help him to deal with his own ambivalence about smoking
pot. Indeed, youngsters often provoke this kind of confrontation to resolve their own conflict and find an excuse they can carry back to their
peers. ("My old man will kill me if I smoke another joint.")

Listening doesn't mean you have to agree with what your son or
daughter says. Marijuana is really a high-risk drug for adolescents. If
pressed, you may have to take a hard-line stand.

It's easy to talk about taking a stand, harder to actually take it. You
may need help, and you can look for it from one of the many parent
groups that have been started up across the country in recent years to
help families like yours. You can usually contact such a group through

your state or local drug abuse agency. You can also look for help from a counselor at a local drug program or at your child's school.

Parents have a lot of muscle. If they are willing to use it, they can usually bring their kids into line. It is not going to be very pleasant around the house if you have to clamp down heavy restrictions and enforce them. But if your youngster is into any heavy or regular use, chances are he hasn't been such a joy to have around anyway.

If it comes to a test of wills over his right to smoke pot, then you are into a fight you cannot easily win without support. You probably need a treatment program, such as the IMPACT program described earlier or another model that involves family participation.

You want to be a part of his treatment, and there may be a lot you can learn from such a program. You might discover just why drugs became such an issue in your home. The point is that you not only want him to get off drugs, you want to learn what you need to know to help him keep off.

9

HALLUCINOGENS

For most drug users, distorted perceptions and hallucinations are a risk of drug-taking. For some, however, they are a goal, and the hallucinogens —a group of otherwise diverse drugs—can all alter perceptions and cause sensory distortion at relatively low doses.

Although much was made of hallucinogens when they appeared on the scene, use of the drugs grew slowly through most of the 1960s, picking up sharply as the decade ended and declining just as rapidly after 1972. A second wave of popularity began several years later, but this proved short-lived; between 1976 and 1979, use of hallucinogens rose and then fell once again.

Natural hallucinogens were among the first psychoactive drugs. In 1600 B.C., the mushroom *Amanita muscaria* was clouding consciousness in India. Peyote cactus (mescaline) and psilocybin mushrooms were used in the New World long before the Spanish arrived. The modern age of hallucinogens began in 1943, when the psychedelic effects and potency of the experimental synthetic drug LSD were discovered. During the years that followed, LSD was studied widely, mostly to learn more about mental illness. Some psychiatrists tried it in treatment, and government research was done on LSD's capacity to aid brainwashing. But it first achieved notoriety in 1963, when Timothy Leary and Richard Alpert, then young psychologists, were fired from Harvard for experimenting with the drug on students.

Most early U.S. users came from the counterculture generation, turning to LSD and the hallucinogens that followed it onto the illicit market (such as DOM, MDA and DMT) for the sensory experience or as a back route to self-knowledge. For some, the drugs were a way to get a different perspective on the real world. As Marcelle Clements wrote in her *Rolling Stone* article, "The Dog Is Us," tripping was "my generation's idea of a good time; to take note of the absurd and to laugh at it." By the later 1960s many of these first-wave users began to switch from synthetic hallucinogens to substances they considered more "organic," mescaline and psilocybin.

The second wave of popular use, from 1976 to 1979, was somewhat different. There were many more adolescent users, but they took less potent doses of the drug with little heavy tripping. However, PCP (phencyclidine), a drug first-wave users had rejected as too disturbing and dangerous, became a second-wave favorite in spite of its extraordinary risks—the possibilities of prolonged psychosis and self-destructive or violent behavior. Indeed, PCP proved to be just the kind of horror drug that marijuana was falsely branded back in the 1930s.

The different natures of the hallucinogens make it difficult to generalize about them, and it is important to recognize just how they differ from each other, what effects and reactions to anticipate, what dangers are involved and what is needed to get off and stay off.

LSD

The hallucinogenic properties of LSD (D-lysergic acid diethylamide) were first noted when the drug's developer, Swiss chemist Albert Hofmann, accidentally absorbed a small amount through the skin of his fingers. "I was seized by a peculiar sensation of vertigo and restlessness," he later recalled. "Objects, as well as the shapes of my associates in the laboratory, appeared to undergo optical changes. I was unable to concentrate on my work. In a dreamlike state I left for home, where an irresistible urge to lie down overcame me. I drew the curtains and immediately fell into a peculiar state similar to drunkenness, characterized by an exaggerated imagination. With my eyes closed, fantastic pictures of extraordinary plasticity and intensive color seemed to surge toward me. After two hours this state gradually wore off."

The best known and most popular of modern hallucinogens, LSD is a synthetic derived from ergot (a fungus that grows on rye and certain members of the sunflower family). Ergot itself will produce hallucinations, and history notes several incidents of widespread ergotism (includ-

Table 5. Hallucinogens

Drug	Duration of Effects	Threshold Dose (Hallucinogenic)	Notes
LSD-type (Indolealkylamines)			
D-Lysergic acid diethylamide (LSD)	8–12 hours	50–100 micrograms (mcg)	One of the most potent psychoactive drugs
Alpha-acetyl LSD (ALD)	8–12 hours	45–90 mcg	The original "orange sunshine"; "speedy trip"
D-Lysergic acid amide (LSA)	8–12 hours	0.5–1.0 mg	Also called ergine; found in morning glory seeds (often commercial seeds are coated to prevent misuse)
Psilocin (psilocybin)	4–6 hours	4–6 mg	In at least 90 different species of mushrooms; effects are described as like LSD but "more gentle"
DMT, DET, DPT (substituted tryptamines)	30–45 minutes for DMT, the "businessman's LSD." Longer for DET and DPT (up to 6 hours)	50 mg (DMT)	Ineffective when taken orally; usually smoked
Mescaline-type (Phenylethylamines and Amphetamine Derivatives)			
Mescaline	8–12 hours	200 mg or 3–5 peyote buttons	1/200 the potency of LSD but more toxic in high doses; *a rare drug for which counterfeits are often sold*
DOM (STP)	16–24 hours or longer	5 mg	Many adverse reactions: panic, paranoia, flashbacks and psychosis
DOB	16–24 hours	1–2 mg	Next to LSD in potency, sometimes an LSD substitute; has bizarre side effects

Table 5. Hallucinogens (*cont.*)

Drug	Duration of Effects	Threshold Dose (Hallucinogenic)	Notes
MDA	8–12 hours	50 mg	"The love drug"— subtle in low doses, like LSD in higher doses. Called XTC or "ecstasy" on illicit market.
MDM	8–12 hours	50 mg	A new drug much like MDA

Dissociative type (Phencyclidines)

Phencyclidine hydrochloride (PCP)	4–6 hours	about 5 mg	Effects begin at lower doses; unpredictable at higher doses

ing a possible outbreak in Salem, Massachusetts, at the time of the witchcraft trials there). One of the most powerful of all psychoactive drugs, LSD's effects can be felt at doses as low as 10 micrograms, or one millionth of a gram.

Effects

The body responds to LSD's impact on central nervous system receptors before the mind does, usually within the first hour after the drug has been taken. Not all users react the same way, and these physiological effects seem less related to dosage than the drug's psychological effects are. Enlarged pupils, rapid heartbeat, slight shakiness and rising blood pressure and temperature are common. Sweating alternates with chills. Breathing becomes rapid at first, then deeper and slower. Users have little appetite, and some experience nausea. In general, early effects follow the pattern of the "fight-or-flight" response to stimulation of the sympathetic nervous system, including agitation and insomnia that may persist after psychological effects diminish. Users often are left with a tense, nervous, "wired" feeling not too different from what amphetamine users feel at the end of a spree.

Forty-five minutes to an hour after taking LSD, the individual starts to undergo mental changes. At very low doses of 10 to 25 micrograms, LSD produces mild euphoria and loss of inhibitions. The "psychedelic" threshold is crossed somewhere between 50 and 100 micrograms, and these effects reach maximum intensity between 400 and 500 micrograms.

Higher doses do not always increase the effects, but they may prolong them.

What individual users experience at doses of 100 micrograms or higher is heavily influenced by their expectations, their mental "set," and the setting (where and with whom the drug is used). Usually, sensory perceptions are heightened. Colors appear brighter, shapes more clearly defined, tastes seem sharper, and sound louder and purer. Users often have the sense of "hearing" color or "seeing" sound. They may see afterimages or "trails" when objects cross their field of vision and leave "streaks" of color. "Psychedelic" patterns may appear. Time seems to stretch and perceptions of space and distance are also distorted. Bizarre bodily sensations are common, feelings of heaviness or "floating." Users become highly suggestible and can be easily manipulated. Spontaneous mood changes may occur rapidly. Hallucinations most often are visual, and usually are limited to "pseudohallucinations" (although the illusions appear real, users are aware of their unreality).

Lost memories tend to resurface. Control over thought diminishes. There is a sense of detachment, as boundaries between the individual and the environment seem to disintegrate. For some, this produces a rewarding sense of "becoming one with the universe." For others, this detachment can be terrifying.

The responses to these effects vary from user to user and change during the course of the trip from withdrawal and introspection to a wary guardedness. When drug effects peak, usually after two or three hours, users may become convinced that they are having a religious or "mystical" experience; for some, this is the goal of the LSD trip.

Patterns of Use

Although it has occasionally been administered intravenously and even in eye drops, LSD is almost always taken orally these days. It is sold on small pieces of paper ("blotter acid"), in colored aspirin-size tablets ("tab acid"), and in tiny, pinhead-size tablets ("microdots").

First-wave users, at the end of the 1960s and during the early 1970s, favored doses between 200 and 300 micrograms—although many took about 500 micrograms and some ventured near the 1,000 microgram range —and consumed the drug on sugar cubes, in squares of gelatin or in tablets. Adverse reactions were frequent, and users tended to trip in private with a lover or a few close friends. Much was made of "preparing" for the trip—finding a comfortable spot, putting each other at ease, selecting tranquil music. Some users went so far as to keep sedatives on hand just in case a "bad trip" ensued.

Much lower doses (35 to 75 micrograms) were the rule with the second wave (from 1976 to 1979), adverse reactions were less common, and many young users tripped in public, at concerts or discotheques. When larger doses were taken and full effects of the drug experienced, these low-dose users were likely to blame "bad acid" or insist that PCP or even a mixture of LSD and strychnine had been substituted.

Although the popularity of LSD has fallen since the end of the 1970s, dosage seems to be rising again, and the average in some areas is now 100 micrograms or higher. Remarkably, LSD remains one of the more trustworthy street drugs. Despite reports of "bad acid" over the years (especially in the late 1960s), you are usually likely to get what you pay for. Even when you are slipped something else, it isn't often likely to be harmful.

Adverse Reactions

A "bad trip" is the most common, and it can range from mere anxiety to a panic reaction or full-blown toxic psychosis that involves loss of identity, severe confusion, paranoia, delusions, and an inability to recognize hallucinations as unreal. Although a large number of LSD users have reported bad trips, some do not view this experience as totally negative and claim, "You can learn something from it." There does not appear to be any way to prevent bad trips at doses high enough to cause psychedelic effects, and even experienced users with a long history of good trips may suddenly have a bad one. But the worst trips, with psychosis that lasts a day or more, seem to happen most often to newer users.

"Talking down" the victim is the classic prescription for this reaction. You've got to explain that he or she has taken a powerful drug and that the effects will pass, which they will as the drug metabolizes and leaves the body. Reassurance, comfort and a quiet, darkened room all help. Doctors sometimes will administer a depressant to induce sleep or may use an antipsychotic to control extreme psychotic reactions.

Longer-lasting (more than forty-eight hours) psychosis is induced by LSD from time to time, but this is a more common reaction to other hallucinogens. However, there is widespread belief among psychiatrists that victims of this kind of psychosis are usually either predisposed to mental illness or have histories of mental illness. In some cases, psychosis may occur some time after an LSD trip has ended. Prolonged psychosis is difficult to relieve, although recent experimental use of a drug that raises levels of serotonin in the central nervous system—LSD's chemical action involves blocking serotonin receptors—has reversed its symptoms.

Although severe, even suicidal depression can follow LSD use, this too is a rare reaction and usually involves some history of mental illness. It is a condition that calls for medical attention and often responds to treatment normally given manic-depressives.

Far more frequent among LSD users is the "flashback," a replay of the hallucinatory experience unprompted by a hallucinogen. It strikes about 5 percent of all users and 80 percent of all frequent users. Symptoms can range from mild distortion of perceptions to episodes so severe medical treatment and sedation are needed. Usually brief, flashbacks rarely last more than a few hours; they may occur only once or repeatedly over a period of months.

Drug experts aren't sure just what causes flashbacks, but many believe a part of the hallucinatory experience is stored in the user's memory and recalled involuntarily when the nervous system becomes highly aroused again (similar to the state induced by the hallucinogen) by stress, anxiety or the use of alcohol or another drug—often marijuana.

Behavioral toxicity must be counted as an adverse reaction to LSD and by far the most life-threatening one. In extreme cases, highly suggestible trippers, suffering from delusions and hallucinations, have died attempting impossible feats, such as flying from a window or stopping oncoming traffic by the force of their will.

Long-Term Effects

Those rare instances of prolonged psychosis may well be the only long-term effects LSD produces. None of the drug's toxic effects damage other organs, and save for behavioral toxicity, none are potentially lethal. Even massive overdose will not prove fatal, but this is not true of more chemically toxic hallucinogens such as MDA and DOM.

Abuse Potential

The tolerance that LSD users develop tends to reduce rather than increase the likelihood of abuse. A rapidly rising tolerance (called tachyphylaxis), it can become so great after three of four days of LSD use that no effect can be achieved no matter how much of the drug is taken. Cross-tachyphylaxis makes it impossible to feel the effects of such similar hallucinogens such as psilocybin or mescaline. Sensitivity to LSD, however, can be regained after a few days of abstinence.

Tachyphylaxis alone is not responsible for LSD's limited abuse potential. Most drug experts consider its use "self-limiting," because the effects tend to become progressively less attractive. Thus, patterns of compulsive LSD-taking rarely develop. There are exceptions. While the "acid heads" of an earlier generation are hardly ever seen these days, some first-wave users, adolescents and emotionally disturbed older users do occasionally trip on a regular basis.

Other LSD-type Hallucinogens

ALD-52 has nine tenths the potency of LSD itself and produces identical effects, although its action starts a bit sooner.

LSA, naturally derived from morning glory seeds and only 5 to 10 percent the strength of LSD, has pronounced side effects (from unrelated alkaloids it contains), including nausea and diarrhea.

Psilocybin and *psilocin* both are found in about ninety species of mushrooms native to Europe and to North and Central America. Psilocybin, which is metabolized by the body into psilocin, is less potent than psilocin itself, which has only 1 percent of LSD's strength. Good-size doses, usually 5 to 10 grams, of dried mushrooms are needed to produce four to six hours of effects somewhat gentler than LSD's.

DMT is not effective taken orally. Most often smoked (usually with marijuana), it can also be injected. Strong effects, felt at 50 milligrams, resemble LSD's but are more intense, start sooner, peak earlier and usually end within forty-five minutes. Because of the brief duration of its action, DMT has become known as "the businessman's high."

DET and *DPT,* both chemical cousins of DMT, have somewhat longer-lasting (rarely more than two hours) but similar effects.

Mescaline and Amphetaminelike Hallucinogens

Mescaline, extracted from peyote and San Pedro cactus, is between three and four thousandths of the strength of LSD. At doses of 200 milligrams—or with three to five peyote "buttons"—LSD-like effects are achieved and last from eight to twelve hours. However, nausea and vomiting often occur; high doses can produce extreme toxic effects, mostly on the digestive system; and a fatal overdose, though unlikely, is still possible.

DOM, known on the street as STP (after the motor oil additive), produces LSD-like effects at doses between 2 and 5 milligrams that can last as long as twenty-four hours. Bad trips occur frequently, overdose can be fatal, and DOM-induced psychosis may persist for years.

DOB, a DOM derivative, is relatively easy to produce. Although one tenth the strength of LSD, it is potent enough to be sold occasionally as LSD, exposing users to DOM-like dangers of toxicity and bad trips.

MDA, called "the love drug" or XTC (for ecstasy), produces effects quite different from LSD's at doses between 50 and 150 milligrams. At these levels, users experience a serene euphoria that increases empathy, prompts self-discovery and intimacy, and seems to encourage feelings of affection. At higher doses (between 150 and 200 milligrams) its effects are closer to LSD's, with vague hallucinations, sweating and tension. There is obvious reinforcement of MDA use and significant potential for abuse. Although bad trips are rare at normal doses, toxic levels (above 200 milligrams) can prove fatal.

MDM is much the same drug as MDA. A somewhat newer substance, its effects and dangers are almost identical.

TMA also has two separate sets of characteristics. At doses of 50 to 100 milligrams, it behaves much the way mescaline does. At doses of about 250 milligrams, its nature changes, and it becomes more of an amphetaminelike substance, often prompting displays of anger and hostility.

PCP (Phencyclidine)

A heavy-hitting and highly toxic drug that does not lend itself to low-risk use, PCP—best known to users as "angel dust"—has only a modest claim to the hallucinogen label. Although it can behave as both a stimulant and a depressant, PCP became popular with young users at the end of the 1970s primarily for its "dissociative effect," the way it allowed them to detach themselves from reality—or as one adolescent user describes it, "making the world look like TV."

Initially developed as an anesthetic, PCP revealed so many frightening side effects—agitation, delirium, hallucinations and convulsions—that research on humans was discontinued in 1965 and legal use restricted to veterinary medicine. Introduced to the street in 1967, the drug first appeared on the West Coast in tablet form—as the Peace Pill—but never caught on. During the early 1970s it reappeared as a powder young users sprinkled on marijuana and smoked. In this form, it spread across the country, and the number of users increased rapidly until, by 1979, 13 percent of the nation's high school seniors had at least sampled PCP. Since then, however, use of the drug has fallen sharply (except in a few locations, such as Los Angeles and parts of New York City), most likely because of the wretched reputation it has earned and the number of PCP "casualties" in the adolescent population.

Effects

When smoked it takes several minutes for PCP's effects to be felt (the less common routes of administration—injection and snorting—are much more rapid), and effects usually last from two to six hours, although they have been known to continue for more than a day. At doses from 1 to 5 milligrams, PCP often seems like very potent marijuana. Above 5 milligrams, effects become much less predictable.

Within the normal dosage range, dizziness and loss of coordination are common. LSD-like visual distortions and illusions can be seen, and users may experience bizarre bodily sensations—often feeling like they are made of rubber and immune to pain—and hallucinations. In addition, they often suffer nausea, vomiting and cramps, may become agitated or depressed, experience insomnia and feelings of paranoia.

Adverse Reactions

The behavioral toxicity of PCP is extreme. Accidental death can result from auto accidents, falls or burns. Drownings are frequent, for PCP elevates body temperature, gives the skin a hot and dry feeling that prompts a desire to bathe or swim. The aggressive behavior and violence sometimes induced by PCP appear to be the result of the massive disorientation and paranoia the drug can cause. In addition to loss of feeling, the diminished pain threshold produced by the drug's anesthetic properties clearly contributes to accidents and self-inflicted injury.

Acute intoxication is marked by high blood pressure, increased heart rate, rapid eye movement, sweating, drooling and loss of body control. Users may become highly agitated and violent. Attempting to "talk them down" can be a high-risk mission. They need medical care, not necessarily because their condition has become life-threatening but because they are capable of injuring themselves and others.

There is a narrow margin between doses that produce the desired effects of PCP and toxic doses, and acute intoxication puts the user on the border of overdose. Toxic effects, both physical and psychological, are difficult to treat, for there is no specific antagonist for PCP and the drug behaves much as THC does, leaving the body reluctantly after storage in fatty tissue and reabsorption. Overdose victims can suffer extreme elevation of blood pressure, prolonged coma and convulsions. Death

Hallucinogens **209**

may result even when timely and competent medical attention is available.

Toxic psychosis, which can be brought about by a single dose of PCP, is often preceded by paranoid delusions and aggressive behavior. Although victims are usually violent, some become catatonic, and symptoms generally mimic those of an acute schizophrenic episode. Treatment with large doses of such benzodiazepine tranquilizers as Valium or Librium or the antipsychotics is generally effective in controlling symptoms. Violent behavior usually ends after several days, although it can take another ten days or two weeks for patients to return to normal.

Long-Term Effects

PCP-induced psychosis may last for long periods, although psychiatrists believe persistent or recurrent psychosis most likely indicates either a predisposition to mental illness or a history of mental illness that predates PCP use. The possibility of permanent brain damage as a result of PCP use remains an issue of concern. Heavy users do show long-lasting mental impairment, including memory gaps, some disorientation, speech impairment and visual disturbance. These "crystalized" users, as they are called on the street, resemble "burned-out" amphetamine users. However, their disabilities usually seem to disappear within six months to a year after drug use ends.

No birth defects have yet been noted in the children of PCP-using mothers. Still, the possibility of birth defects cannot be discounted, since PCP is such a toxic drug, has so many side effects and is retained in the body for so long.

Abuse Potential

A good many PCP users do increase the amounts they take, but there is no clear evidence of tolerance to the drug. Nor has physical dependence been demonstrated, although PCP's chemical structure suggests the possibility and physical dependence in laboratory animals has been induced with high doses. Psychological dependence, however, is created, and a number of users experience withdrawal symptoms—some physical distress, lack of energy, depression—when they discontinue PCP use.

Danger Signs

Any *regular* or *prolonged* use of a hallucinogen is high-risk. *Any* use of PCP is. There are few subtle behavioral clues to danger, but there are clear warnings to stop—frequent flashbacks, incidents of aggressive behavior or violence, and toxic reactions. Repeated bad trips are a clear signal. If you use hallucinogens in public, you are raising risks well above a rational level, and the need to stop should be evident if you have suffered injury or been involved in an accident while under the influence of hallucinogens.

Starting Off

First, you've got to recognize just what drug you are getting off. Hallucinogen users often take other drugs too, and may take these drugs more often and more regularly than hallucinogens. It isn't useful to think of yourself as essentially a hallucinogen user at this point if you have developed a dependency on opioids, depressants or stimulants, or are using alcohol or marijuana compulsively.

No matter what drug it is that determines how you go about getting off (and you have to get off *all* of them), your first stop should be the doctor's office. You may be malnourished or suffering from injuries or illness your drug use has been masking. If you have been using LSD or a similar hallucinogen, you are not going to have withdrawal symptoms. But if use has been prolonged—if you stayed with the drug long past the point where most other users quit—then your doctor is likely to recommend a psychiatric evaluation.

If PCP has been your hallucinogen of choice, and you have been a heavy or regular user, then you can expect some withdrawal symptoms —a measure of physical discomfort, loss of energy and depression. Try not to anticipate too much distress, for withdrawal has a way of living up to expectations. Remember, too, that a good many drug researchers aren't convinced PCP actually does produce an abstinence syndrome. (Doctors at the Community Health Project in Los Angeles, however, have noted the symptoms and recently began using the tricyclic antidepressant desipramine to help withdraw PCP users over a five-to-ten-day period.)

Treatment Alternatives

Treatment needs vary from individual to individual and from drug to drug. For most adult hallucinogen users—but not users of PCP—the following drug involvement test (when used with the personal resources test in Chapter 2) will indicate what kind of treatment might be appropriate.

Drug Involvement Test

Answer each question as honestly as you can, but don't trust yourself too much. Remember, honest self-assessment is not your strong suit. Ask someone close to you—your husband or wife, friend or lover—to check and correct your answers.

	YES	NO
1. Are you frequently confused, or do you have trouble concentrating, or have you ever been hospitalized because of hallucinogen use?	—	—
2. Do you use hallucinogens more than five times a month?	—	—
3. Do you use them at least twice a month? (Answer yes even if you have responded affirmatively to the previous question.)	—	—
4. Have you used hallucinogens a total of fifty or more times?	—	—
5. Have you used them more than ten times? (Answer Yes even if you have replied affirmatively to the previous question.)	—	—
6. Do you use any drugs to compensate for hallucinogenic effects?	—	—
7. Do you use any other drugs in combination with hallucinogens?	—	—
8. Do you use any other drugs three or more times a week?	—	—
9. Do you suffer flashbacks?	—	—
10. Do you occasionally have adverse reactions (bad trips, aggressive behavior, paranoid feelings)?	—	—
11. Has your use of hallucinogens increased during the past three months?	—	—

A Yes answer to Question 1 or 2 or a total of more than five Yes answers indicates *profound* involvement. Three to five Yes answers indicate *serious* involvement, and less than three *moderate* involvement.

For PCP, any regular use should be considered *profound* involvement. If your drug involvement is profound and your personal resources less than strong, then you should probably consider *residential treatment,* at least at the outset. If you have regularly been using other drugs, have few family responsibilities and no compelling reason to keep your present job or if you are unemployed, then long-term treatment in a therapeutic community may be your best bet.

If your personal resources are strong or on the strong side of the limited range and your drug use is less than profound, then an *outpatient, drug-free* (OPDF) program may provide all the help you will need. The point is to find the form of treatment that works best for you without disrupting your life more than is necessary. Both residential and outpatient treatment and the points to consider when choosing a program are covered fully in Chapter 2.

Individual psychotherapy can also benefit the heavy or longtime hallucinogen user. If your doctor recommends psychiatric evaluation that leads to therapy, then you should consult your therapist about any additional treatment needs.

Individual Efforts

Most hallucinogen use is not habitual, and former users normally need not worry about the cues that prompt drug-taking behavior. But cues may prove a problem if hallucinogen use has been prolonged or regular, and will almost definitely trouble recovering users of PCP. All former hallucinogen users will miss the drug experience, however, and should seek new activities and associations, avoid the sites and situations that are associated with drug use and find alternatives to drug use (these "individual efforts" are covered more fully in Chapter 2). Activities that offer other routes to self-knowledge or spiritual and mystical experiences are particularly useful for recovering hallucinogen users. Yoga and meditation are obvious choices, but so are more traditional church involvement and studies in religion or philosophy. If you have been using PCP, then you may have little energy and feel depressed when you quit. For you, the need to get moving is vital, and exercise is the best way you can start to overcome lethargy and raise mood levels.

Staying Off

Adult hallucinogen users who have not been taking other drugs should anticipate little difficulty avoiding future drug involvement. Heavy adult users who have not already started psychotherapy should probably consider it after other treatment ends. All PCP users and younger, low-dose users of other hallucinogens may need continued support to remain drug-free. Programs for youth often offer aftercare services and allow youngsters to stay in touch with counselors. For adults, a Twelve-Step program, like the one offered by Alcoholics Anonymous (see Chapter 7), can provide long-term support.

Notes for the Hallucinogen User's Parents

While few youngsters are into heavy tripping, many use hallucinogens in low doses, and PCP has a special attraction for youngsters. This kind of drug involvement is not something parents can expect to handle themselves. While your family doctor should be consulted, a counselor at a local drug abuse program or at your child's school may provide more practical advice about what kind of treatment to seek.

There are a number of treatment options for adolescents these days. The most effective usually demand family participation, which not only benefits the youngster involved, but can also increase the family's ability to cope with drug problems. Look over the descriptions of treatment methods in Chapter 2 and the treatment alternatives and notes for parents sections of Chapter 8 on Marijuana.

10

OTHER DRUGS

The drugs of abuse in this chapter do not fit comfortably into other categories. Inhalants—volatile solvents and aerosols, amyl and butyl nitrite, and nitrous oxide—form a class of their own, while the deliriants and ketamine are hallucinogens of limited use with special characteristics. Although abuse of prescribed antidepressants is rare, a brisk street trade in Elavil exists in some areas.

Volatile Solvents and Aerosols

The most physically threatening of all psychoactive drugs, the volatile solvents and aerosols are technically anesthetics that have a short-lived stimulant effect before depressing the central nervous system. The solvents are generally liquid at room temperature but rapidly evaporate. They are found in cleaning fluid, model glue, plastic cement, and a good many other common household products.

The first solvent used as a drug of abuse, gasoline, was being sniffed during the 1950s. Model glue became popular soon after, and aerosols were used almost as soon as spray cans appeared. Just about every kind of aerosol product has been tried (insecticides and disinfectants, as well as hair spray, furniture polish, glass chillers and vegetable pan coaters). Volatile substances are used mostly by the young (preteens through early

Table 6. Volatile Substances of Abuse

Drugs Present in Volatile Substances	Representative Compound in Drug Class	Toxic Effects	Duration of Action	Potential for Causing Physical Dependence
Alcohols (found in paint thinner, degreasers, model cements, aerosol sprays)	Methyl alcohol ("wood alcohol")	Headaches, weakness, delayed blindness (6–30 hours after use), death	5–45 minutes	Possible
Aliphatic hydrocarbons (found in gasoline, paint thinner, adhesives and rubber cement, model cements)	Hexane	Anemia, nerve degeneration, muscle weakness, loss of touch sensation in patches, muscle atrophy	Up to 2 hours	Possible
Anesthetics (found in paint thinner, degreasers, aerosol sprays, foam and cream dispensers)	Trichloroethylene	Liver damage, kidney damage, and damage to the optic nerve and other major cranial nerves. (Note: many of these have caused deaths)	Up to 2 hours	Possible
Aromatic hydrocarbons (found in gasoline, paint thinner, degreasers, adhesives and rubber cement, model cements, aerosol sprays)	Toluene	Nausea, stomach pain, loss of appetite, jaundice and enlarged liver, urinary dysfunction, kidney damage, mental dulling, tremors, emotional disturbances, staggering, nerve and brain damage.	Up to 2 hours	Possible
Esters (found in paint thinner, degreasers)	Ethyl acetate	Severe eye, skin and mucous membrane irritation (known as "sniffers" or "huffers" syndrome), marked depression of central nervous system	5–45 minutes	None
Ketones (found in paint thinner, degreasers, adhesives and rubber cement, model cements)	Acetone	Same as esters but *highly flammable*	About one hour	Possible

adolescence) and the poor, and are particularly popular among Hispanic and Native American youngsters. A fairly steady amount of abuse has persisted through the past decade and shows no sign of declining. Among high school seniors surveyed during 1982, some earlier use of volatile substances was reported by 13 percent. Although adult use is rare, it is not uncommon in prisons and other institutions where alcohol and other drugs are hard to come by.

Solvents can be poured onto cloths and sniffed. They can also be dumped into plastic bags (called "bagging") and either sniffed or "huffed" (inhaled by mouth). Aerosols are either sprayed into containers or inhaled straight from the can.

Effects are felt almost immediately. A brief euphoria, lasting from just a few moments to an hour or more, is accompanied by excitement, a sense of anticipation and delusions of strength and power. During the high, users experience visual distortions, loss of coordination and judgment, slurred speech and giddiness. With high doses, hallucinations may occur.

Toxic effects include memory loss and the inability to concentrate. Behavioral toxicity is high, for the volatile substances prompt recklessness and their disinhibiting effects often let aggressions loose. They are among the drugs most likely to induce violence, though there is only a brief opportunity for it before intoxication passes and most users fall asleep. Accidents are common during this period. Users have died of asphyxiation in their plastic bags or smothered in solvent-impregnated cloths. Solvent overdose has caused respiratory arrest, and the propellants in aerosols are blamed for SSD ("sudden sniffing death"), the result of physical exertion following inhalation that causes erratic heart rhythm and cardiac arrest.

Regular users often suffer headaches, drowsiness and irritability. Prolonged use can do permanent damage to the brain and the peripheral nervous system. It can lead to kidney and liver failure, destroy bone marrow, cause digestive disorders, anemia, convulsions and certain types of leukemia.

Tolerance to volatile substances can be created by regular use, and while there is little evidence of physical dependency, psychological dependency does develop. In spite of attempts to control abuse by restricting the sale of solvents to adults and the addition of irritants to certain of the substances, the drugs remain popular, generally accessible and cheap. Although young people in certain communities are under peer pressure to try these drugs, most experimenters do not go on to become regular users. Those who do are likely to "mature out" in late adolescence, giving up the drug but then turning to either alcohol or depressants.

Adolescent users are unlikely to generate a strong commitment to quit by themselves, and youngsters who use volatile substances compulsively often are emotionally disturbed or come from disorganized homes or families. Many are insecure, with strong feelings of inferiority.

Parents should make sure a young abuser sees a doctor and has a complete examination to determine whether any physical damage has been done by the drug. A doctor may well recommend further psychiatric evaluation for many of these youngsters.

Abuse of volatile substances is not a problem parents can handle as a disciplinary matter. Treatment is necessary. Various alternatives for adolescents are covered in Chapter 9 and in the "treatment alternatives" section of Chapter 8, on marijuana. Keep in mind that parent participation is a major factor in successful treatment of adolescents.

Amyl and Butyl Nitrite

These are two quite similar inhalants. Volatile, inflammable liquids that decompose when exposed to air, they are vasodilators (they cause blood vessels to expand). For more than a hundred years, until longer-acting remedies were available, amyl nitrite was used to relieve the symptoms of angina pectoris by lowering the resistance of blood vessels and relieving demand on the heart.

When amyl nitrite ceased to be a prescription drug, in 1960, nonmedical use picked up sharply, and a number of adolescents discovered it. It quickly gained a reputation for enhancing sex. "Poppers," as ampules of amyl nitrite were called, were crushed and the drug inhaled just before orgasm to create a sensation of prolonged climax. In 1969, amyl nitrite was returned to the prescription category by the Food and Drug Administration, but its nonprescription cousin, butyl nitrite (and isobutyl nitrite, another family member), became available, first as an "under-the-counter" drug, later as a perfectly legal room deodorizer sold in head shops under such names as Locker Room, Rush, Kick and Bullet.

Plastic bags are sometimes used to inhale butyl nitrite (which now comes in small bottles), although sophisticated users carry their own sniffing devices. Effects are felt within ten to thirty seconds and last two or three minutes. Mostly, users feel light-headed and giddy. There is some distortion of perception. Time seems to stretch and sensory stimulation appears more intense. The drug has disinhibiting effects and sometimes causes displays of aggressiveness.

The downside of butyl nitrite includes dizziness and nausea, flushing, and occasional loss of consciousness. Among its more toxic effects are vomiting, a weakened pulse rate, and loss of control over bodily functions. Expansion of blood vessels serving the brain can cause throbbing headaches. There have been reports of strokelike incidents following use of the drug.

Butyl nitrite became increasingly popular during the 1970s. Today, it is used mostly by adolescents for a cheap and legal high. When used with alcohol, there is a real chance of adverse reactions. Drugs of considerable risk, the volatile nitrites pose severe dangers for users with low blood pressure or glaucoma (since they increase intraocular pressure) or for those who have recently suffered head injuries.

Although tolerance to amyl and butyl nitrite can be acquired, the drugs do not cause true physical dependency. Psychological dependency can be developed, and younger users are particularly vulnerable. Parents should deal with their children's abuse of these drugs much as they would with abuse of any other volatile substance.

Nitrous Oxide

The heyday of nitrous oxide as a drug of abuse came in the middle of the nineteenth century when "laughing gas" was a popular recreational drug. Although classed with inhalants, nitrous oxide is an anesthetic (a relatively weak one, but with powerful analgesic properties) still used in medicine and particularly dentistry. It has industrial and commercial applications, too, the most familiar being its use as a propellant for aerosol whipped cream. Since it is not a controlled substance, head shops can sell the small metal cylinders of the gas—called "Whippets" and made for use with whipped-cream dispensers—as well as the balloons experienced users use to inhale it.

Nitrous oxide goes to work within seconds after being inhaled. Users feel exhilarated, and sometimes laugh and sing. In the middle of the high, which lasts only two or three minutes, they will lose consciousness for several seconds, but may experience sensations of floating or flying before they go under and sometimes experience sensory distortion as consciousness returns. Some users find the brief trip a mystical experience; others can be distressed by insights that surface while they are high.

The aftermath of the drug-taking experience is characterized by a sense of well-being that can last as long as several hours. However, some users feel a diminished sense of identity after the high. Mild nausea and a dry throat are just about the only physical side effects.

Although nitrous oxide is nontoxic, it is dangerous, and users have injured themselves and even died, by taking the drug in stupid ways.

"Nitrous frostbite" occurs when they attempt to draw gas directly from the cylinder. Since expanding gas reaches extremely low temperatures, users have frozen noses, lips, mouths, throats and vocal cords this way. They have also injured themselves in "dead-weight" falls after inhaling the drug and either losing their balance or passing out from a standing position.

More serious outcomes result from strapping on an anesthetic mask to take the drug. Because nitrous oxide does not provide all the oxygen the brain requires (anesthesiologists make sure that a mixture of no less than 30 percent pure oxygen is used when administering it), users have lost consciousness and either suffocated or suffered brain damage this way.

Deliriants

A group of unrelated natural psychoactives and their chemical derivatives, the deliriants are the less popular and more toxic members of the hallucinogen class, most of which can induce delirium at well below toxic levels. They are very high-risk drugs with unattractive features that generally makes use self-limiting. "Drugs of opportunity" rather than "drugs of choice," they are taken because they are available, not necessarily because they are desirable—which makes dependency unlikely and treatment for abuse generally unnecessary.

Scopolamine, Atropine, and Other Related Alkaloids

The plants of the nightshade family—deadly nightshade *(Atropa belladonna)* and jimsonweed or "locoweed" *(Datura stramonium),* along with henbane and mandrake—are the sources of these drugs, the most powerful of which is scopolamine. Used medically to dry secretions in the nose and mouth, scopolamine also has mild sedative effects. Until recently, small amounts were allowed in over-the-counter sleep aids and pills for motion sickness. No controls were exercised over scopolamine because it was assumed the drug was simply too terrifying to be misused.

However, nonmedical use of scopolamine and the other atropine alkaloids, while not widespread, is far from rare. Users can get substantial amounts by smoking jimsonweed or brewing jimsonweed or mandrake tea. Adolescents are the most frequent users and their source of supply is often the jimsonweed that grows in vacant lots, abandoned fields and garbage dumps all across the country. Outbreaks of jimsonweed "freak-out" or poisoning occur regularly.

The effects of the drugs—which are sometimes taken with alcohol—can be terrifying. Hallucinations seem real. Users lose touch with reality. They see "monsters and giant bats" and are involved in violent encounters. Often, they remember little of the experience, for the drugs tend to blur memory. True toxic psychosis may result, with prolonged hallucinations and wildly excited delirium. Victims often must be restrained, but are rarely sedated because their physical symptoms can be so erratic.

These drugs induce severe thirst and the skin becomes hot and dry; pupils dilate, making bright lighting uncomfortable. As toxicity rises, so do temperature and heart rate. Users have difficulty urinating or ejaculating (effects that can last for twelve to forty-eight hours) and fit the classic description of belladonna poisoning victims: "Hot as a hare, red as a beet, and mad as a hatter." Overdose can result in death from respiratory failure.

But it is behavioral toxicity that most often proves fatal. Users, suffering headaches, blurred vision and loss of coordination along with delirium, are often victims of accidents and falls. Thirst, rising temperature, and hot, dry skin draw them to pools, lakes, beaches and bathtubs, where they often drown.

Amanita Muscaria

The least poisonous member of the most deadly mushroom genus *Amanita,* muscaria is sometimes known as "fly agaric," for it was long believed to draw and kill flies if set out in a bowl of water. Easily recognized by its bright red cap and white "warts," muscaria grows brightest and largest—and most psychoactively potent—in the West. The farther east one travels, the paler muscaria appears, and the Eastern variety, light yellow or even white, looks remarkably like muscaria's more deadly relatives.

An old drug, muscaria is believed to be the psychedelic substance called "soma" in India's ancient Vedic texts. For hundreds of years, native Siberian tribes have made an intoxicating broth of muscaria. Today, just about the only users of the mushroom, aside from some native Siberians, are a few adventurous Westerners.

It is a hard-hitting drug. Within fifteen or twenty minutes after taking it—and often before any psychedelic reaction—users may become severely confused or have difficulty breathing. Visual distortions are common, along with color displays, vivid dreams and delirium. Physical effects include loss of coordination, muscle spasms, and impairment of speech. As the effects wear off, some users may twitch for several hours and suffer muscle pains for a few days.

The toxicity of muscaria varies from region to region. Because toxic ingredients are often more heavily concentrated in one part of the same mushroom than in another, no standard or safe dose can be determined. Overdose will produce extremely high temperatures and prolonged delirium leading to convulsions, deep coma and even death as a result of cardiac arrest.

Nutmeg and Mace

Not in the same toxic league with other deliriants and having only mild hallucinogenic effects, these common kitchen spices are true "drugs of opportunity." Although they once enjoyed some popularity among sailors and are now occasionally tried by college students, most users are confined in prisons or similar institutions. Both nutmeg (from the seed of the East Indian nutmeg tree) and mace (the nutmeg's outer covering) will produce marijuanalike effects, often followed by a severe hangover that can last twelve to eighteen hours. Although far from toxic in normal amounts and even in the sizable doses used to induce a high, nutmeg has proven fatal to women attempting to induce abortion by consuming massive amounts of the spice.

Ketamine

A close relative of PCP, ketamine is an injected anesthetic that is given when a mask is impractical or for brief surgical procedures that can be performed in a surgeon's office. Feelings of dissociation (of being separated from the environment) occur within fifteen seconds after injection, and the patient is unconscious after thirty seconds. Unconsciousness lasts only ten to fifteen minutes, but amnesia persists for an hour or two and patients recall nothing they experience even after regaining consciousness. Vivid and disagreeable dreams, as well as hallucinations, occur as the drug wears off.

At doses well below those needed for anesthesia, the effects of ketamine resemble LSD's or PCP's. There is a strong tendency to experience a sense of disconnection from the real world and sensations of floating or suspension in space.

In recent years, ketamine—known as "Special K" or "The Green," because of its color—has become a street drug of limited but growing popularity in some areas. Sold as a powder, it is usually either sniffed or smoked by street users and preferred to PCP for its briefer action and less devastating adverse effects.

Antidepressants

There are a great many antidepressants on the market these days, and although they can elevate mood and produce a measure of euphoria for men and women who suffer depressions of biological origin, these drugs are rarely abused. Most have unpleasant side effects and many are effective only after an extended period of use. The one exception to the "rarely abused" rule is the tricyclic antidepressant amitriptyline (Elavil), for which there is considerable demand on the street in a number of urban areas.

While it would seem reasonable for some drug users to seek stimulation and mood elevation from this drug, what they actually are after is a "down"—the depressant effect amitriptyline has on normal users. But it is not all that pleasant a down. Its side effects make users light-headed and clumsy; they feel tired and often suffer blurred vision and dry mouth. For users who do not have an endogenous depression, Elavil tends to increase rather than reduce anxiety. After taking the drug for several days, these users also begin to have difficulty concentrating or thinking clearly. Still, Elavil is a popular drug of abuse in several places, and it is often abused by methadone maintenance patients who claim it enhances their methadone "glow."

Some authorities feel that tolerance to Elavil can be developed and that sustained use may result in both psychological and physical dependency. Getting off the drug should be handled much the way getting off a depressant is handled (see Chapter 6). Doctors generally recommend detoxification for amitriptyline abusers before further treatment.

11

SPECIAL PROBLEMS

Most of the problems of drug use have already been discussed in this book. This chapter focuses more closely on several that threaten nearly all users—new and more potent products, drug deceptions and drug interactions. It also notes special dangers to certain users, and looks at the most recently recognized risk of drug abuse—acquired immune deficiency syndrome (AIDS).

New and More Potent Psychoactives

During the summer and fall of 1979, California agents of the Drug Enforcement Administration (DEA) kept hearing about a new and powerful narcotic on the street called "China White." Their informants couldn't say if high-grade Asian heroin once known by that name had reappeared on the illicit market or if some hitherto unknown substance had been introduced by dealers in the Los Angeles area. Whatever it was, China White was credited with a growing number of overdose deaths.

Not until the following January did the DEA get hold of the drug, after two tiny packets were found on overdose victims. Forensic chemists at the agency's regional laboratory in San Diego discovered that all but about 1 percent of the minuscule samples (neither weighed as much as a postage stamp) was lactose, simple milk sugar. Not knowing what to make of the remainder, they shipped the samples off to DEA's main laboratory outside of Washington, D.C.

There, the China White project got top priority. Chemists separated bits of the active ingredient and began trying to map its mysterious molecule. Although they were thrown off the trail any number of times by impurities in the sample, the DEA chemists eventually learned that what they had was a molecule much like fentanyl (a short-acting synthetic narcotic, most often used with other drugs in anesthetic combinations). Only, the China White molecule seemed to have a wrinkle all its own— an attached methyl (CH_3) group. It turned out that this fentanyl-with-amethyl combination was not unknown; it had been developed and patented by a pharmacologist at the University of Mississippi but was never produced commercially.

After comparing samples from Mississippi with China White, DEA officials concluded that some back-street chemist, using descriptive material from the professional literature, had reproduced the synthetic drug, which is about eighty times more potent than morphine. Word of China White's origins, along with sample material, went back to California, where DEA agents were able to explain to police why so many packets of white powder seized during the preceding year showed no traces of heroin and seemed instead to contain only milk sugar.

The anonymous fabricator of China White belongs to that band of "basement" or "bathtub" chemists—often unqualified and usually ill-equipped—who turn out drugs for the illicit market. But the backroom boys only follow—sometimes with fatal sloppiness—where their more respected colleagues lead, for interest in new psychoactive drugs runs high in university and commercial laboratories. Improved technology has meant greater manipulation of natural substances and the creation of synthetic drugs of awesome strength and amazing specificity—drugs tailor-made to produce a narrow range of effects.

Today, the road from simple opium to morphine (a natural derivative) to semisynthetic heroin (still using natural ingredients) runs on not only to synthetic narcotics such as fentanyl but also to more sophisticated semisynthetics such as etorphine, nearly a thousand times stronger than morphine. Among hallucinogens, the semisynthetic LSD opened the door for a whole wave of new drugs.

Advances in agriculture, too, have upped the muscle of psychoactive drugs. Modern methods of plant breeding and cultivation, including the use of halide lights, have raised the average concentration of THC (pot's primary psychoactive component) from well below 1 percent in the 1960s to between 3 and 5 percent today. In new seedless varieties and such special strains as *indica,* THC levels now run as high as 10 percent. As for PCP, there are now at least thirty derivatives of it, many of which are sold on the illicit market as "angel dust" but which may produce even more unanticipated and adverse reactions.

Dangers mount as drug potency increases, and today's users also have ways of strengthening and enhancing the effects of drugs. There are various smoking implements that help direct more concentrated blasts of marijuana to the lungs, and there are also devices for home treatment of marijuana that can raise THC levels and even extract "hash oil." Cocaine users can convert their drug to freebase for smoking. The abuse potential—and the likelihood of compulsive use—however, rises with increased potency.

Drug Deceptions

A problem inherent in any illicit enterprise, deception in the drug market poses more of a threat to users than simply the possibility of being "burned" or cheated. There is also the danger of unexpected or toxic effects that may result from some of following deceptive practices.

Dilution, the addition of an inactive substance to increase bulk and reduce purity, is common. Potent and costly drugs are almost always "cut" before distribution to street dealers. Cocaine, for example, when bought by the gram, is rarely more than 20 percent pure. Most often it is cut with inert materials, such as talc, flour or cornstarch, or with sugars (mannitol, lactose, dextrose, sucrose or inositol). Although these additives have no psychoactive effects, they may well cause physical side effects. For example, abrasive additives can aggravate the damage cocaine does to the nasal passages, and additives can create great risk for the intravenous drug user.

Adulteration involves cutting the drug with an active, not an inert, ingredient. Caffeine can perk up low-powered (already diluted) amphetamine. Local anesthetics, such as lidocaine, benzocaine and tetracaine, and stimulants, such as ephedrine, are often added to cocaine to make it seem more pure. But adulterants may be even more toxic than the drug to which they are added. Although marijuana is generally a reliable street drug, it is sometimes "spiked" with PCP (angel dust) and passed off as higher-quality or more powerful pot. What the buyer gets, of course, is PCP's rough trip and unattractive side effects.

Substitution is simple misrepresentation. One drug or a combination of drugs is sold as another and often goes unrecognized by buyers (particularly young and inexperienced users). Hallucinogens are frequently mislabeled on the street market. LSD is sold as psilocybin; and LSD, PCP, or a combination of the two are sold as mescaline. Most "amphetamines" now are look-alike capsules filled with over-the-counter stimulants (caffeine, ephedrine), or various controlled substances such as pemoline (Cylert). While there's little harm done when a user gets a less powerful drug than he bargained for (except a false notion of how much of the real stuff he can handle), there is real risk when he gets a *more* powerful substitute. Overdose, as discussed earlier, was common among buyers of synthetic China White who thought they had scored heroin.

Contamination, not a deception so much as a hazard of illicit drug purchases, most often results when basement chemists get sloppy. Street drugs often contain the residue of chemical reagents, like the potassium cyanide used to manufacture both PCP and methamphetamine. Recently, several buyers of "synthetic heroin" in California were struck down by this kind of laboratory slipup.

Drug Interactions

The risks of drug use rise when more than one substance is used, and psychoactives work together or oppose each other in several ways. Potentiation, for example, occurs when two similar-acting drugs are taken together and produce a combined effect greater than the total of their individual effects. Overdose is frequently the result of this interaction when two depressants are taken, or when a depressant and an opioid are used together, or a depressant is combined with alcohol.

Most drug users are aware of this kind of interaction. Few, however, realize the problems that can be created by the interaction of psychoactive with nonpsychoactive drugs. There are a good many ways drugs inhibit or enhance each other. Several of the barbiturates appear to speed the metabolism of other drugs in the liver, reducing their effect and duration of action. High levels of alcohol will reduce metabolism and increase another drug's impact and length of action. Interaction also can occur in the bloodstream, in the intestinal tract, and at receptor sites in the central nervous system.

Various kinds of medication may interact with popular drugs of abuse, including antifungal agents, anticoagulants, some cortisone drugs and digitalis. This means you mustn't keep your drug use a secret from your doctor when you are ill. He or she must know what the prescribed substances are going to run into when you take them. You can expect your doctor to tell you that eating milk products, drinking alcohol or taking aspirin will alter effects of medication. You can't expect him to add a cautionary note about unprescribed barbiturates, amphetamine or LSD.

High-Risk Users

Not all drug users run the same risks. Age, health, individual resources, and emotional well-being affect the way you use drugs and the likelihood of abuse. In addition, there are special risks associated with certain conditions.

Heart disease adds an extra degree of danger to the use of drugs that induce stress, such as hallucinogens, and drugs that impose stressful withdrawal. Prolonged use of alcohol, which damages heart muscle and coronary arteries and can cause irregular heart rhythm, is plainly a bad idea. So is smoking marijuana, which raises heart rate and can precipitate angina pectoris.

Epilepsy also increases the risk of alcohol use. Although alcohol will suppress convulsions, its antiepileptic effects are reversed when drinking ends, and users become more susceptible to seizures. Depressants can cause complications if anticonvulsant medication is used. They may intensify effects of the medication and make seizures likely during withdrawal.

Pregnancy does not increase risks to expectant mothers from drug use, but drug use during this period can impose risks on unborn children, for most drugs easily cross the placental barrier. What's more, the danger of birth defects is hard to detect. It took several years of widespread use and repeated gross deformities before the danger of Thalidomide was recognized. For many drugs, a tendency to increase the incidence of a common birth defect is not easily noted, and many defects may not be visible at birth. What expectant mothers should bear in mind is that the fetus is most vulnerable to malformation during the first ninety days of pregnancy.

Alcohol is an obvious danger to the unborn. Fetal alcohol syndrome (see Chapter 7) can afflict newborns with severe birth defects. Other depressants also pose dangers. Use of most (including prolonged use of certain tranquilizers) will cause withdrawal symptoms in newborn children, and there is some association of barbiturates with malformation. There is also some evidence that stimulants can cause heart defects and abnormalities in the digestive system.

Children of opioid-using mothers display withdrawal symptoms at birth and may be below normal size or weight. Some opioids can also induce respiratory depression in the newborn. Although there is no evidence yet that hallucinogens cause birth defects, they are considered likely to endanger infants (see Chapter 9). Marijuana has been shown to damage embryos in animal studies, and some newborn human infants suffer symptoms of depressant withdrawal. The possible dangers of marijuana to human infants are discussed in Chapter 8.

Adolescence is also a "condition" that raises drug risk. There are simple physical reasons for this, including the vulnerability of rapidly growing tissue to the toxic effects of drugs and the added impact of drug-induced hormonal changes during puberty. Other reasons for heightened risk include the normal stresses of adolescence, the influence of peer pressure, social and sexual insecurities, the lure of risk-taking, as well as uncertain values and limited judgment. Most significant perhaps is the impact of drug use on development (discussed in Chapter 8) and the tendency of many users to revert to infantile self-involvement, forestalling maturation.

AIDS
(Acquired Immune Deficiency Syndrome)

A new danger to drug users, AIDS was first noted in 1981 and initially believed to occur exclusively among homosexual men. AIDS prevents the immune system from protecting the body against certain previously rare "opportunistic" tumors and infections, such as Kaposi's sarcoma (a form of cancer) and *Pneumocystis carinii* pneumonia. Symptoms of AIDS include fever, diarrhea and weight loss, swollen glands and fatigue. There is no known treatment as yet, and mortality is at least 50 percent. It may well be much higher, for victims who recover from an initial infection remain vulnerable to others.

Drug users who administer drugs intravenously were the second group of potential AIDS victims identified. Other populations have subsequently been found at risk.

Early in the spring of 1983, there were some twenty-five hundred reported cases of AIDS, nearly half of them in New York City, with significant numbers in San Francisco, Los Angeles, Miami, and Newark, New Jersey. At the start of 1984, there were still no definite answers to such questions as cause and means of transfer of AIDS. But it was clear that drug users who employ intravenous injection were among the most vulnerable to AIDS.

PART THREE

Some Final Thoughts
on
How to Get Off Drugs

Getting off and staying off drugs is tough. It requires real effort and can involve both physical and psychological pain. Still, it is not hard to find help. More types of treatment exist now than ever before—residential and outpatient, chemically assisted and drug-free. In addition, our knowledge of how drugs work in the body keeps growing, and researchers are working on new treatment forms and variations of old ones. So, if you really want to get off, you should be able to locate a treatment plan or program that is right for you.

In the end, of course, stopping drug use means just that—stopping. And only you can do that. Treatment can help. It can ease you through whatever physical or psychological discomfort quitting entails. It can offer support during the difficult early days of abstinence and will probably increase your chances of remaining drug-free. But the real work of getting off is up to you. No matter what kind of treatment you opt for, you will have to make the effort for yourself.

To get off drugs, with help or without, means making real changes in your life. These should leave you with new attitudes and new values. But the changes to be made start with overcoming conditioning and breaking the pattern of stimulus and response that triggers drug-taking. They include restoring your body, taking care of it and strengthening it, using and enjoying it in new ways; finding alternative activities, interests and associations; learning to handle anxiety and depression without drugs;

233

and dealing with relationships that have suffered because of your drug use—and which may further change because of your abstinence.

No matter who you are or what kinds of drugs you have used, you will need to take the same four steps to get off:

1. Recognize that you have a problem and decide to do something about it;
2. Actually quit and get through whatever withdrawal is involved;
3. Make the changes in your life that will enable you to remain drug-free;
4. Cope with whatever problems subsequently arise.

There are the steps *everyone* with a drug problem must take. A teenager using marijuana compulsively may have little in common with an adult dependent on barbiturates, and a middle-class cocaine user is probably different in dozens of ways from an inner-city narcotic addict. Nevertheless, their dependency is much the same, and they all must go through essentially the same process to get off and stay off drugs.

Certainly, different drugs are taken for different reasons, produce different effects and impose different penalties. It is also true that strong personal resources increase the chance of quitting successfully. But there are no guarantees where drugs are concerned. You may have a job you find fulfilling, a good education, a comfortable home and strong family ties. But all this does not by itself ensure that you will be any more successful than someone with weaker personal resources.

What is important to remember is that the various forms of drug abuse are more similar than different, and (with a few notable exceptions) the process of getting off and staying off is much the same for all users—no matter what their personal resources or drug of choice.

Finally, you should keep in mind the basic points that have reappeared through the book.

- Drugs exact a price from all users. Sooner or later, the bill comes due, and costs can run high—permanent physical damage, social or emotional dysfunction, and drug dependency. To some people, the price may *seem* small. But the reality is that you often cannot recognize how much your career or relationships have suffered because of your drug use.
- You are not alone. If you become dependent upon drugs, you are not the first nor will you be the last to do so. You should know others have become dependent and have succeeded in getting off. This knowledge can strengthen you. You also need help and can

get it not only from professionals but also from those who love you. But you must be willing to ask for help and ready to accept it.

- You should consult a doctor who has had some experience with drug dependency when you decide it's time to quit. A physician can discover if drugs have done any physical damage or masked illness and will help you locate the treatment you need.
- Treatment that best meets your needs should be minimally intrusive and disturb your life no more than necessary. But it is most important to choose a potent enough alternative—one that can do the job and enable you to achieve abstinence. It is also important to feel comfortable with a program you have chosen, to trust the staff and recognize a common basis of experience with other participants.
- Withdrawal can be difficult, but it tends to live up to expectations. If you anticipate a hard time, then that is what you are likely to have. But, whether you have a difficult time or an easy one, the real challenge of getting off drugs comes after withdrawal is past.
- Boredom is the enemy. Once you've quit, you've got to get moving, finding new interests, activities and associations. Inactivity leaves you vulnerable to depression and drug cravings. It is a sure route to relapse.

No matter what kind of professional help you get or how much your loved ones support you, quitting drugs is something you do for yourself. You got yourself on, and you must get yourself off. The rewards of a drug-free life must be earned.

APPENDIX

INFORMATION AND REFERRAL SOURCES

There are a great many sources of up-to-date information about drugs, drug abuse prevention and drug abuse treatment. These include:

National Clearinghouse for Drug Abuse Information (NCDAI)
An arm of the National Institute on Drug Abuse, the clearinghouse provides information at no cost and can supply a considerable variety of materials, from treatment directories to technical monographs. Address:

> P.O. Box 416
> Kingston, Maryland 20795
> (301) 443-6500

National Clearinghouse for Alcohol Information
Similar to NCDAI, this is a service of the National Institute on Alcohol Abuse and Alcoholism and provides information on issues of alcoholism and treatment resources. Address:

> P.O. Box 2345
> Rockville, Maryland 20852
> (301) 468-2600

Phoenix House Foundation
The nation's largest multiservice drug abuse agency, Phoenix House is based in New York but operates treatment facilities in California as well and provides information on drug abuse problems, prevention and treatment. Address:

> 164 West Seventy-fourth Street
> New York, New York 10023
> (212) 595-5810

The American Council on Drug Education (ACDE)
This group, formerly known as the American Council on Marijuana, publishes and distributes materials on drug abuse issues and will respond to requests for information. Address:

> 6193 Executive Boulevard
> Rockville, Maryland 20852
> (301) 984-5700

Pyramid
An information sharing and technical assistance organization supported by the National Institute on Drug Abuse, Pyramid's primary concern is drug abuse prevention. Address:

> 39 Quail Court, Suite 201
> Walnut Creek, California 94596
> (800) 277-0438 or
> (415) 939-6666

Compcare
A nationwide network of private treatment programs, Compcare agencies treat all forms of alcohol and drug abuse. Address:

> P.O. Box 27777
> Minneapolis, Minnesota 55427

Alcoholics Anonymous
Contact with AA can be made 24 hours a day at a number listed in your local telephone directory. To find an AA group in your area, you can also write to:

> Alcoholics Anonymous
> P.O. Box 459
> Grand Central Station
> New York, New York 10017

Al-Anon Family Groups
To contact a family support group in your area, write:

> Al-Anon Family Groups
> P.O. Box 182
> Madison Square Station
> New York, New York 10159

National Self Help Clearinghouse
This organization will put you in touch with a group that can help you with any kind of drug abuse problem or provide information about starting your own group. You should explain the exact nature of your problem so that they can recommend the most appropriate group; enclose a stamped, self-addressed envelope when you write. Address:

33 West Forty-second Street
Room 1206-A
New York, New York 10036

You can call the Clearinghouse at (212) 840-7607, but if you are not in New York, they will call back collect when they have assembled the information you need.

Single-State Agencies

Each state has a special state agency that oversees drug abuse services, including prevention, treatment, and rehabilitation programs (many have a separate agency for alcohol abuse services). They are the best places to start learning what programs or other services are available in your area. The following is a list of state drug abuse agencies as of September 1983:

ALABAMA

Department of Mental Health
Division of Mental Illness and
  Substance Abuse Community
  Programs
200 Interstate Park Drive
P.O. Box 3710
Montgomery, Alabama 36193
(205) 271-9253

ALASKA

Department of Health and Social
  Services
Office of Alcoholism and Drug Abuse
Pouch H-05-F
Juneau, Alaska 99811
(907) 586-6201

ARIZONA

Department of Health Services
Division of Behavioral Health
  Services
Bureau of Community Services
Alcohol Abuse and Alcoholism
  Section
2500 East Van Buren
Phoenix, Arizona 85008
(602) 255-1238

Department of Health Services
Division of Behavioral Health
  Services
Bureau of Community Services
Drug Abuse Section
2500 East Van Buren
Phoenix, Arizona 85008
(602) 255-1240

ARKANSAS

Department of Human Services
Office on Alcohol and Drug Abuse
  Prevention
1515 West Seventh Avenue, Suite 310
Little Rock, Arkansas 72202
(501) 371-2603

CALIFORNIA

Department of Alcohol and Drug
  Abuse
111 Capitol Mall
Sacramento, California 95814
(916) 445-1940

COLORADO

Department of Health
Alcohol and Drug Abuse Division
4210 East Eleventh Avenue
Denver, Colorado 80220
(303) 320-6137

CONNECTICUT

Alcohol and Drug Abuse Commission
999 Asylum Avenue, Third Floor
Hartford, Connecticut 06105
(203) 566-4145

DELAWARE

Division of Mental Health
Bureau of Alcoholism and Drug Abuse
1901 North Dupont Highway
Newcastle, Delaware 19720
(302) 421-6101

DISTRICT OF COLUMBIA

Department of Human Services
Office of Health Planning and
　Development
601 Indiana Avenue, NW, Suite 500
Washington, DC 20004
(202) 724-5641

FLORIDA

Department of Health and
　Rehabilitative Services
Alcoholic Rehabilitation Program
1317 Winewood Boulevard, Room
　187A
Tallahassee, Florida 32301
(904) 488-0396

Department of Health and
　Rehabilitative Services
Drug Abuse Program
1317 Winewood Boulevard, Building
　6, Room 155
Tallahassee, Florida 32301
(904) 488-0900

GEORGIA

Department of Human Resources
Division of Mental Health and Mental
　Retardation
Alcohol and Drug Section
618 Ponce de Leon Avenue, NE
Atlanta, Georgia 30365
(404) 894-4785

HAWAII

Department of Health
Mental Health Division
Alcohol and Drug Abuse Branch
1250 Punchbowl Street
P.O. Box 3378
Honolulu, Hawaii 96801
(808) 548-4280

IDAHO

Department of Health and Welfare
Bureau of Preventive Medicine
Substance Abuse Section
450 West State
Boise, Idaho 83720
(208) 334-4368

ILLINOIS

Department of Mental Health and
　Developmental Disabilities
Division of Alcoholism
160 North La Salle Street, Room 1500
Chicago, Illinois 60601
(312) 793-2907

Illinois Dangerous Drugs Commission
300 North State Street, Suite 1500
Chicago, Illinois 60610
(312) 822-9860

INDIANA

Department of Mental Health
Division of Addiction Services
429 North Pennsylvania Street
Indianapolis, Indiana 46204
(317) 232-7816

IOWA

Department of Substance Abuse
505 Fifth Avenue
Insurance Exchange Building, Suite
　202
Des Moines, Iowa 50319
(515) 281-3641

KANSAS

Department of Social Rehabilitation
  Service
Alcohol and Drug Abuse Services
Biddle Building
2700 West Sixth Street
Topeka, Kansas 66606
(913) 296-3925

KENTUCKY

Cabinet for Human Resources
Department of Health Services
Substance Abuse Branch
275 East Main Street
Frankfort, Kentucky 40601
(502) 564-2880

LOUISIANA

Department of Health and Human
  Resources
Office of Mental Health and Substance
  Abuse
655 North Fifth Street
P.O. Box 4049
Baton Rouge, Louisiana 70821
(504) 342-2565

MAINE

Department of Human Services
Office of Alcoholism and Drug Abuse
  Prevention
Bureau of Rehabilitation
32 Winthrop Street
Augusta, Maine 04330
(207) 289-2781

MARYLAND

Alcoholism Control Administration
201 West Preston Street, Fourth Floor
Baltimore, Maryland 21201
(301) 383-2977

State Health Department
Drug Abuse Administration
201 West Preston Street
Baltimore, Maryland 21201
(301) 383-3312

MASSACHUSETTS

Department of Public Health
Division of Alcoholism
755 Boylston Street, Sixth Floor
Boston, Massachusetts 02116
(617) 727-1960

Department of Public Health
Division of Drug Rehabilitation
600 Washington Street
Boston, Massachusetts 02114
(617) 727-8617

MICHIGAN

Department of Public Health
Office of Substance Abuse Services
3500 North Logan Street
P.O. Box 30035
Lansing, Michigan 48909
(517) 373-8603

MINNESOTA

Department of Public Welfare
Chemical Dependency Program
  Division
Centennial Building
658 Cedar Street, Fourth Floor
Saint Paul, Minnesota 55155
(612) 296-4614

MISSISSIPPI

Department of Mental Health
Division of Alcohol and Drug Abuse
1102 Robert E. Lee Building
Jackson, Mississippi 39201
(601) 359-1297

MISSOURI

Department of Mental Health
Division of Alcoholism and Drug
  Abuse
2002 Missouri Boulevard
P.O. Box 687
Jefferson City, Missouri 65102
(314) 751-4942

MONTANA

Department of Institutions
Alcohol and Drug Abuse Division
1539 11th Avenue
Helena, Montana 59620
(406) 449-2827

NEBRASKA

Department of Public Institutions
Division of Alcoholism and Drug
  Abuse
801 West Van Dorn Street
P.O. Box 94728
Lincoln, Nebraska 68509
(402) 471-2851, ext. 415

NEVADA

Department of Human Resources
Bureau of Alcohol and Drug Abuse
505 East King Street
Carson City, Nevada 89710
(702) 885-4790

NEW HAMPSHIRE

Department of Health and Welfare
Office of Alcohol and Drug Abuse
  Prevention
Hazen Drive
Health and Welfare Building
Concord, New Hampshire 03301
(603) 271-4627

NEW JERSEY

Department of Health
Division of Alcoholism/Narcotic and
  Drug Abuse
129 East Hanover Street, CN 362
Trenton, New Jersey 08625
(609) 292-8949

NEW MEXICO

Health and Environment Department
Behavioral Services Division
Substance Abuse Bureau
725 Saint Michaels Drive
P.O. Box 968
Santa Fe, New Mexico 87503
(505) 984-0020, ext. 304

NEW YORK

Division of Alcoholism and Alcohol
  Abuse
194 Washington Avenue
Albany, New York 12210
(518) 474-5417

Division of Substance Abuse Services
Executive Park South
Box 8200
Albany, New York 12203
(518) 457-7629

NORTH CAROLINA

Department of Human Resources
Division of Mental Health, Mental
  Retardation and Substance Abuse
  Services
Albemarle Building
325 North Salisbury Street
Raleigh, North Carolina 27611
(919) 733-4670

NORTH DAKOTA

Department of Human Services
Division of Alcoholism and Drug
  Abuse
State Capitol Building
Bismarck, North Dakota 58505
(701) 224-2767

OHIO

Department of Health
Division of Alcoholism
246 North High Street
P.O. Box 118
Columbus, Ohio 43216
(614) 466-3543

Department of Mental Health
Bureau of Drug Abuse
65 South Front Street
Columbus, Ohio 43215
(614) 466-9023

OKLAHOMA

Department of Mental Health
Alcohol and Drug Programs
4545 North Lincoln Boulevard
Suite 100, East Terrace
P.O. Box 53277
Oklahoma City, Oklahoma 73152
(405) 521-0044

OREGON

Department of Human Resources
Mental Health Division
Office of Programs for Alcohol and
   Drug Problems
2575 Bittern Street, NE
Salem, Oregon 97310
(503) 378-2163

PENNSYLVANIA

Department of Health
Office of Drug and Alcohol Programs
Commonwealth and Forster Avenues
Health and Welfare Building
P.O. Box 90
Harrisburg, Pennsylvania 17108
(717) 787-9857

RHODE ISLAND

Department of Mental Health, Mental
   Retardation and Hospitals
Division of Substance Abuse
Substance Abuse Administration
   Building
Cranston, Rhode Island 02920
(401) 464-2091

SOUTH CAROLINA

Commission on Alcohol and Drug
   Abuse
3700 Forest Drive
Columbia, South Carolina 29204
(803) 758-2521

SOUTH DAKOTA

Department of Health
Division of Alcohol and Drug Abuse
523 East Capitol
Joe Foss Building
Pierre, South Dakota 57501
(605) 773-4806

TENNESSEE

Department of Mental Health and
   Mental Retardation
Alcohol and Drug Abuse Services
James K. Polk Building, Fourth Floor
505 Deaderick Street
Nashville, Tennessee 37219
(615) 741-1921

TEXAS

Commission on Alcoholism
809 Sam Houston State Office
   Building
Austin, Texas 78701
(512) 475-2577

Department of Community Affairs
Drug Abuse Prevention Division
2015 South Interstate Highway 35
P.O. Box 13166
Austin Texas 78711
(512) 443-4100

UTAH

Department of Social Services
Division of Alcoholism and Drugs
150 West North Temple, Suite 350
P.O. Box 2500
Salt Lake City, Utah 84110
(801) 533-6532

VERMONT

Agency of Human Services
Department of Social and
  Rehabilitation Services
Alcohol and Drug Abuse Division
103 South Main Street
Waterbury, Vermont 05676
(802) 241-2170

VIRGINIA

Department of Mental Health and
  Mental Retardation
Division of Substance Abuse
109 Governor Street
P.O. Box 1797
Richmond, Virginia 23214
(814) 786-5313

WASHINGTON

Department of Social and Health
  Service
Bureau of Alcohol and Substance
  Abuse
Office Building—44 W
Olympia, Washington 98504
(206) 753-5866

WEST VIRGINIA

Department of Health
Office of Behavioral Health Services
Division on Alcoholism and Drug
  Abuse
1800 Washington Street East
Building 3, Room 451
Charleston, West Virginia 25305
(305) 348-2276

WISCONSIN

Department of Health and Social
  Services
Division of Community Services
Bureau of Community Programs
Alcohol and Other Drug Abuse
  Program Office
1 West Wilson Street
P.O. Box 7851
Madison, Wisconsin 53707
(608) 226-2717

WYOMING

Alcohol and Drug Abuse Programs
Hathaway Building
Cheyenne, Wyoming 82002
(307) 777-7115, ext. 7118

GUAM

Mental Health and Substance Abuse
  Agency
P.O. Box 20999
Guam 96921

PUERTO RICO

Department of Addiction Control
  Services
Alcohol Abuse Programs
P.O. Box B-Y Rio Piedras Station
Rio Piedras, Puerto Rico 00928
(809) 763-5014

Department of Addiction Control
  Services
Drug Abuse Programs
P.O. Box B-Y Rio Piedras Station
Rio Piedras, Puerto Rico 00928
(809) 764-8140

VIRGIN ISLANDS

Division of Mental Health, Alcoholism
  and Drug Dependency Services
P.O. Box 7329
Saint Thomas, Virgin Islands 00801
(809) 774-7265

AMERICAN SAMOA

LBJ Tropical Medical Center
Department of Mental Health Clinic
Pago Pago, American Samoa 96799

TRUST TERRITORIES

Director of Health Services
Office of the High Commissioner
Saipan, Trust Territories 96950

Veterans Administration Medical Centers

For veterans, a great many excellent drug abuse programs are available at VA hospitals. The following is a list of hospitals as of September 1983:

ALABAMA

Veterans Administration Medical
  Center
Alcohol Dependence Treatment
  Program
700 South Nineteenth Street (116A)
Birmingham, Alabama 35233
(205) 933-8101, ext. 6905

Veterans Administration Medical
  Center
Alcohol Dependence Treatment
  Program
Tuscaloosa, Alabama 35401
(205) 553-3760

ARIZONA

Veterans Administration Medical
  Center
Alcohol Dependence Treatment
  Program
Phoenix, Arizona 85012
(602) 277-5551 ext. 652

Veterans Administration Medical
  Center
Alcohol/Drug Dependence Treatment
  Program, Room 116A3
Prescott, Arizona 86313
(602) 445-4860, ext. 331

Veterans Administration Medical
  Center
Alcohol Dependence Treatment
  Program

South Sixth Avenue at Ajo Way
  (116A1)
Tucson, Arizona 85723
(602) 792-1450, ext. 558

CALIFORNIA

Veterans Administration Medical
  Center
Alcohol Dependence Treatment
  Program
2615 East Clinton Avenue (116D)
Fresno, California 93703
(209) 225-6100, ext. 461

Veterans Administration Medical
  Center
Alcohol Dependence Treatment
  Program
11201 Benton Street (116)
Loma Linda, California 92357
(714) 825-7084

Veterans Administration Medical
  Center
Alcohol Dependence Treatment
  Program
5901 East Seventh Street, Ward K2
Long Beach, California 90822
(213) 498-1313, ext. 2156

Veterans Administration Medical
  Center
Drug Dependence Treatment Program
  Administration
425 South Hill Street (136AQ)
Los Angeles, California 90013
(213) 688-2896

Veterans Administration Medical
Center
Alcohol/Drug Dependence Treatment
Program Administration
11301 Wilshire Boulevard (116A3)
Los Angeles (Brentwood), California
90073
(213) 478-3711

Veterans Administration Medical
Center
Alcohol/Drug Dependence Treatment
Program
150 Muir Road
Martinez, California 94553
(415) 228-6800, ext. 501

Veterans Administration Medical
Center
Alcohol/Drug Dependence Treatment
Program
3801 Miranda Avenue (116A3)
Palo Alto, California 94304
(415) 493-5000, ext. 5780

Veterans Administration Medical
Center
Alcohol Dependence Treatment
Program
3350 La Jolla Village Drive
San Diego, California 92161
(619) 453-7500, ext. 3665

Veterans Administration Medical
Center
Alcohol/Drug Dependence Treatment
Program
4150 Clement Street (116 Elm)
San Francisco, California 94121
(415) 750-2075

Veterans Administration Medical
Center
Alcohol/Drug Dependence Treatment
Program
16111 Plummer Street
Sepulveda, California 91343
(213) 891-2344

COLORADO

Veterans Administration Medical
Center
Alcohol/Drug Dependence Treatment
Program
1055 Clermont Street
Denver, Colorado 80220
(303) 399-1454, ext. 151

Veterans Administration Medical
Center
Alcohol Dependence Treatment
Program, Building 6
Fort Lyon, Colorado 81038
(303) 456-1260, ext. 331

CONNECTICUT

Veterans Administration Medical
Center
Alcohol Dependence Treatment
Program
West Spring Street (116A3)
West Haven, Connecticut 06516
(203) 932-5711, ext. 351

DISTRICT OF COLUMBIA

Veterans Administration Medical
Center
Alcohol/Drug Dependence Treatment
Program
50 Irving Street, NW
Washington, DC 20422
(202) 745-8160

FLORIDA

Veterans Administration Medical
Center
Alcohol Dependence Treatment
Program
Bay Pines, Florida 33504
(813) 391-9644, ext. 401

Veterans Administration Medical
   Center
Alcohol Dependence Treatment
   Program
Archer Road
Gainesville, Florida 32602
(904) 376-1611, ext. 6764

Veterans Administration Medical
   Center
Alcohol/Drug Dependence Treatment
   Program Administration
900 NW Seventh Avenue
Miami, Florida 33125
(305) 324-4455, ext. 3330

GEORGIA

Veterans Administration Medical
   Center
Alcohol Dependence Treatment
   Program
Building 12
Augusta, Georgia 30910
(404) 724-5116, ext. 1547

Veterans Administration Medical
   Center
Alcohol/Drug Dependence Treatment
   Program
1670 Clairmont Road (116A3)
Decatur, Georgia 30033
(404) 321-6111, ext. 451

Veterans Administration Medical
   Center
Drug Dependence Treatment Program
   Administration
1670 Clairmont Road
Decatur, Georgia 30033
(404) 321-6111, ext. 451

ILLINOIS

Veterans Administration Medical
   Center
Alcohol Dependence Treatment
   Program
820 South Damen Avenue (116A4)
Chicago, Illinois 60612
(312) 666-6500, ext. 2944

Veterans Administration Medical
   Center
Drug Dependence Treatment Program
   Administration
820 South Damen Avenue, P.O. Box
   8195
Chicago, Illinois 60680
(312) 666-6500, ext. 2289

Veterans Administration Medical
   Center
Alcohol Dependence Treatment
   Program
1900 East Main Street
Danville, Illinois 61832
(217) 442-8000, ext. 516

Veterans Administration Medical
   Center
Alcohol Treatment and Education
   Center, Dept. 116A1
Hines, Illinois 60141
(312) 261-6700, ext. 2086

Veterans Administration Medical
   Center
Drug Dependence Treatment Program
   Administration
Building 53 MP (116C)
Hines, Illinois 60141
(312) 261-6700, ext. 2087

Veterans Administration Medical
   Center
Alcohol/Drug Dependence Treatment
   Program
North Chicago (Downey), Illinois
   60064
(312) 689-1900, ext. 2605

INDIANA

Veterans Administration Medical
   Center
Alcohol Dependence Treatment
   Program
Unit 116J
Indianapolis, Indiana 46222
(317) 267-8795

Veterans Administration Medical
Center
Drug Dependence Treatment Program
Administration
2601 Cold Spring Road
Indianapolis, Indiana 46222
(317) 635-7401, ext. 1744

Veterans Administration Medical
Center
Alcohol Dependence Treatment
Program
Building 12
Marion, Indiana 46952
(317) 674-3321, ext. 277

IOWA

Veterans Administration Medical
Center
Alcohol Dependence Treatment
Program
Thirtieth and Euclid Streets
Des Moines, Iowa 50310
(515) 255-2173, ext. 468

Veterans Administration Medical
Center
Alcohol Dependence Treatment
Program
Knoxville, Iowa 50138
(515) 842-3101, ext. 426

KANSAS

Veterans Administration Medical
Center
Alcohol/Drug Dependence Treatment
Program
Building 122, 116C
Leavenworth, Kansas 66048
(913) 682-2000, ext. 566

Veterans Administration Medical
Center
Alcohol/Drug Dependence Treatment
Program
2200 Gage Boulevard, Building 2

Topeka, Kansas 66622
(913) 272-3111, ext. 203

KENTUCKY

Veterans Administration Medical
Center
Alcohol Dependence Treatment
Program
Leestown Road
Lexington, Kentucky 40507
(606) 233-4511, ext. 310

LOUISIANA

Veterans Administration Medical
Center
Alcohol Dependence Treatment
Program
1601 Perdido Street (116A)
New Orleans, Louisiana 70146
(504) 568-0811, ext. 5833

Veterans Administration Medical
Center
Drug Dependence Treatment Program
Administration
2001 Canal Street, Suite 416
New Orleans, Louisiana 70140
(504) 589-0811, ext. 251

Veterans Administration Medical
Center
Alcohol Dependence Treatment
Program
510 E. Stoner Avenue, Tenth Floor,
10W12
Shreveport, Louisiana 71130
(318) 221-8411, ext. 6495

MAINE

Veterans Administration Medical
Center
Alcohol Dependence Treatment
Program
VAMROC
Togus, Maine 04330
(207) 623-8411, ext. 531

MARYLAND

Veterans Administration Medical
  Center
Alcohol/Drug Dependence Treatment
  Program
3900 Loch Raven Boulevard
Baltimore, Maryland 21218
(301) 467-9932

Veterans Administration Medical
  Center
Drug Dependence Treatment Program
31 Hopkins Plaza
Baltimore, Maryland 21201
(301) 962-3301

Veterans Administration Medical
  Center
Alcohol Dependence Treatment
  Program
Fort Howard, Maryland 21052
(301) 477-1800, ext. 280

MASSACHUSETTS

Veterans Administration Medical
  Center
Alcohol/Drug Dependence Treatment
  Program
200 Springs Road
Bedford, Massachusetts 01730
(617) 275-7500

Veterans Administration Medical
  Center
Alcohol/Drug Dependence Treatment
  Program, Outpatient Clinic
125 Lincoln Street
Boston, Massachusetts 02111
(617) 223-6424

Veterans Administration Medical
  Center
Alcohol/Drug Dependence Treatment
  Program
150 South Huntington Avenue
Boston, Massachusetts 02130
(617) 232-9500

Veterans Administration Medical
  Center
Alcohol/Drug Dependence Treatment
  Program
940 Belmont Street
Brockton, Massachusetts 02401
(617) 583-4500, ext. 494

Veterans Administration Medical
  Center
Alcohol Dependence Treatment
  Program
Northampton, Massachusetts 01060
(413) 584-4040, ext. 347

MICHIGAN

Veterans Administration Medical
  Center
Alcohol Dependence Treatment
  Program
Southfield Road Outer Drive (116A)
Allen Park, Michigan 48101
(313) 562-6000, ext. 781

Veterans Administration Medical
  Center
Alcohol/Drug Dependence Treatment
  Program
Battle Creek, Michigan 49016
(616) 966-5600, ext. 3661

Veterans Administration Medical
  Center
Drug Dependence Treatment Program
  Administration
1151 Taylor Street, Building 7
Detroit, Michigan 48202
(313) 872-7044

MINNESOTA

Veterans Administration Medical
  Center
Alcohol/Drug Dependence Treatment
  Program
Fifty-fourth Street and Forty-eighth
  Avenue South
Minneapolis, Minnesota 55417
(612) 725-6767, ext. 6866

Veterans Administration Medical
 Center
Alcohol Dependence Treatment
 Program
Saint Cloud, Minnesota 56301
(612) 252-1670, ext. 311

MISSISSIPPI

Veterans Administration Medical
 Center
Alcohol Dependence Treatment
 Program
Pass Road (116A)
Biloxi, Mississippi 39501
(601) 863-1972, ext. 185

Veterans Administration Medical
 Center
Alcohol Dependence Treatment
 Program
Jackson, Mississippi 39216
(601) 362-4471, ext. 1154

MISSOURI

Veterans Administration Medical
 Center
Alcohol Dependence Treatment
 Program
4801 Linwood Boulevard
Kansas City, Missouri 64128
(816) 861-4700, ext. 557

NEBRASKA

Veterans Administration Medical
 Center
Alcohol Dependence Treatment
 Program
600 South Seventieth Street (116A)
Lincoln, Nebraska 68510
(402) 489-3802

Veterans Administration Medical
 Center
Alcohol Dependence Treatment
 Program
4101 Woolworth Avenue

Omaha, Nebraska 68105
(402) 346-8800, ext. 578

NEW HAMPSHIRE

Veterans Administration Medical
 Center
Alcohol Dependence Treatment
 Program
718 Smyth Road, Building 5
Manchester, New Hampshire 03104
(603) 624-4366, ext. 368

NEW JERSEY

Veterans Administration Medical
 Center
Alcohol/Drug Dependence Treatment
 Program
Tremont Avenue
East Orange, New Jersey 07019
(201) 676-1000

Veterans Administration Medical
 Center
Alcohol Dependence Treatment
 Program
Building 57AS
Lyons, New Jersey 07939
(201) 647-0180, ext. 513

NEW MEXICO

Veterans Administration Medical
 Center
Alcohol Dependence Treatment
 Program
2100 Ridgecrest Drive SE
Albuquerque, New Mexico 87108
(505) 265-1711, ext. 2474

NEW YORK

Veterans Administration Medical
 Center
Alcohol/Drug Dependence Treatment
 Program
113 Holland Avenue
Albany, New York 12208
(518) 462-3311, ext. 363

Veterans Administration Medical
Center
Alcohol Dependence Treatment
Program
130 West Kingsbridge Road (151G)
Bronx, New York 10468
(212) 584-9000, ext. 1343

Veterans Administration Medical
Center
Alcohol/Drug Dependence Treatment
Program Administration
800 Poly Place
Brooklyn, New York 11209
(212) 836-6600

Veterans Administration Medical
Center
Alcohol/Drug Dependence Treatment
Program
3495 Bailey Avenue
Buffalo, New York 14215
(716) 834-9200

Veterans Administration Medical
Center
Alcohol Dependence Treatment
Program
Fort Hill Avenue, Building 7
Canandaigua, New York 14424
(716) 394-2000, ext. 153

Veterans Administration Medical
Center
Alcohol Dependence Treatment
Program
Building 28
Montrose, New York 10548
(914) 737-4400, ext. 2193

Veterans Administration Medical
Center
Alcohol/Drug Dependence Treatment
Program Administration
440 First Avenue
New York, New York 10010
(212) 686-7500, ext. 683

NORTH CAROLINA

Veterans Administration Medical
Center
Alcohol Dependence Treatment
Program
1601 Brenner Avenue (116A3)
Salisbury, North Carolina 28144
(704) 636-2351, ext. 334

OHIO

Veterans Administration Medical
Center
Alcohol Dependence Treatment
Program
17273 State Route 104
Chillicothe, Ohio 45601
(614) 773-1141

Veterans Administration Medical
Center
Alcohol Dependence Treatment
Program
Building 3, Second Floor, MDP 116A7
Cincinnati, Ohio 45220
(513) 559-5027, ext. 448

Veterans Administration Medical
Center
Drug Dependence Treatment Program
Administration
3200 Vine Street
Cincinnati, Ohio 45220
(513) 861-3100, ext. 4775

Veterans Administration Medical
Center
Alcohol/Drug Dependence Treatment
Program Administration
10000 Brecksville Road
Cleveland, Ohio 44141
(216) 526-3030

OKLAHOMA

Veterans Administration Medical
Center
Alcohol/Drug Dependence Treatment
Program
921 NE Thirteenth
Oklahoma City, Oklahoma 73104
(405) 272-9876

Veterans Administration Medical
Center
Alcohol/Drug Dependence Treatment
Program Administration
635 West Eleventh Street
Tulsa, Oklahoma 74127
(918) 581-7127

OREGON

Veterans Administration Medical
Center
Alcohol Dependence Treatment
Program
Garden Valley Boulevard
Roseburg, Oregon 97470
(503) 672-4411, ext. 315

Veterans Administration Medical
Center
Alcohol Dependence Treatment
Program
White City, Oregon 97503
(503) 826-2111, ext. 317

PENNSYLVANIA

Veterans Administration Medical
Center
Alcohol/Drug Dependence Treatment
Program (116A5)
Coatesville, Pennsylvania 19320
(215) 384-7711, ext. 477

Veterans Administration Medical
Center
Alcohol/Drug Dependence Treatment
Program Administration
University and Woodland Avenues
Philadelphia, Pennsylvania 19104
(215) 823-5808

Veterans Administration Medical
Center
Drug Dependence Treatment Program
Administration
University Drive C (116A)
Pittsburgh, Pennsylvania 15240
(412) 683-3000, ext. 421

RHODE ISLAND

Veterans Administration Medical
Center
Alcohol/Drug Dependence Treatment
Program Administration
Davis Park
Providence, Rhode Island 02908
(401) 273-7100

SOUTH CAROLINA

Veterans Administration Medical
Center
Alcohol Dependence Treatment
Program
109 Bee Street
Charleston, South Carolina 29403
(803) 577-5011, ext. 260

Veterans Administration Medical
Center
Alcohol Dependence Treatment
Program
William Jennings Bryan Dorn
Veterans Hospital
Columbia, South Carolina 29201
(803) 776-4000, ext. 549

SOUTH DAKOTA

Veterans Administration Medical
Center
Alcohol Dependence Treatment
Program
Building 148 Ward E
Fort Meade, South Dakota 57741
(605) 347-2511, ext. 370

Veterans Administration Medical
Center
Alcohol Dependence Treatment
Program
Hot Springs, South Dakota 57747
(605) 745-4101, ext. 217

TENNESSEE

Veterans Administration Medical
Center
Alcohol/Drug Dependence Treatment
Program Administration
1030 Jefferson Avenue
Memphis, Tennessee 38104
(901) 523-8990

Veterans Administration Medical
Center
Alcohol Dependence Treatment
Program
Johnson City
Mountain Home, Tennessee 37684
(615) 926-1171, ext. 7714

Veterans Administration Medical
Center
Alcohol Dependence Treatment
Program
Lebanon Road, Building 7A
Murfreesboro, Tennessee 37130
(615) 893-1360, ext. 3253

TEXAS

Veterans Administration Medical
Center
Alcohol Dependence Treatment
Program
2400 Gregg Street (116)
Big Spring, Texas 79720
(915) 263-7361, ext. 355

Veterans Administration Medical
Center
Alcohol/Drug Dependence Treatment
Program Administration
4500 South Lancaster Road

Dallas, Texas 75216
(214) 376-5451

Veterans Administration Medical
Center
Alcohol Dependence Treatment
Program
7400 Merton Minter Boulevard (116A)
San Antonio, Texas 78284
(512) 696-9660, ext. 254

Veterans Administration Medical
Center
Alcohol Dependence Treatment
Program
Memorial Drive (116)
Waco, Texas 76703
(817) 752-6581, ext. 385

UTAH

Veterans Administration Medical
Center
Alcohol/Drug Dependence Treatment
Program
500 Foothill Boulevard
Salt Lake City, Utah 84148
(801) 582-1565

VERMONT

Veterans Administration Medical
Center
Alcohol Dependence Treatment
Program
North Hartland Road, 116C
White River Junction, Vermont 05001
(802) 295-9363, ext. 451

VIRGINIA

Veterans Administration Medical
Center
Alcohol Dependence Treatment
Program
Hampton, Virginia 23667
(804) 722-9961, ext. 635

Veterans Administration Medical
Center
Alcohol/Drug Dependence Treatment
Program Administration
1201 Broadrock Boulevard
Richmond, Virginia 23249
(804) 231-9011, ext. 203

Veterans Administration Medical
Center
Alcohol Dependence Treatment
Program
Salem, Virginia 24153
(703) 982-2463, ext. 2585

WASHINGTON

Veterans Administration Medical
Center
Alcohol Dependence Treatment
Program
4435 Beacon Avenue South (116A)
Seattle, Washington 98108
(206) 762-1010, ext. 451

Veterans Administration Medical
Center
Drug Dependence Treatment Program
Administration
1520 Third Avenue, Suite 200
Seattle, Washington 98101
(206) 622-4081

Veterans Administration Medical
Center
Alcohol/Drug Dependence Treatment
Program
American Lake
Tacoma, Washington 98493
(206) 582-8440

Veterans Administration Medical
Center
Drug Dependence Treatment Program
Administration
Fourth Plain and ''O'' Streets
Vancouver, Washington 98661
(206) 696-4061, ext. 226

WEST VIRGINIA

Veterans Administration Medical
Center
Alcohol Dependence Treatment
Program
Martinsburg, West Virginia 25401
(304) 263-0811, ext. 480

WISCONSIN

Veterans Administration Medical
Center
Alcohol Dependence Treatment
Program
116A81
Tomah, Wisconsin 54660
(608) 372-3971, ext. 354

Veterans Administration Medical
Center
Alcohol/Drug Dependence Treatment
Program Administration
500 West National Avenue
Wood, Wisconsin 53193
(414) 384-2000

WYOMING

Veterans Administration Medical
Center
Alcohol Dependence Treatment
Program
Sheridan, Wyoming 82801
(307) 672-3473, ext. 356

PUERTO RICO

Veterans Administration Medical
   Center
Alcohol Dependence Treatment
   Program
GPO Box 4867
Rio Piedras, Puerto Rico 00936
(809) 764-4545, ext. 577

Veterans Administration Medical
   Center
Drug Dependence Treatment Program
GPO Box 4867
San Juan, Puerto Rico 00936
(809) 764-4545, ext. 590

Canada: Provincial Agencies

The following agencies, from a list provided by the Addiction Research Foundation of Toronto, Ontario, can direct users to local treatment programs.

ALBERTA

Alberta Alcoholism and Drug Abuse
   Commission
10909 Jasper Avenue, Sixth Floor
Edmonton, Alberta T5J 3M9
(403) 427-7301

BRITISH COLUMBIA

Alcohol and Drug Program
Information and Services Division
1775 West Broadway, Suite 201
Vancouver, British Columbia B6J 4S5
(604) 731-9121

MANITOBA

Alcoholism Foundation of Manitoba
1031 Portage Avenue
Winnipeg, Manitoba R3G OR9
(204) 786-3831

NEW BRUNSWICK

Alcoholism and Drug Dependency
   Commission of New Brunswick
103 Church Street, P.O. Box 6000
Fredericton, New Brunswick
   E3B 5H1
(506) 453-2136

NEWFOUNDLAND

Alcohol and Drug Dependency
   Commission of Newfoundland and
   Labrador
Royal Trust Building
139 Water Street, Fifth Floor
St. Johns, Newfoundland A1C 1B1
(709) 737-3600

NORTHWEST TERRITORIES

Department of Social Services,
Alcohol and Drug Program
Government of the Northwest
   Territories
Yellow Knife, Northwest Territories
   X1A 2L9
(403) 873-7155

NOVA SCOTIA

Nova Scotia Commission on Drug
   Dependency
5675 Spring Garden Road, Suite 314
Halifax, Nova Scotia B3J 1H1
(902) 424-4270

ONTARIO

Addiction Research Foundation
33 Russell Street
Toronto, Ontario M5S 2S1
(416) 595-6000

PRINCE EDWARD ISLAND

Queens County Addiction Services
P.O. Box 1832
Charlottetown, Prince Edward Island
  C1A 7N5
(902) 892-4265

QUEBEC

Ministry of Social Affairs
1075 Chemin Ste. Foy
Quebec City, Quebec G1S 2M1
(418) 643-6024

SASKATCHEWAN

Saskatchewan Alcoholism
  Commission
3475 Albert Street
Regina, Saskatchewan S4S 6X6
(306) 565-4085

YUKON

Royal Canadian Mounted Police, M
  Division
N.C.O. in Charge, Drug Section
4100 Fourth Avenue
White Horse, Yukon Y1A 1H5
(403) 667-5577

INDEX

ABOUT THE AUTHORS

IRA MOTHNER, who writes frequently on social issues, was a senior editor of *Look,* executive assistant to New York's Mayor John V. Lindsay and the editor of *EPO,* a magazine for public officials. He has been writing about drug abuse since 1968 and is the coauthor (with Dr. Mitchell S. Rosenthal of Phoenix House) of *Drugs, Parents and Children: The Three-Way Connection.*

ALAN WEITZ is a senior editor of *Rolling Stone* magazine. He was formerly editor of the *Soho Weekly News* and managing editor of the *Village Voice.*